# Copy Rights

Copyright © 2019 by Wajid Hassan

All rights reserved. No part of this publication may be reproduced, distributed, or transmitted in any form or by any means, including photocopying, recording, or other electronic or mechanical methods, without the prior written permission of the publisher, except in the case of brief quotations embodied in critical reviews and certain other non-commercial uses permitted by copyright law. For permission requests, write to the publisher, addressed "Attention: Permissions Coordinator," at the address below.

# About the Author

Wajid Hassan technical expertise spawns several years in building new Products and Solutions for IT Services, Telecommunications and Network Infrastructure verticals. He has been a forceful proponent of Network Automation.

In the past he has worked at Tier 1 Telecommunication companies including AT&T as a Solution Architect and at US Government (USDA) developing and deploying innovative mobility and networking solutions. He has command on Mobility, Software Defined Networking, Virtualization, OpenStack, Linux Containers and VMware technologies. Having sound knowledge on the evolution of Cloud and market directions, on a day to day basis he provides technical solutions with practical approach.

Highly motivated in research, he has developed experimental Networking, Virtualization and Cloud Computing lab, provides guidance and mentors researchers in Networking, Cloud and Virtualization domains. He is a great proponent of Research & Development and is considered to be an excellent mentor in nurturing the new talent and building a high performing team. He has hands on experience in Python Scripting and Cisco, Juniper, Ericsson and Nokia equipment.

He has a Master of Science degree in Electrical Engineering with emphasis on Digital Communication and Networking from Wichita State University. He is currently a PhD fellow at Indiana State University with specialization in Digital Communication. His PhD Dissertation is in Software Defined Networking, Machine Learning, Network Automation and Analytics,

He is an author of a research-oriented book. He has several technical research papers published to his credit. He has dual Cisco Certified Internetwork Expert (CCIE) in Service Provider and Data Centre. He has also served as a visiting faculty member at Bellevue College and taught at Indiana State University and Wichita State University. His undergraduate work on communication satellites earned him the 2008 IEEE-P Gold Medal Award. He has published several research papers. His two patents are pending approval.

# Contacting the Author

I'd be very interested to hear your comments and get your feedback on this book. Feel free to let me know what you think about the book or what additional items you would like to see in the next version of this book by sending me an email at wajid@logicfinder.net.

Customer feedback is critical to the success of this book; If you think you have found a technical error in this book, please send an email to wajid@logicfinder.net

# Acknowledgements

I would like to acknowledge the support or my associates and friends and family who have helped in making this book successful.

I would like to thank my wife Aiman, son Humza, My parents Khalid and Shahnaz, my brother Samad and sister Amber in their continuous support and for their encouragement.

Many of my associates have tested the code, read the manuscript and guided in helping to develop a network engineering better book. In no order the following individuals have been a great support as Python script testers, motivators and active contributors Debashish Dash, Rakesh Kumar, Dr. Patrick Appiah-Kubi, Pooja Thacker, Omar Azeemi, Larry Vongkhamchanh , Trung Vu, Hina Mumtaz, Fiza Khaliq, Ammara Siddiqui, Muhamad Naeem, Qamar Mahmood.

# Contents at a Glance

Preface

Chapter 1: Introduction

Chapter 2: Elements of Programming

Chapter 3: Collections and Sequences

Chapter 4: Conditional Statements

Chapter 5: Loops (FOR loop, WHILE loop, DO-WHILE loop)

Chapter 6: Functions   (Classes and Object Oriented Programming)

Chapter 7: Errors and Exceptions

Chapter 8: Well Known Python Network Libraries

Chapter 9: Practice Programs for Python Network Scripting

Chapter 10: Network Automation Tools

Appendix 1:  Online Courses and Books in Python

Appendix 2:  Selected Bibliography

# Preface

Network Automation addresses some of the most urgent, critical and complex network challenges. In the past the tedious process of network configuration and management has resulted in slowed growth and slowed fixing of the networks. Similar to the prevalent server automation which helps systems administrators diminish configuration issues and spares their time to focus on more strategic projects, network automation improves the efficiency of network engineers. Most of the enterprises still administer networks manually, even though manual network administration is cost inefficient and requires a lot of time. When easy accessibility to open source tools is available, network automation becomes easier to run an organization easily. It is high time for network teams to focus on becoming more agile. To stay competitive network management teams need to quickly fold novel advancements into organizations. This is possible by using Python Scripting for Automation.

Today Network Automation can be used for provisioning, configurations, identifying rogue devices, mitigating security attacks, compliance, audits, capacity planning, and scores of other activities. It has helped in enhancing network visibility and have empowered the network engineers to make faster, smarter network decisions, optimize uptime, efficiency, and performance, enhance security, and enable innovation instead of spending endless cycles in bringing the network

Automation has introduced faster and easier methods to achieve productivity goals, in a similar way if the network is not fully automated then it remains vulnerable to unplanned outages, traffic spikes, slow performance, and security risks.

Proprietary vendor automation solutions are becoming better but do not support a multi-vendor environment. Python Scripting has come to rescue and has deploy the blazing fast, high-availability, agile network was always wanted by the Network Administrators and Managers.

With Python Scripting, network engineers can reduce the likelihood of human error while configuring network devices, resulting in not only better-functioning networks, but more secure ones as well. Network automation has been difficult because networks are not usually the same, they are designed and evolve based on the need of the organization. The complex nature of business results in various needs of the users resulting in even complex networks, to manage such networks, network automation is needed

Programming was not much used in Network Engineering uphill 5 years ago however long and complicated lines of Network Configuration and with the advent of Software Defined Networking, it has become imperative to use scripting.

This book has been written for Network Engineers who are starting to explore network automation to build better computer Networks. This book is a good starting point for Network Engineers who learnt Programming in their earlier academic or work career and haven't used it in a long time or those Network Engineers who are learning Programming and Automation for the first time. The book has example Python Scripts which readers can practice and improve their job potential and make the networks more resilient and scalable.

# What does this book cover?

This book contains an introduction to the concepts of programming and approaches to network automation, management and scaling by demonstrating various kinds of network challenges, easibility of various learning tasks and the capabilities of python scripting, and examples of practical applications of machine learning to real-world problems.

Where possible, the chapters have been written to be readable in any sequence. However, some interdependence is unavoidable. If this is being used as a course text for a beginner level network scripting course, we recommend first covering Chapter 1 through Chapter 8. Following these six chapters, the remaining chapters 9 and 10 can be read in nearly any sequence.

A one-semester course in network automation using Python Scripting might cover the first six chapters, followed by whichever additional chapters are of greatest interest and experience level of the class. Below we present a brief survey of the chapters.

**Chapter 1**   **Introduction**

The chapter introduces the Python as a scripting language of choice, discusses the IDE/Software used to compile the Python scripts and gives ideas about the Network Libraries, APIs and tools which are used today in industry such as Ansible, Pramiko and Netmiko.

**Chapter 2**   **Elements of Programming**

This chapter discusses the basics of programming such as Numbers, variables, strings. It also introduced Data Structures which is later elaborated in Chapter 3.

**Chapter 3**   **Collections and Sequences**

Collections and Sequences chapter's gets you started on List, Tuples, Strings, Dictionary and Sets. It helps sets the foundation on how to sort information and manipulate results obtained as a result of gathered data

**Chapter 4**   **Conditional Statements**

This chapter introduces an important aspect of programming such as If, If Else and Nested conditional statements. These are important to make decisions in programming based on an input or a desired output

**Chapter 5**   **Loops (FOR loop, WHILE loop, DO-WHILE loop)**

This Chapter introduces you to subnetting. You will be able to subnet a network in your head after reading this chapter if you really want to. Plenty of help is found in this chapter if you do not skip the written labs and review questions.

**Chapter 6**   **Functions**

Functions help to decrease the size the overall program and reduce complexity by not having to repeat the same code which is used many times. In this chapter, we introduce how the Functions are created and how they can be called over and over in a script. The same chapter discusses the concept of Classes and Object Oriented Programming. With the help of numerous examples, it's easier to understand Functions and simplifying the Python Scripts that you will write.

| | |
|---|---|
| **Chapter 7** | **Errors and Exceptions** |

This is an important chapter for the novice scripting programmers as it helps explains different kinds of logical errors and how to handle them. Exceptions are errors which are deducted during runtime and prevents normal execution of a program. These are also known as "run time errors". These are logical errors and may cause the program to crash or not produce the expected results. In this chapter we discuss how to handle Exceptions and Errors.

| | |
|---|---|
| **Chapter 8** | **Well Known Python Network Libraries** |

Python libraries are significant in network engineering automation tasks as these can save tremendous amount of time by doing small tricks. For example, you might spend only 1 hour in writing a data script and running it. We discuss libraries such as NMAP, Diesel, pyopenssl, Scappy , Pramiko. We further demonstrate the use of each Python Network library by providing some examples scripts showcasing their usage.

| | |
|---|---|
| **Chapter 9** | **Practice Programs for Python Network Programming** |

The more you practice Python Scripting the better you become. In this chapter we have listed several practice programs so that you can brainstorm the solutions however we have also provided a working script for each. We encourage the readers to use the working scripts as baseline and use the practice programs as an example to write a different script and try their approach in handling a networking issue.

Python libraries are very crucial aspect in the world of software developers and engineers because one it contains maintainable and readable codes that enables developers to focus on the quality work they are to produce avoiding syntax errors. For example, when using construct that enables you to construct or deconstruct what has been created. Python also has multiple paradigms for programming that will support object oriented and structured programming fully the matplotib does in histogram coding. Python libraries are also compatible with major systems and platforms like ubuntu, Linux and windows. This allows you to run multiple programming increasing development time. Python also has a well-known standard library that outcompetes other programming language. This allows you to choose from a wider range of library randy from scapy, scipy, nmap, numpy and many more. Finally, python simplifies complex software development as they have library that facilitate visualization data analysis. This makes everything effective.

| | |
|---|---|
| **Chapter 10** | **Network Automation Tools** |

There are many Network automation tools that augment the learning of Python Script Development, we discuss some of those cool Network automation tools which are prevalent in the Network and Systems Engineering tasks.

These tools not only make life easier but also are better approaches to solving the network and Systems automation.

**Appendix 1:** **Online Courses and Books in Python**

We feel that there is very good information available online and some of these books and online courses will help the novice programmer get a deeper understanding of programming in general and Python in particular such as Algorithms and various different ways to approach the same problem. The different approach may help in reducing the time to execute the program or make the results more desirable or prefer a particular method of network configuration.

**Appendix 2:** **Bibliography**

Listed here are the various resources that we have used including blogs, books, articles, white papers and research papers.

# What skills do you need to master Network Automation?

Network Automation is a complex task and is intended to be achieved in a gradual and consistent manner. Automatic Network Status Report generation is the first step. As next generation of "hybrid engineers" is in huge demand in order to translate traditional network domain engineers into software/application developers, a number of skills are needed to master network automation.

To master it, a network engineer should have DevOps Mindset along with fair grip on some programming languages such as C, Java and Python. Similarly, a good understanding of operating systems, virtualization, hypervisors, applications, and databases is also needed.

In this book we give you tools to learn the basics of Programming and Python Scripting to get started assuming you have basic Network Engineering knowledge including TCP/IP, Interior Routing Protocol, Security Protocols and have worked on Layer 2 and Layer 3 devices.

As networker responsibilities are growing, systems will become less about deployment and more about optimization. So, specialization in a specific field will become crucial such as Network Routing and Switching, Security or other key Network functions.

# Official Website and Blog

This book is primarily written as a guide to learn Network Automation using Python. It is mainly targeted for newbies however seasoned and experience programmers can also take advantage of this book. We also offer an online interactive course that compliments the book. The blog on the website also provides updates and new content.

Our official website is https://www.logicfinder.net/python
Our official blog is https://netfv.wordpress.com

# How to Use This Book

If you want a solid foundation to master Python Scripting leading to Network Automation and hence reliable and secure networks. Execute exercises provided in each chapter by hand and practice the programs in Chapter 9 before analysing the solutions given in the same chapter for these complex Python Scripts. Mostly likely, you will come up with a different solution than the solution provided in the book, this will give you an opportunity to rethink and analyse which of the two codes will perform better in a real scenario.

I have spent hundreds of hours putting together this book with the intention of helping you to build Automated Networks which are easier to configure and manage.

This book is loaded with valuable information, and you will get the most out of your studying time if you understand how it was put together.

# Warning and Disclaimer

The author has made every effort to ensure the accuracy of the contents of this paper and do not accept responsibility for any omission and errors, as it is not deliberate.

# Feedback and Errata Information

Reader's feedback is a natural continuation of this process, if you have any comments regarding how we could improve the quality and content of this book, or otherwise provide comments, you can contact us through email at wajidh55@gmail.com. Please make sure to include the book title and ISBN in your message.

# Table of Contents

Copy Rights ................................................................................................................. 1
About the Author ........................................................................................................ 2
Contacting the Author ................................................................................................. 3
Acknowledgements ..................................................................................................... 3
Contents at a Glance ................................................................................................... 4
Preface ........................................................................................................................ 5
    What does this book cover? ................................................................................... 6
    What skills do you need to master Network Automation? .................................... 8
    Official Website and Blog ....................................................................................... 9
    How to Use This Book ............................................................................................ 9
    Warning and Disclaimer ........................................................................................ 9
    Feedback and Errata Information .......................................................................... 9
Table of Contents ...................................................................................................... 10
List of Figures ........................................................................................................... 21
List Of Tables ........................................................................................................... 23
Chapter 1 : Introduction to Network Automation ..................................................... 24
    1.1    Objectives ................................................................................................... 24
    1.2    Introduction ................................................................................................ 24
    1.3    Why Python Scripting is a MUST learn Network Engineer? .................... 24
    1.4    Give Specific Examples where Python Scripting is being used for Network Automation ... 25
    1.5    Network automation tools: Should you build or buy? ............................... 26
    1.6    Automation Tools and Languages ............................................................. 26
    1.7    Proprietary Automation Tools .................................................................... 27
        1.7.1    Cisco Prime Infrastructure ................................................................ 27
        1.7.2    Cisco Crosswork for Service Providers ........................................... 27
        1.7.3    SolarWinds ........................................................................................ 27
        1.7.4    WeConfig .......................................................................................... 27
    1.8    What is Scripting? ...................................................................................... 28
    1.9    What is the difference between Perl vs. Python? ...................................... 28
    1.10    Battle of Python Versions ......................................................................... 29
    1.11    Important Differences between Python 2 and Python 3 ......................... 29
    1.12    Python IDE ............................................................................................... 30
    1.13    Complete IDE ........................................................................................... 31
        1.13.1    PyCharm ......................................................................................... 32
        1.13.2    WingIDE ......................................................................................... 32

1.13.3 PyDev ........................................................................................................ 33
1.13.4 PyScripter .................................................................................................. 33
1.13.5 Eric Python IDE ........................................................................................ 34
1.14 Online python IDE ............................................................................................ 35
1.14.1 repl.it ........................................................................................................ 35
1.14.2 Python Anywhere ..................................................................................... 35
1.14.3 CodeSkulptor ........................................................................................... 36
1.14.4 IDEONE .................................................................................................. 37
1.14.5 Other online IDEs/Interpreters for python programming ....................... 37
1.15 Conclusion ........................................................................................................ 38
1.16 Summary ........................................................................................................... 38
1.17 Assignment Questions ...................................................................................... 39
Assignment . 1 .............................................................................................................. 39
Chapter 2 Elements of Programming ................................................................................. 40
2.1 Objectives ......................................................................................................... 40
2.2 Introduction ....................................................................................................... 40
2.3 Writing a simple Program in Python ................................................................ 40
2.3.1 Python Variables ....................................................................................... 40
2.3.2 Assigning Values to Variables .................................................................. 41
2.3.3 Multiple Assignment ................................................................................ 41
2.4 Python Standard Data Types ............................................................................. 42
2.4.1 Python Numbers ....................................................................................... 42
2.4.2 Named constant ........................................................................................ 42
2.5 Numeric Data Types and Operators .................................................................. 43
2.5.1 Multiplication operator ............................................................................. 43
2.5.2 Division operator ...................................................................................... 44
2.5.3 Modulus operator ..................................................................................... 45
2.5.4 Assignment operator ................................................................................ 45
2.5.5 Comparison operators .............................................................................. 46
2.5.6 Logical operators ...................................................................................... 48
2.6 Python Strings ................................................................................................... 48
2.6.1 Printing the length of a string ................................................................... 49
2.7 Data Structures .................................................................................................. 51
2.8 Lists ................................................................................................................... 51
2.9 Sets .................................................................................................................... 53
2.9.1 Changing sets in Python ........................................................................... 54

  2.9.2  Removing items from the set .................................................................. 55  
 2.10  Tuples ...................................................................................................... 56  
  2.10.1  Creating a Tuple in Python ................................................................. 56  
  2.10.2  Creating a non-empty tuple ................................................................. 57  
 2.11  Differences between Tuples and Lists ................................................... 58  
 2.12  Dictionaries ............................................................................................. 58  
  2.12.1  Accessing items in a dictionary .......................................................... 58  
  2.12.2  Creating and adding values to a dictionary ........................................ 59  
  2.12.3  Counting and looping through Python dictionary .............................. 59  
 2.13  Difference between a list and a dictionary ............................................. 60  
 2.14  Conclusion .............................................................................................. 60  
 2.15  Summary ................................................................................................. 60  
 2.16 Assignment Questions ................................................................................... 61  
  Assignment No. 1 ............................................................................................ 61  
  Assignment No. 2 ............................................................................................ 61  
  Assignment No. 3 ............................................................................................ 63  
  Assignment No. 4 ............................................................................................ 64  
Chapter 3 Collection and Sequences ........................................................................ 65  
 3.1  Objectives ................................................................................................ 65  
 3.2  Introduction ............................................................................................. 65  
 3.3  Collections .............................................................................................. 65  
  3.3.1  Types of Collections ............................................................................ 66  
 3.4  Sequences ................................................................................................ 67  
  3.4.1  Lists ...................................................................................................... 69  
  3.4.2  List Slicing ........................................................................................... 73  
  3.4.3  Functions that are used to control and edit the data stored in a list ..... 74  
  3.4.4  More List Operations ........................................................................... 77  
  3.4.5  Tuple .................................................................................................... 80  
  3.4.6  Strings .................................................................................................. 85  
 3.5  Escape sequences .................................................................................... 93  
  3.5.1  String formatting .................................................................................. 95  
  3.5.1.1  Components of formatting: ................................................................ 95  
 3.6  Mappings ................................................................................................. 97  
 3.7  Dictionaries ............................................................................................. 97  
  3.7.1  Modification of dictionaries ................................................................ 99  
  3.7.2  Constructor .......................................................................................... 102

|   |   |   |
|---|---|---|
| | 3.7.3 More on Dictionaries | 104 |
| | 3.7.3.1 Akin to Java Maps | 104 |
| | 3.7.3.2 Lookup: | 104 |
| | 3.7.3.3 Delete, insert, overwrite: | 105 |
| | 3.7.3.4 Keys, values, items: | 105 |
| | 3.7.3.5 Presence check: | 106 |
| | 3.7.4 Reason for key Immutability: | 106 |
| 3.8 | Sets | 107 |
| 3.9 | Summary | 108 |
| 3.10 | Conclusion | 108 |
| 3.11 | Assignment Questions | 109 |
| | Assignment No. 1 | 109 |
| | Assignment No. 2 | 109 |
| | Assignment No. 3 | 110 |
| | Assignment No. 4 | 111 |

## Chapter 4 Conditional Statements in Python .................. 112

| | | |
|---|---|---|
| 4.1 | Objectives | 112 |
| 4.2 | Introduction | 112 |
| 4.3 | Variables in python | 112 |
| 4.4 | Types, Values, and Expressions | 113 |
| 4.5 | Boolean comparisons | 114 |
| 4.6 | Logical operators | 117 |
| 4.7 | Generating Random Numbers | 118 |
| 4.8 | Properties of a good random number generator | 118 |
| 4.9 | Flow Chart, Symbols and usage | 120 |
| | 4.9.1 Start symbol: | 121 |
| | 4.9.2 Process symbol | 121 |
| | 4.9.3 Decision symbol | 121 |
| 4.10 | Conditional statements in Python | 122 |
| | 4.10.1 IF Statements | 123 |
| | 4.10.2 Two-Way if-else Statements | 124 |
| | 4.10.3 Nested if and Multi-Way if-elif-else Statements | 126 |
| | 4.10.4 Common Errors in Selection Statements | 127 |
| 4.11 | Logical Operators | 128 |
| | 4.11.1 Operator Precedence and Associativity | 133 |
| 4.12 | Conclusion | 134 |

13

4.13 Summary .................................................................................................... 134
4.14 Assignment Questions ............................................................................... 135
    Assignment No. 1 ............................................................................................. 135
    Assignment No. 2 ............................................................................................. 135
    Assignment No. 3 ............................................................................................. 136
    Assignment No. 4 ............................................................................................. 138

# Chapter 5 Loops ............................................................................................... 139
5.1 Objectives ..................................................................................................... 139
5.2 Introduction to Loops .................................................................................. 139
    5.2.1    FOR Loop ............................................................................................ 139
    5.2.2    While loop ........................................................................................... 141
    5.2.3    Do - While loop: .................................................................................. 142
5.3 Difference between a FOR loop and a WHILE loop ................................ 146
    5.3.1    Syntax Comparison ............................................................................. 147
5.3 Comparing "The Do-While loop" with other Looping structures ......... 148
5.4 Difference between the do while loop and the while loop ....................... 150
5.5 Conclusion .................................................................................................... 151
5.6 Summary ....................................................................................................... 151
5.7 Assignment Questions ................................................................................. 152
    Assignment No. 1 ............................................................................................. 152
    Assignment No. 2 ............................................................................................. 152
    Assignment No. 3 ............................................................................................. 153

# Chapter 6 Functions in Python Scripting ...................................................... 154
6.1 Objectives ..................................................................................................... 154
6.2 Introduction ................................................................................................. 154
    6.2.1    Functions ............................................................................................. 154
    6.2.2    Object-oriented programming ........................................................... 155
    6.2.3    Classes ................................................................................................. 155
6.3 Program Components in Python ............................................................... 156
6.4 Python Built-in Functions .......................................................................... 156
6.5 User Defined Function ................................................................................ 161
6.6 Calling a Function ....................................................................................... 162
6.7 Functions with/without Return Values ..................................................... 163
    6.7.1    Python functions without return values ........................................... 163
    6.7.2    Python functions without return none .............................................. 164
    6.7.3    Python functions with return values ................................................. 164

| 6.8 | Positional and Keyword Arguments | 164 |
| --- | --- | --- |
| 6.9 | Passing Arguments by Reference and by Values | 166 |
| 6.10 | Modularizing Code | 166 |
| 6.11 | Important Functions used in Network Scripting | 167 |
| 6.12 | Case Study: Converting Decimals to Hexadecimal | 168 |
| 6.13 | The Scope of Variables | 170 |
| 6.13.1 | Global variables | 170 |
| 6.13.2 | Local variables | 170 |
| 6.14 | Default Arguments | 171 |
| 6.15 | Returning Multiple Values | 173 |
| 6.15.1 | Using object | 173 |
| 6.15.2 | Using tuple | 174 |
| 6.15.3 | Using a list | 175 |
| 6.15.4 | Using a dictionary | 175 |
| 6.16 | Oriented Programming (and how it is used in Python) | 176 |
| 6.17 | Characteristics and features of OOP | 176 |
| 6.18 | What Is a Class (in Python)? | 177 |
| 6.18.1 | Making Your Own Classes | 178 |
| 6.19 | Conclusion | 181 |
| 6.20 | Summary | 181 |
| 6.21 Assignment Questions | | 182 |
| Assignment No. 1 | | 182 |
| Assignment No. 2 | | 182 |
| Assignment No. 3 | | 184 |
| Assignment No. 4 | | 185 |
| Chapter 7 Errors and Exceptions in Python | | 186 |
| 7.1 | Objectives | 186 |
| 7.2 | Introduction | 186 |
| 7.3 | What are Exceptions? | 186 |
| 7.4 | Handling Simple Exceptions: | 187 |
| 7.5 | Classes of Exception: | 191 |
| 7.6 | Creating and Raising an Exception Object | 194 |
| 7.7 | Creating custom Exception Classes | 194 |
| 7.8 | Accessing Properties of the Raised Exception | 196 |
| 7.9 | Implementing Complex Error handling | 198 |
| 7.10 | Using traceback if All Else Fails: | 200 |

| 7.11 | Exception chaining and Tracebacks | 203 |
|---|---|---|
| 7.12 | Conclusion | 204 |
| 7.13 | Summary | 205 |
| 7.14 Assignment Questions | | 206 |
| Assignment 1 | | 206 |

## Chapter 8 Well Known Python Libraries ............................................. 209

| 8.1 | Objectives | 209 |
|---|---|---|
| The main objective of this chapter is to: | | 209 |
| 8.2 | Introduction | 209 |
| 8.3 | Installing Libraries in Python Environment | 209 |
| 8.4 | Python Libraries | 209 |
| 8.4.1 | NTPLIB | 210 |
| 8.4.2 | Diesel 3.0.24 | 211 |
| 8.4.3 | Python NMAP | 213 |
| 8.4.4 | Scapy | 215 |
| 8.4.5 | Netifaces | 217 |
| 8.4.6 | netaddr | 220 |
| 8.4.7 | pyOpenSSL | 222 |
| 8.4.8 | Pygeocoder | 225 |
| 8.4.9 | Pyyaml | 227 |
| 8.4.10 | Request | 229 |
| 8.4.11 | Feedparser | 232 |
| 8.4.12 | Paramiko | 235 |
| 8.4.13 | Fabric | 238 |
| 8.4.14 | Supervisor | 240 |
| 8.4.15 | Xmlrpclib | 241 |
| 8.4.16 | Construct | 243 |
| 8.4.17 | Pandas | 245 |
| 8.4.18 | Matplotib | 247 |
| 8.4.19 | SOAPpy | 249 |
| 8.5 | Conclusion | 249 |
| 8.6 | Summary | 249 |
| 8.7 Assignment Questions | | 251 |
| Assignment 1 | | 251 |
| Assignment 2 | | 251 |

## Chapter 9 Practice Programs and Scripts Network Automation ............................... 257

| 9.1 | Objectives: | 257 |
|---|---|---|
| 9.3.1 | Interacting with HTTP Services as a Client | 257 |
| 9.2 | Introduction | 260 |
| 9.3 | Network Automation Scripts and Programs | 260 |
| 9.3.1 | Setting up a Simple HTTP Server | 260 |
| 9.3.2 | Creating a TCP Server and TCP Client | 261 |
| 9.3.3 | Creating a UDP Server and UDP Client | 264 |
| 9.3.4 | Generating a Range of IP Addresses from a CIDR | 264 |
| 9.3.5 | Waiting for a remote network service | 266 |
| 9.3.6 | Finding the IP address for a specific interface on your machine | 267 |
| 9.3.7 | Using the socket function, changing a socket to the blocking/non-blocking mode | 268 |
| 9.3.7.1 | Blocking socket | 268 |
| 9.3.7.2 | Non – blocking socket | 269 |
| 9.3.8 | Ping 15 servers sequentially 192.158.10.1 - 192.168.10.15 | 270 |
| 9.3.9 | Pool the services enabled on a server 192.168.1.5 (Interrupt ) | 272 |
| 9.3.10 | When the service goes down (outage) on a server | 276 |
| 9.4 | More Advanced Network Automation Scripts and Programs | 277 |
| 9.4.1 | Finding whether an interface is up on your machine | 277 |
| 9.4.2 | Enumerating interfaces on your machine | 279 |
| 9.4.3 | ARP Monitoring | 279 |
| a. | Using Scapy to monitor ARP traffic | 279 |
| 9.4.4 | Write a short Firewall Program in Python | 281 |
| 9.4.5 | Sniffing packets on your network | 283 |
| 9.4.6 | Write a Python Script that can work as a packet sniffer | 284 |
| 9.4.7 | Implementing Network Service Involving Sockets | 286 |
| 9.4.8 | Identifying Bouncing Interfaces on a Network Device | 288 |
| 9.4.9 | NetConf Agent Implementation | 288 |
| 9.5 | Ideas for Additional Network Scripts and Programs | 290 |
| 9.5.1 | Authenticating Clients | 290 |
| 9.5.2 | Perform health check on a router | 291 |
| 9.5.3 | ASIC errors on a network device | 294 |
| 9.5.4 | Generate configlets for Juniper routers | 295 |
| 9.5.5 | Collecting Logs from Juniper Devices | 299 |
| 9.5.6 | Reporting errors on Connected Router Interfaces | 300 |
| 9.5.7 | Detecting Configuration changes using SNMPv3 | 304 |
| 9.5.8 | Detecting Man-in-the-middle attack | 304 |

17

| 9.5.9 | Using NetFlow to track utilization | 305 |
| 9.5.10 | Server's Virtualization Parameters | 307 |
| 9.5.11 | Querying OIDs using SNMP | 309 |
| 9.5.12 | Monitor Network using Python | 315 |
| 9.5.13 | Playing with ciscoconfparse Python Library | 316 |
| 9.5.14 | Monitoring windows registry Changes | 316 |
| 9.5.15 | Assignment Questions | 318 |
| | Assignment 1 | 318 |

## Chapter 10 Network Automation and Automation tools .................................................. 319

| 10.1 | Objectives | 319 |
|---|---|---|
| 10.2 | Introduction | 319 |
| 10.3 | What kind of networks can be automated? | 319 |
| 10.3.1 | Network automation categories | 319 |
| 10.4 | Reasons and benefits for network automation | 319 |
| 10.5 | What Makes Automation Of Network A Possibility? | 321 |
| 10.6 | How to automate network management? | 321 |
| 10.7 | Steps to achieve a fully automated network | 322 |
| 10.8 | Using Python and its libraries for network automation | 323 |
| 10.9 | Should you build or buy network automation tools? | 323 |
| 10.10 | Do we need expensive tool to do meaningful automation? | 324 |
| 10.11 | Outstanding automation tools and libraries vendor specific APIs: | 324 |
| 10.11.1 | Ansible | 324 |
| 10.11.2 | Puppet | 324 |
| 10.11.3 | Chef | 325 |
| 10.11.4 | NetConf | 325 |
| 10.11.5 | Salt | 325 |
| 10.11.6 | Git / GitHub / Gitlab | 325 |
| 10.11.7 | Jenkins | 325 |
| 10.11.8 | NETMIKO | 325 |
| 10.11.9 | REST | 326 |
| 10.11.10 | REST | 326 |
| 10.11.1 | SOAP | 326 |
| 10.11.2 | JSON | 327 |
| 10.11.3 | YAML | 327 |
| 10.11.4 | NAPALM | 327 |
| 10.12 | Vendor specific Automation Tools and APIs | 328 |

- 10.12.1 Cisco Prime Infrastructure .................................................................. 328
- 10.12.2 Juniper PyEZ .......................................................................................... 330
- 10.12.3 Cisco CrossWorks for Service Providers ............................................. 330
- 10.12.4 PYCSCO ................................................................................................. 331
- 10.12.5 Cisco pyIOSXR ..................................................................................... 331
- 10.12.6 Arista EOS API eAPI ............................................................................ 331
- 10.13 PYTHON ENVIRONMENTS AND PROJECTS USED FREQUENTLY WITH NETWORK AUTOMATION TOOLS ................................................................. 332
  - 10.13.1 Modules and Packages ...................................................................... 332
  - 10.13.2 Python Modules .................................................................................. 332
  - 10.13.3 Python Packages ................................................................................ 332
  - 10.13.4 Pip ....................................................................................................... 332
  - 10.13.5 Virtualenv ........................................................................................... 333
  - 10.13.6 Anaconda ............................................................................................ 333
- 10.14 Other Tools Used to Support Network Automation ................................. 333
  - 10.14.1 CFEngine ............................................................................................ 333
  - 10.14.2 Prometheus ......................................................................................... 333
  - 10.14.3 Vagrant ............................................................................................... 335
  - 10.14.4 Rancher ............................................................................................... 335
  - 10.14.5 Solar Winds ........................................................................................ 335
- 10.15 Conclusion .................................................................................................... 336
- 10.16 Summary ....................................................................................................... 337
- 10.17 Assignment Questions ................................................................................. 338
  - Assignment 1 ...................................................................................................... 338
  - Assignment 2 ...................................................................................................... 338

## Appendix 1: Online Courses and Books in Python ......................................... 339
- A. Online Courses Teaching General Python Programming Scripting ......... 339
- B. Network Automation Courses using Python .............................................. 340
- C. General Python Learning Books ................................................................ 340
- D. Books on Network Automation .................................................................. 341

## Appendix 2: Selected Bibliography ................................................................... 342
- Chapter 1 ............................................................................................................. 342
- Chapter 2 ............................................................................................................. 343
- Chapter 3 ............................................................................................................. 344
- Chapter 4 ............................................................................................................. 344
- Chapter 5 ............................................................................................................. 344
- Chapter 6 ............................................................................................................. 344

Chapter 7 ........................................................................................................................... 345
Chapter 8 ........................................................................................................................... 345
Chapter 9 ........................................................................................................................... 346
Chapter 10 ......................................................................................................................... 347

# List of Figures

Figure 1-1 Standard Python IDE ........................................................................................... 30
Figure 1-2 PyCharm IDE ...................................................................................................... 32
Figure 1-3 Wing IDE ............................................................................................................ 33
Figure 1-4 PyDev ................................................................................................................. 33
Figure 1-5 PyScriptter ........................................................................................................... 34
Figure 1-6: Eric Python IDE ................................................................................................. 34
Figure 1-7 repl.it IDE ............................................................................................................ 35
Figure 1-8 Pyton Anywhere ................................................................................................. 36
Figure 1-9 code skulptor ....................................................................................................... 36
Figure 1-10 IDEONE IDE .................................................................................................... 37
Figure 2-1 Multiplication code in Python ............................................................................. 41
Figure 2-2 Display of the above code in CMD ..................................................................... 41
Figure 2-3 Script for multiple assignments ........................................................................... 41
Figure 2-4 Display of script in CMD .................................................................................... 42
Figure 2-5 Demonstrating numbers in Python ...................................................................... 42
Figure 3-1 Defining Collections ........................................................................................... 65
Figure 3-2 Diagram presenting mapping types .................................................................... 66
Figure 4-1 Flowchart symbols .............................................................................................. 120
Figure 4-2 Symbol of "Start" ................................................................................................ 121
Figure 4-3 Symbol for "Process" .......................................................................................... 121
Figure 4-4 Symbol for "Decision" ........................................................................................ 121
Figure 4-5 Flow chart ............................................................................................................ 122
Figure 4-6 Flow chart ............................................................................................................ 122
Figure 4-7 General representation of if statement ................................................................ 123
Figure 4-8 General representation of if then else statement ................................................. 123
Figure 4-9 Code snippet ........................................................................................................ 125
Figure 4-10 working code snippet ........................................................................................ 126
Figure 4-11 Code demonstration of if-else statement ........................................................... 126
Figure 4-12 Code snippet for demonstrating common errors in selection statement ........... 127
Figure 4-13 Running code presenting typing errors ............................................................. 128
Figure 4-14 Screenshot of the running program ................................................................... 130
Figure 4-15 Code snippet displaying random number game ................................................ 130
Figure 6-1 Code demonstration of creating a function ......................................................... 154
Figure 6-23 output in python ................................................................................................ 159
Figure 6-35 output in python ................................................................................................ 160
Figure 6-49 output in python ................................................................................................ 161
Figure 6-5 Code snippet demonstrating my-function() ........................................................ 162
Figure 7-15 Code snippet demonstrating exception handling .............................................. 190
Figure 7-2 Code snippet of the program stated above .......................................................... 199
Figure 7-3 Code snippet ........................................................................................................ 199
Figure 8-1 Installing NTP Library ........................................................................................ 210
Figure 8-2 Outcome of the script .......................................................................................... 210
Figure 8-3 Output of the code ............................................................................................... 210
Figure 8-4 Code snippet to show the use of PyGeocode in a script ..................................... 226

Figure 8-5 Installing Construct Python Library ................................................................. 243
Figure 8-66 Code for Construct Library .......................................................................... 245
Figure 9-1 Output of interacting with HTTP Services as a client ..................................... 257
Figure 9-2 Output of interaction with rest API ................................................................. 258
Figure 9-3 Output to interact with rest API ...................................................................... 259
Figure 9-4 Output of testing weather ............................................................................... 260
Figure 9-5 Output of setting up a simple HTTP server .................................................... 261
Figure 9-6 Representation of all files in a drive ............................................................... 261
Figure 9-7 Output of client code ...................................................................................... 263
Figure 9-8 Output of creating a UDP server and UDP client .......................................... 264
Figure 9-9 Output of creating a UDP client ..................................................................... 264
Figure 9-10 Code of generating a range of IP addresses from a CIDR ......................... 265
Figure 9-11 Output of the code stated above ................................................................. 265
Figure 9-12 Output of the code to generate IP's ............................................................. 266
Figure 9-13 Output of non-blocking client ....................................................................... 270
Figure 9-14 Output of the code after pinging the service ............................................... 272
Figure 10-1 Impacts of Automation on the Business ...................................................... 321
Figure 10-2 Pictorial presentation .................................................................................... 322
Figure 10-3 Code snippet ................................................................................................ 326
Figure 10-4 Code snippet ................................................................................................ 327
Figure 10-5 Cisco Prime Infrastructure ........................................................................... 328
Figure 10-6 Code snippet ................................................................................................ 331
Figure 10-7 Code snippet of uploading Pip package ..................................................... 332
Figure 10-8 Architecture of Prometheus server .............................................................. 334

# List Of Tables

Table 1 Logical Operators .................................................................................. 47
Table 2 Logical Operators .................................................................................. 48
Table 3 Comparison of List, Sets, Dictionary and Tuple.................................... 67
Table 4 Positions of Item numbers ..................................................................... 72
Table 5 Command with results ........................................................................... 72
Table 6 More list Operations .............................................................................. 77
Table 7 Operators with their descriptions .......................................................... 80
Table 8 String Functions..................................................................................... 91
Table 9 Escape Sequences .................................................................................. 93
Table 10 String Methods..................................................................................... 94
Table 11 Conversion Types ................................................................................ 95
Table 12 String Conversion Types...................................................................... 96
Table 13 Functions and their demonstration .................................................... 107
Table 14 Boolean Comparison operators.......................................................... 115
Table 15 Logical Operators .............................................................................. 117
Table 16 Logical Operators .............................................................................. 128
Table 17 Operators and their description ......................................................... 133
Table 18 Comparison table of Looping structures ........................................... 146
Table 19 Steps and their description ................................................................ 322
Table 20 Codes and their functions.................................................................. 327

# Chapter 1 : Introduction to Network Automation

## 1.1 Objectives

There is a dramatical change in the networking industry which is driving the networking professionals and organizations to utilize the concepts and idea of network programmability and automation. To cater the need of organizational competitiveness, it is high time for networking professionals to learn the new scripting languages and protocols as new service delivery models require new skillsets. Both businesses and networking professionals need to be more agile and flexible to strive in this new network automation world. This chapter discusses and explains both the need and demand of networking professionals to be skilful in the domain of network automation by helping them analyse why they should learn Python scripting.

## 1.2 Introduction

Python is a modern and a powerful computer programming language that was developed by Guido van Rossum (Rivers & Koedinger, 2017). Python is a programming language that resembles Java. The language is, however, cleaner and easier to read than Java. Python has become a scripting language for choice for Network Engineering tasks. In the following sections, we will discuss and elaborate why Network Engineers need to learn Python, although, chances are, if you are reading this you are already motivated to learn Python language and discuss the ecosystem of Python. The below narrative will help solidify your thinking and give you tools to get started on the journey to learning Python Scripting for Network Engineers

## 1.3 Why Python Scripting is a MUST learn Network Engineer?

This is a beginner level book to learn Python Scripting and perfect for those Network Engineers who have too little experience with respect to programming and scripting. Those Network Engineers can get most benefit out of this discussion who are confused concerning to learning a programming skill as part of their network engineering career. Network engineers who are opting for career path related to Data Center, Security, Voice, or Wireless will also find this book useful as Network Automation has sweeping impact in every Networking Engineering domain.

Managing networks seems antiquated. Some are the problems that many of us have faced over the years:

- Not opening that 500-entry access-list in dread that it may cause some unanticipated and network shattering problems.
- Figuring out the undocumented 1000-line running configuration
- One of the most unfulfilled promises made by my networking vendor(s) was about diverse product families sold to me. It was claimed that they will eventually have a common configuration and management interfaces (APIs). Due to lack of good APIs, management GUI exposed half of what my hardware was able to do.
- And finally, the slow performance as device management GUIs must connect via SSH/Telnet as well as use CLI parsing or screen scraping as compensation of the lack of common management APIs.

We, as network engineers, are experienced in designing customer networks, network scalability, learning about product capabilities, operations, and network management. Among all, network operations, is the one aspect of networking that takes a lot of time concerning to maintenance, escalations, supporting P1 cases and performing complex troubleshooting. With Network Automation it is now possible to simplify these time consuming tasks.

However, many of the Network Engineers are of the perception that programming is difficult and unexciting. They also recall getting bored while programming because of your past experience in programming. Let us clear one thing. The new modern languages are powerful, comparatively simple to learn, and understand and it is quite easy to write code or understand already written code. If you understand OSPF or BGP, then you can easily comprehend Python Scripting

In recent times, the novel concepts in the market are about Software Defined Networking, Network Overlays, and Network Virtualization. Software Defined Networking and Network Virtualization offers a comprehensive set of tools to support customers for network automation, simplicity of management and orchestration. All of these require knowledge of Scripting.

Learning a modern programming language is also efficient as it easy to learn a programming language instead of learning several different CLIs. In case of Cisco, Checkpoint, Palo Alto, Juniper, Fortinet, you are required to deploy each of these along with several switches and routers. In these scenarios, scripting language is more useful and efficient to serve the purpose of network deployment with several vendors.

At the moment, in the networking industry, almost each and everything is altering swiftly. Together with this, every new networking project comprise of several devices for configuration or automation. In this case, it becomes difficult to set these up box by box and scripting serves the purpose.

Network engineers have come to an agreement that we need to learn continuously to evolve our understanding, skills and jobs. With this mindset, it is hard for deliberately overlook a new way to manage and configure networks i.e. via scripting. Be adaptable as, for network engineers, adaptability is synonymous to survival.

## 1.4 Give Specific Examples where Python Scripting is being used for Network Automation

As python scripting is a handy tool for network automation, typical manual tasks that can be automated are:

- Configuring switches
- Configuring routers
- Configuration changes
- Configuration management
- Troubleshooting

We need automation in networking to create a more efficient networking environment, improved network uptime and prevent mistakes. Network Automation is helping to solve:

- Mistakes due to human error in configuring the devices
- Repetitive tasks such as changing device logging credentials or time-based ACLs
- Allows to reproduce and dispose of logs which may cause devices to crash
- Deliver bug free code on time

## 1.5 Network automation tools: Should you build or buy?

Network Engineers are always in a dilemma if they should create Network Automation tools or if they should purchase an automation solution from a well-known networking vendors.

In a small enterprise environment with limited time and human resources, tasks such as updating port settings, modifying access control lists, and altering administrative passwords are time consuming for network engineers. It is well settled that a set of python scripts can be used to automate such recurrent network and systems tasks hence building customized tools helps controlling the entire network automation process which is designed according to the needs of the enterprise.

For a small organization, building network automation tool is better as network mostly needs a bit of addition, deletion or alteration of some commands.

On contrary, a large organization should purchase network automation tool for several reasons. Primarily, script designed by a network engineer may be safe until there is no organizational change, if there are big organization change, a new network engineer may need take a lot of time to understand a "person-specific" script therefore buying "personalized" solution is a wiser option.

It should be noted that often network automation tools which are purchased can become very expensive and complicated when a new networking vendor or a new hardware model is used.

## 1.6 Automation Tools and Languages

Python is the main topic of this book which can be used for network automation on its own, but it's frequently used with other network automation software tools for automating network monitoring, configurations and maintenance activities. Some of such tools are Ansible, Puppet, Chef, SatlStack, Github-Git, and Jenkins which are discussed below, briefly.

Ansible is an open source software that helps to automate software configuration, management and application deployment. It can be used to configure routers, switches and various types of servers.

Similarly, another open source software, Puppet, is a good tool for configuration management. It runs on Microsoft Windows, numerous Unix-like systems, and have its own declarative language too for system configuration description.

Chef is another tool for configuration management, written in Ruby and Erlang. Its build on a DevOps model and can help in building reliable scalable systems.

A Python-based open source configuration management software, SatlStack, serves as a remote execution engine. As it uses the "Infrastructure as Code" methodology for deployment and cloud management, it is a competitive tool and can be used in replacement of Puppet, Ansible, and Chef.

GitHub is a sort of web-based hosting service used for version control by means of Git as Git is a version-control system to track modifications in computer files. Git also coordinates activities of multiple people who work on same files.

Another open source automation software, Jenkins, can also be used for network automation and can automate the non-human fragment. Thus, it helps for continuous development and continuous integration. It is written in Java.

## 1.7 Proprietary Automation Tools

Several networking gear providers have developed automation tools geared specifically to automate networks based on their hardware and software such as Cisco, Arista and Juniper. There are other well-known Network Solution providers who have developed tools to simplify network automation such as SolarWinds. We will discuss some of these tools in brief here.

### 1.7.1 Cisco Prime Infrastructure

One of such tool is Cisco Prime Infrastructure. It helps administrating both wireless and wired networks. It provides "One Management," assurance from the branch to the data center. Due to single point of control, both networking and computation becomes easy. Along with this, it consolidates products, manages the network for mobile cooperation, simplifies intelligent WAN administration, and extends administration to the Data Center. Cisco Prime Infrastructure also offers Device Packs and Technology Packs. Device Packs provides ongoing support of new Cisco devices along with software releases. It helps in eradicating gaps regarding management operations, particularly concerning to troubleshooting and service availability. On the other hand, Technology Packs provides new features regarding releases.

### 1.7.2 Cisco Crosswork for Service Providers

Cisco Crossworks is helpful in transforming mass scale network operations. It helps to plan, implement, and operate, the process along with monitoring and optimization services for network automation. Along with this, it helps in gaining the mass awareness and pre-emptive control for data driven network automation. Mass awareness helps gathering information from every single corner of network in real time while augmented intelligence helps to constantly evaluate the gathered data. In this way, it helps finding the red flags and soon-to-be red flags which keeps the network in a stable state without any active alerts. Another feature of Cisco CrossWorks Proactive control makes networks more efficient and secure, helps staying ahead of things.

### 1.7.3 SolarWinds

SolarWinds Network Configuration Manager enables clients to achieve automated change management that form the crux of network automation. Its specification includes configuration, multi-vendor support, notifications for events both pre-defined and customizable events, and automation to ease scripting by abating monotonous tasks. Multi-vendor support eases the working procedure with a range of devices from multiple providers. SolarWinds performs network automation in the following ways. Firstly, automated change management save time as it uses change management for standardized configuration changes and does so in minutes. Secondly, automated change tracking advance reliability by means of configuration monitoring. In this way, it detects and reverse any sort of unwanted changes in configuration. Thirdly, automated compliance auditing upholds policy compliance by continuous configuration auditing. Lastly, automated configuration backups abates device downtime using automating configuration backups.

### 1.7.4 WeConfig

Another simple yet powerful tool, WeConfig, provides customization, scripting, graphical interface, and multiple options for settings. It is quite a lightweight tool; however, have limited compatibility. It adjusts network address assignments, monitors failures and provides feedback. Tough, its compatibility is limited, it works well in apposite environment.

## 1.8 What is Scripting?

Any programming language that supports a script is known as scripting language. It helps programmers in order to write programs for a distinct environment to automate the execution of a number of tasks which could otherwise be executed manually by a human operator, one-by-one. Thus, scripting is baseline of network automation.

Python which is the subject of this book is a high-level programming language which was first released in 1991 and still competing fairly because of its efficient design philosophy. It is a general-purpose programming language which underscores code readability by means of significant whitespace.

Some popular ad useful scripting languages are JavaScript, PHP, Perl, Ruby, Tcl, Lua. Among these, Lua is one of the most powerful, swift, and light-weight scripting languages.

## 1.9 What is the difference between Perl vs. Python?

Python and Perl are both frequently referred to as "scripting languages." Both can be used for network automation and network programming, but Perl is a difficult code to run. Perl is increasingly being given up by novice programmers in favor of Python and here is why:

Python is more user friendly and it is much easier to write and understand code in it

1. **Clarity:** Python, by design, forces to write clean code. Perl scripts are often messy (it takes me a while to understand my own scripts.) Resulting in a Python is a much more readable code.
2. **Flexibility:** Python is better than Perl. Python is light on syntax. Python's syntax is cleaner; its object-oriented type system is more modern and consistent, and its libraries are more consistent.
3. **Indentation:** It is important in the Python. Unlike other programming languages, Python uses indentation to identify blocks of code. This in turn is helpful in organizing the code.
4. **Usability:** Python can be used for writing reusable code. Object Oriented in Perl is a little odd and find Python to be more consistent. For example, it is easier to create modules in Python. You can borrow publicly available code that has already been developed and simply import it into your program. Because Perl has been around for much longer than Python, there are several modules available for you to use. Perl, therefore, is extremely powerful and versatile. Python may be a better choice for the novice programmer who wants to accomplish simple tasks. Python commands and keywords are intuitively related to their functions, which makes the language easy to learn
5. **User community:** Python is more popular and has a larger active user community. Appeal to popularity is a fallacy, but you can't just dismiss mindshare and 3rd party support either.

Here are some other few key points to bear in mind when deciding whether to use Perl or Python.

1. Python code is easy to use for beginners due to its intuitive design.
2. Python is unlike other programming languages uses indentation to identify blocks of code.
3. Perl is a much older language with a wider range of modules available.

## 1.10 Battle of Python Versions

What's the difference between Python 2 and Python 3? Or more specifically Python 2.7 and Python 3.3.

One should start with Python 2 and more specifically Python version 2.7 if they are learning today, in 2019. We do believe it is wise to start off with 2.7 as a beginner for the main reason that there is far more documentation and libraries to help you along the way. However, do note that Python 3.3 is better than Python 2.7, but it is not ready yet for mass scale and network automation purposes.

In this course, all of the programs have been written and tested with Python 2.7 having said that many of the programs will work with Python 3.3 as well.

The main advantage of 3.x is that it is still in the active development stage, so all the new features will be implemented in that rather than being added to 2.x. The other thing you may want to consider is that it is the common Python of the future, so looking a couple of years down the line, this will be the mature branch that people go to.

Python 3 is a nicer and more consistent language, but there is very limited third-party module support for it. This is likely to be true for at least a couple of years more. So, all major frameworks still run on Python 2, and will continue to do so for a significant time. Therefore, if you learn Python today, you should learn Python 2, because that is the version you are going to end up actually using.

## 1.11 Important Differences between Python 2 and Python 3

Our focus in this book remains on Python 2.7 as most of the network libraries are well developed and well tested in Python 2.7. Python 3 which is the newer version of Python language has some significant differences and improvement over Python 2. We will discuss some of these differences here:

**Print:** In Python 2, "print" is a statement instead of a function hence you are not required to wrap the text in parentheses that you intend to print; though, if you want so, you can. Usually, several other actions use functions for which arguments need to be placed inside parentheses; it can be puzzling and can lead to unanticipated results as if you want to print, you can place parentheses around a list of items separated by comma. On the other hand, Python 3, unequivocally, considers "print" as a function; it means you need to pass the items, required to be printed, in parentheses. Not doing it in the standard way will lead you to a syntax error. This change may irritate Python 2 programmers, nevertheless, it helps to prevent errors.

**Integer Division:** The numbers that are typed without any digits after the decimal point, Python 2 treats these as integers. It may lead to some unanticipated results during division. For instance, typing an expression 5 / 2, in Python 2 code, will give a result of 2 instead of 2.5. The reason is that Python 2 undertakes that the result required by you is to be an integer, so it rounds off the resulted number to the nearest whole number. To get 1.5 as result, you need to write 5.0 / 2.0 to convey Python that you need a floating number. Python 3 assesses 5 / 2 as 2.5 by default which is a bit more natural for new programmers.

**List Comprehension Loop Variables:** In early versions of Python, to give the variable same name as a global variable, iterated over in a list comprehension, could alter the value of the global variable which is unwanted. In Python 3, this irksome bug has been fixed. Now, a variable name, used already for the control variable in list comprehension, can be used again without upsetting about it as, in the rest of your code, it will not leak out or mess with the values of the variables.

**Unicode Strings:** In Python 3, strings are stored as Unicode by default. However, in Python 2, you are needed to mark a string with a "u" in order to store it as Unicode. These strings are more useful than ASCII strings, which are the Python 2 default. This is because Unicode strings can store letters from foreign languages, emoji, the standard Roman letters as well as numerals. If you want to be certain that your Python 3 code is compatible with Python 2 or not, you can label Unicode strings with a "u."

**Raising Exceptions: In** Python 3, different syntax is needed to raise exceptions. In case, if you want to deliver an error message to the user, the syntax should be:

*raise IOError("your error message")*

This syntax also works well in Python 2. However, the following code will only work in Python 2:

*raise IOError, "your error message"*

There are several other cases of minor dissimilarities in syntax between Python 2 and Python 3. You can use a cheat sheet of key syntax differences that is accessible from Python-Future to aid you in writing code having compatibility with both versions of Python. There are some other significant differences such as how the two versions of Python handle strings. Both Python 2.7 and Python 3.3 executes at almost same speed, however, new language is considered much faster according to some benchmarks measure.

## 1.12 Python IDE

Python programming can be done from the command line, but an IDE (Integrated development environment) makes writing scripts much easier. With several options out there, which one should you use? To help you decide, we have tested several Python editors which all are freely available.

Python has been more of a Linux programming language however the last few years have seen its increasing use on Windows, so many of these five IDE are cross-platform.

Python IDE is the standard Python development environment. Its name is an acronym of "Integrated Development Environment." It works well on both Unix and Windows platforms.

It has a Python shell window, which gives you access to the Python interactive mode. It also has a file editor that lets you create and edit existing Python source files.

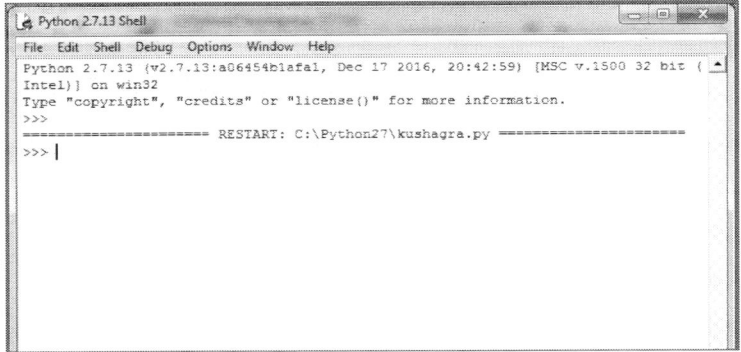

Figure 1-1 Standard Python IDE

During the following discussion of IDE's features, its best to start IDE and try to replicate these simple codes.

Python code can be directly typed into this shell, at the '>>>' prompt. Whenever a complete code fragment is entered, it will be executed. For instance, typing:

>>> print "hello world"

And pressing Enter will cause the following to be displayed:

hello world

IDE can also be used as a calculator:

>>> 4+4
8

Addition, subtraction, and multiplication operators are built into the Python language. This means these operators can be used right away. If you want to use a square root in your calculation, you need to import the math module. Do not worry about what it means right now; we will cover this later during the course. Below is an example of square root calculation:

>>> import math
>>> math.sqrt(16)
4.0

Math module allows you to do several useful operations:

>>> import math
>>> math.pow(3, 2)
9.0
>>> math.cos( 0 )
1.0

## 1.13  Complete IDE

To reduce the complexity and time-consumption of the work done by a developer, a lot of sophisticated Python tools are available. As these tools make the job speedier a lot of developers turn to integrated development environments (IDEs). IDEs help in managing workflows, a single dashboard to access a suite of development tools and decrease the chances to make errors. If a cross-platform and complete IDE is needed, following IDE are well established in industry and can be readily used

1. PyCharm (Community Edition)
2. WingIDE
3. PyDev
4. PyScripter
5. Eric Python IDE

There are of course other IDEs available too such as Microsoft Visual Studio. My IDE of choice is PyCharm. It is very good already and because its developers keep improving it, I have no doubt PyCharm is going to be even better in the future. It's a stable platform.

Both PyCharm and WingIDE are well-priced and have personal and academic licenses, plus free licenses for classroom use and open source developers. PyDev is free and LiClipse license is of $50, which is a no-brainer if you need to work with Eclipse.

You can't go wrong with WingIDE as well. It has outstanding features and a remarkable debugger. WingIDE developers know that it needs some UI improvement and keep launching new versions.

I have a lot of respect for PyDev's developer as well. It gives you the power of the Eclipse editor plus code folding. The only disadvantage is that Eclipse can be a bit of a memory hog. But if you're used to it, PyDev is a no brainer.

We will discuss each of these IDE's in more detail now

### 1.13.1 PyCharm

This is the community free version of the JetBrains IDE. JetBrains is well known for Resharper and other development tools, and there's a professional version of PyCharm, as well. PyCharm feels a little like Eclipse. It's very slick with the usual JetBrains attention to detail. Though it's nowhere near as full-featured as the commercial version, the free IDE includes refactoring, code inspection, integration with Git, Mercurial, CVS, Subversion, GitHub, and of course debugging. It's slick and polished.

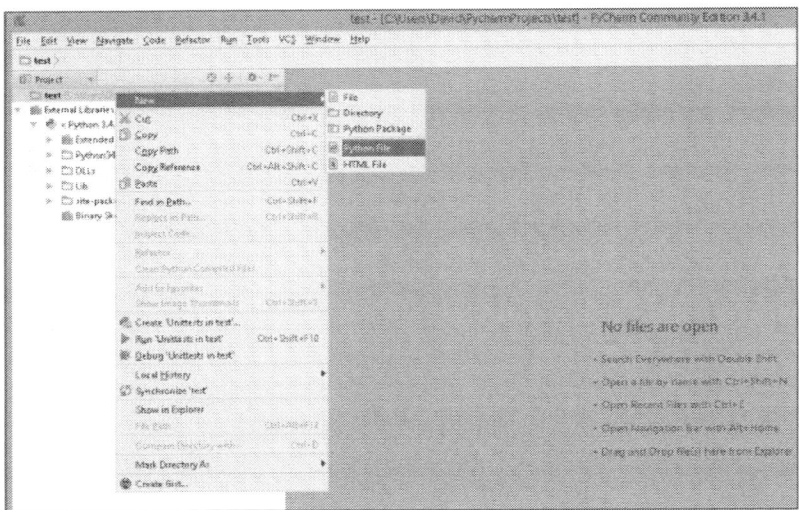

Figure 1-2 PyCharm IDE

### 1.13.2 WingIDE

WingIDE is a solid IDE from Wingware that has been in development since 1999. It has many advanced features such as a first-rate debugger, code intelligence, and it can be extended in Python.

WingIDE's debugger is super powerful and allows you to set breakpoints, step through code, inspect data, debug remotely, and debug Django templates. It has support for matplotlib where the plots are updated automatically.

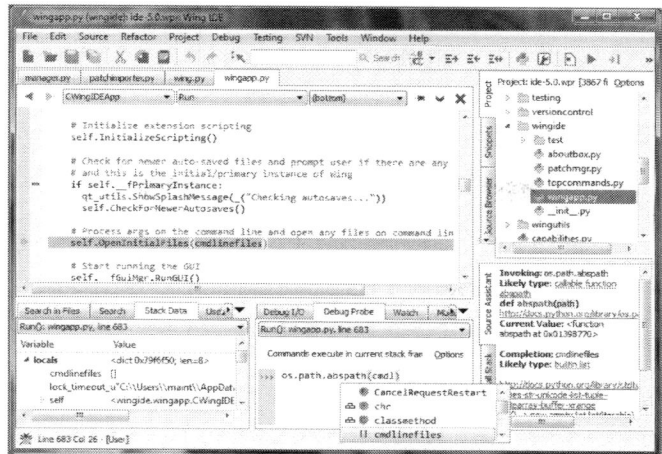

Figure 1-3 Wing IDE

### 1.13.3 PyDev

PyDev supports Python, Jython and IronPython (the .NET Python). It gives you the power of the Eclipse editor plus code folding, matching brackets and many more features. Most important is its debugging tools—you get expression watch, breakpoints and lots more. Plugins allow you to extend the platform with Myllyn for task management and Subclipse for subversion. The only con is that Eclipse can be a bit of a memory hog. But if you're used to it, PyDev is a no brainer.

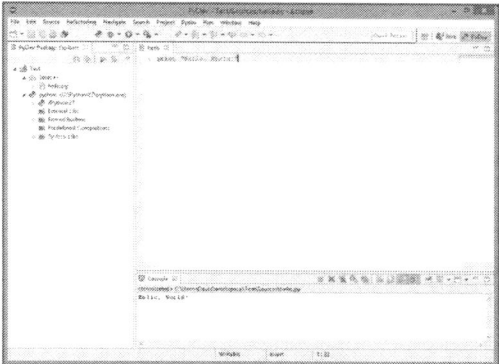

Figure 1-4 PyDev

### 1.13.4 PyScripter

Developed by Kiriakos Vlahos, PyScripter is the only package here that's restricted to Windows (it's written in Delphi). It's a nice, snappy IDE that supports projects, editing files and debugging. It's not as complicated or powerful as Eric (see below), but if you're just starting to learn Python on Windows you may find it a lot less intimidating and a great way to start. By default, it picks up the Python 2.7 installation (it needs Python installed first), and it's easy enough to switch paths to Python 3.4.

33

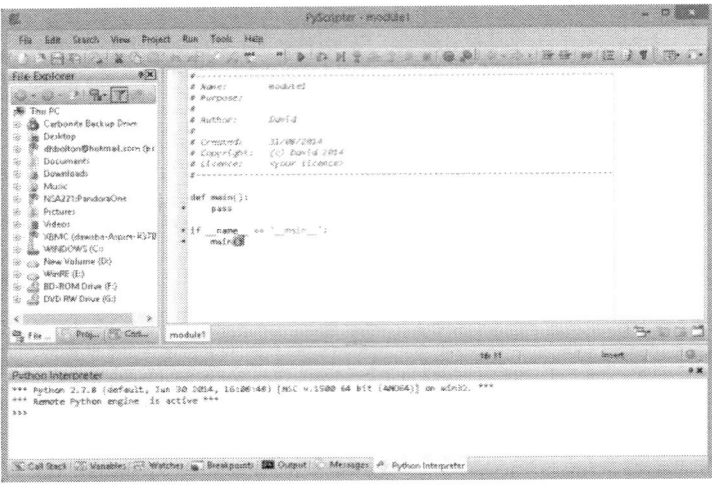

Figure 1-5 PyScriptter

## 1.13.5 Eric Python IDE

Eric—named for the Monty Python team member Eric Idle—is a cross platform IDE for Python and Ruby. It comes in two flavours: Eric 4 for Python 2.x and Eric 5 for Python 3. Before you can run it, you need to install PyQt, which is a quick 30 MB download. After that, the installer builds and installs Eric for you. My first impression is that it gives Visual Studio and Eclipse quite a challenge. Because of editing and debugging capabilities, it has project management, plugin support. Over all, it is a nice Python shell and lots more.

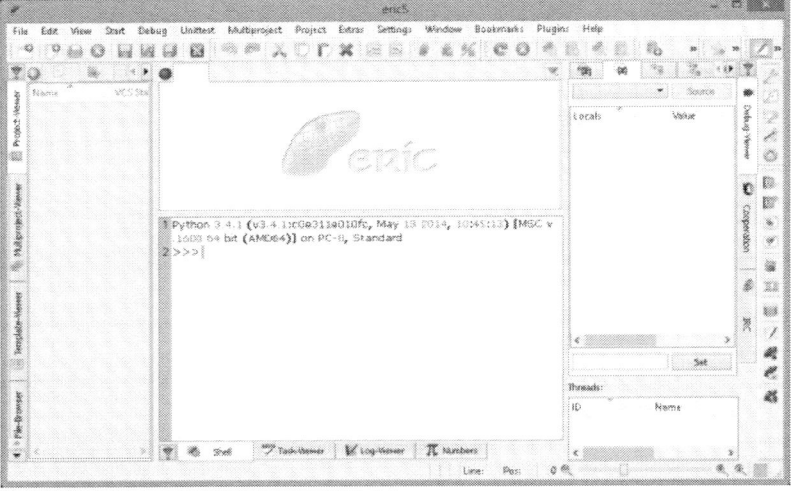

Figure 1-6: Eric Python IDE

## 1.14 Online python IDE

In some cases, it might be a good idea to use online Python IDE. We have tried only a couple as its preferred to use python installed on your own local system for larger and complex project.

Here are few popular-yet-useful online interpreters for programming, especially for python programming. Some of these are not full blown IDE, but python shells.

### 1.14.1 repl.it

This online IDE is by far the best, without a doubt. It is quite easy to use it as it is simple, saves and runs your code online as well as has a better command prompt interface to allow the programmer to interact with the code from a terminal. In addition, it also supports Python 2.7, Python 3 and several other languages. I urge ever programmer to check it out.

The URL to access repl.it is *URL: https://repl.it/languages/python3*

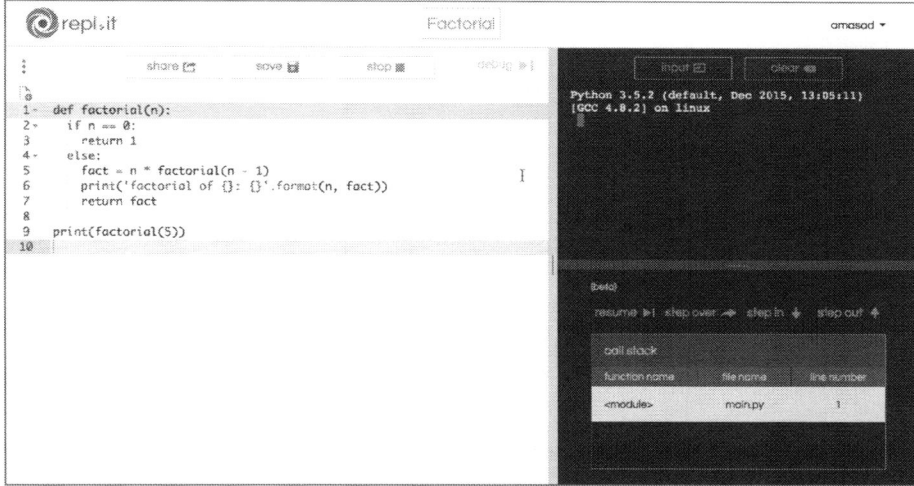

Figure 1-7 repl.it IDE

### 1.14.2 Python Anywhere

Although it is not an IDE, nevertheless it is based upon online Python environment for both development and execution. It offers the following feature :

- An editor to highlight syntax with built-in pyflakes syntax and error checking
- You can use Python 2 or 3, zsh, Bash, bpython, ipython in a console environment. I addition, source control tools like git, mercurial/hg, vim or emacs can also be used in a console environment
- A browsable online files system
- A system to plan and arrange recurring tasks
- A complete web app hosting platform to build a website using django, web2py, flask or python/wsgi framework. Python host it for clients to manage their load and for scaling etc.

All the above mentioned stuff is incorporated in a free plan. If more power or advanced hosting material is needed, then payment is needed. Python Anywhere possesses great support by developers.

The URL to access Python Anywhere is http://www.PythonAnywhere.com.

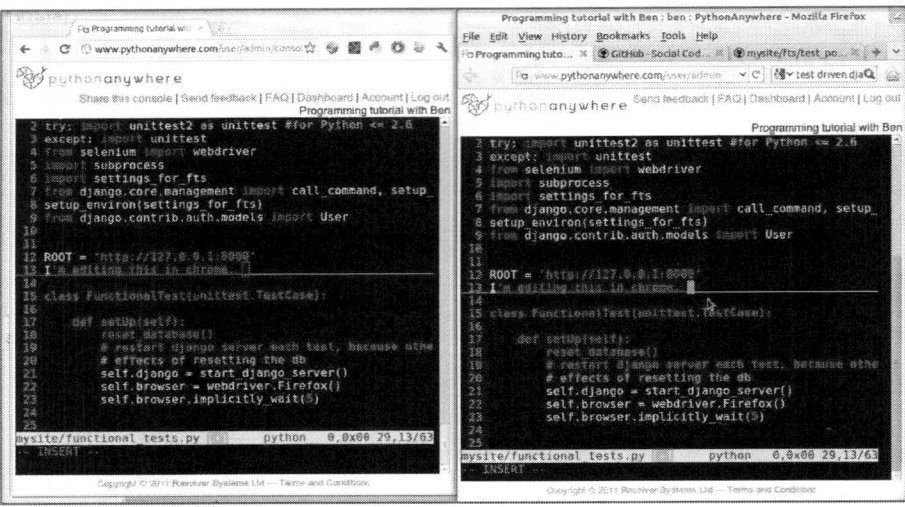

Figure 1-8 Pyton Anywhere

### 1.14.3 CodeSkulptor

Developed by Professor Scott Rixner at Rice University, this is a browser-based IDE. I found CodeSkulptor great. Especially for code testing. It's simple, well-documented, no need for a sign-up, and straight to the point. I've included it because it's how I learned Python online and you never forget your first time. It's for Python 2.6. The IDE is a Web page with code on the left and output messages on the right. Just click the run button (top left) and it either picks up your mistakes or runs it.

Figure 1-9 CodeSkulptor

36

## 1.14.4 IDEONE

IDEONE is another great option. It is an online compiler and debugger that allows programmers to compile source code as well as execute it online. You can execute the source code in more than 60 programming languages. All you need to do is choose a programming language, then enter the source code. You can also enter optional input data.

The URL to access IDEONE is www.www.ideone.com

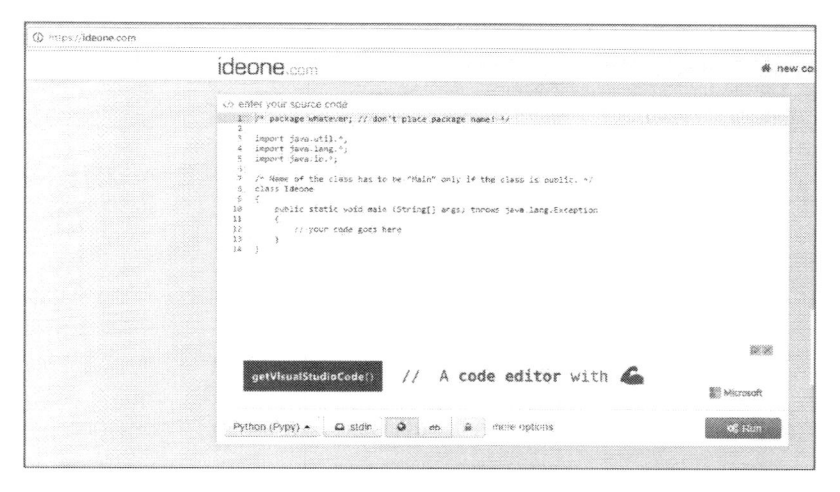

Figure 1-9 IDEONE IDE

## 1.14.5 Other online IDEs/Interpreters for python programming

Several online IDEs/Interpreters for python programming are listed below for completeness; we have not tested these IDEs. Many of these online interpreters support both python 2.x and python 3.x, separately.

- codeacademy
- codingground by tutorial-point
- Codepad
- ideone
- Skulpt
- PythonTutor
- Python Interpreter by holycross
- learnpython
- SourceLair
- TryPython
- Python Cloud IDE
- techmums Python Interpreter
- Rextester
- CodeEnvy
- CodeLinster
- Interactive python shell by Google App Engine
- PythonAnywhere

## 1.15 Conclusion

It can be concluded that it is high time to learn Python as a language to stay ahead of competition in the field of network automation. If network engineers were confused whether they should learn Python or not, I hope, now, they have clear idea why Python is key to network automation and how it can better serve the purpose of automation easily because of the availability of IDEs. This book introduces the Programming concepts with special focus on Python.

## 1.16 Summary

This chapter gets network professionals familiarized with the need of network automation together with the importance of Python in this context. It also introducing the Python as a scripting language.

Chapter discusses Python IDEs and Network Automation Software which share the burden of a network professional to let him learn Python quickly and help him work in swift environment. These IDEs are used to compile the Python scripts and provide insight of the Network Libraries and tools that are essential to learn Python.

Network Automation Software discussed are Ansible, Puppet, Chef, SatlStack, Github-Git, and Jenkins which are a must to survive in the quickly changed networking world.

Differences between Python 2 and Python 3 are also discussed briefly to give an overview. It is encouraged to use Python 2.7 for Network Automation.

## 1.17 Assignment Questions

## Assignment . 1

- **1.1.** What is Network Automation?
- **1.2.** What is Scripting?
- **1.3.** What are the different Python IDE's?
- **1.4.** What are the differences between List and Tuple?
- **1.5.** What are the tools used for network automation?
- **1.6.** Give some examples where python scripting can be used for network automation?
- **1.7.** What is the difference between Python 2 and Python 3?
- **1.8.** What are classes, methods and constructors?
- **1.9.** Give some of differences between Perl and Python?
- **1.10.** Describe some of the network automation software ?

# Chapter 2
# Elements of Programming

## 2.1 Objectives

The main objective of this chapter is to discuss:

- Variables and how variables are assigned different values
- Python numbers, named constants, numeric data types and operations on these data types as well as several mathematical operators.
- Discusses lists, sets, tuples and dictionaries in Python programming language.

## 2.2 Introduction

This chapter focuses on the elements of the Python programming language that are needed to write a program or a script. Python has many elements that facilitate the programming operations. Python has different data types, sets, strings, lists and dictionaries that are important elements in the programming activities of programmers (Dolomanov, et al, 2009). Python programming uses a number of these elements to effectively implement programs useful in several fields and applications. Lists store sequence of objects in an order and iterate over the list. Lists are mutable, unlike dictionaries which are not mutable. The major discussion of this chapter will be focused on the variables, constants, strings, lists, sets, tuples and dictionaries in Python.

Variables in Python mainly refer to the storage location. These variables can be assigned one or more values. Python also has several data types including numeric data types and named constants. There are also a set of characters called strings that are contained in Python.

Lists in Python are sequences of ordered elements that are mutable. Sets, on the other hand, are Python collection of unordered elements that are immutable. Tuples are also Python elements that describe immutable objects but uses parenthesis. The main focus of this chapter is on these elements and how they are applied in Python programming and simple program codes to demonstrate how they work.

## 2.3 Writing a simple Program in Python

### 2.3.1   Python Variables

A variable is a storage location in a computer memory associated with a symbolic name and a value (Bergstra, et al, 2011). In the Python language, there is no specific command that is used to declare a variable. A variable in Python is only declared when it is first assigned a value. A variable can have a short name or a descriptive name. The main rules for naming variables in Python include;

A variable name can only start with underscore character or a letter

A variable name cannot begin with a number

Variable names are case-sensitive

### 2.3.2 Assigning Values to Variables

The code below creates a variable name "a" and assigns it an integer 5. The program also creates a variable name "b" and assigns it a character name "John". The program finally prints the variables "a" and "b".

**Sample code:**

```
1   a = 5
2   b = "John"
3   print(a)
4   print(b)
5
```

Figure 2-1 Multiplication code in Python

```
C:\Users\btaze\AppData\Local\Programs\Python\Python37\python.exe
5
John

Process finished with exit code 0
```

Figure 2-2 Display of the above code in CMD

### 2.3.3 Multiple Assignment

Multiple assignments involve assigning the same variable to more than one value (Kraft, Vaché, Frede & Breuer, 2011). One variable can have one value in one instance and a different value in the second instance. The code below creates a variable name "x" and assigns it an integer value "76" then prints the value. The program then reassigns the variable "x" to a character value of "Sammy" and prints the variable.

**Sample Python code:**

```
1   #Assign x to be an integer
2   x = 76
3   print(x)
4
5   #Reassign x to be a string
6   x = "Sammy"
7   print(x)
```

Figure 2-3 Script for multiple assignments

```
C:\Users\btaze\AppData\Local\Programs\Python\Python37\python.exe
pydev debugger: process 7208 is connecting

Connected to pydev debugger (build 183.5912.18)
76
Sammy
```

Figure 2-4 Display of script in CMD

## 2.4 Python Standard Data Types

### 2.4.1   Python Numbers

Python has three main numeric types (Dalcın, et al, 2008). These include integer, float and complex. These types are determined by the value assigned to the variable. Sample code and code snippet are shown below. The code creases three variables name "x", "y" and "z" which are integer, float and a complex number respectively.

**Python Code:**

```
x = 1           # int
y = 2.8         # float
z = 1j          # complex
CONST_NAME = "Name"  # constant declaration in Python
print(x);
print(y)
print(z)
print(CONST_NAME)
```

Figure 2-5 Demonstrating numbers in Python

```
C:\Users\btaze\AppData\Local\Programs\Python\Python37\python.exe
1
2.8
1j
Name

Process finished with exit code 0
```

Figure 2-6  pynumbers output

**Examples:**

### 2.4.2   Named constant

Constants in Python are memory locations whose values never change during program execution. They are created and called every time they are needed in the program code. They are declared with the type FINAL in Python to show they cannot be changed in any other part of the program.

**Sample codde**

```
1  CONST_NAME = "Name";
2  print(CONST_NAME)
3  CONST_NAME = "JOHN";
4  print(CONST_NAME)
5  CONST_NAME = "PARIS";
6  print(CONST_NAME)
7
```

Figure 2-7 Demonstrating constants in Python

```
C:\Users\btaze\AppData\Local\Programs\Python\Python37\python.exe
pydev debugger: process 9964 is connecting

Connected to pydev debugger (build 183.5912.18)
Name
JOHN
PARIS
```

Figure 2-8 Constpy output

## 2.5 Numeric Data Types and Operators

As discussed earlier Numeric data types can be integers, float or complex numbers. The main operators in Python which work on Numeric data include multiplication, Division, Subtraction, addition and modulus. Here we will discuss the important operators.

### 2.5.1 Multiplication operator

Multiplication is a Python operation that is used to multiply values in the form of numeric data or variable on either side of the operator.

### 2.5.1 Example:

```
1  x = 4
2  y = 5
3  product = x * y
4  print (product)
```

Figure 2-9 Demonstrating multiplication in Python

```
C:\Users\btaze\AppData\Local\Programs\Python\Python37\python.exe
20

Process finished with exit code 0
```

Figure 2-10 Output multiplication

43

### 2.5.2 Example:

```
a = 4
b = float(a)
c = 5
d = float(c)
div = b / d
z = float(div)
print (div)
```

Figure 2-11 Demonstrating division in Python

```
C:\Users\btaze\AppData\Local\Programs\Python\Python37\python.exe
0.8

Process finished with exit code 0
```

Figure 2-12 output division

### 2.5.3 Example:

```
x = 9
y = 5
mod = x % y
print (mod)
```

Figure 2-13 code in python

```
C:\Users\btaze\AppData\Local\Programs\Python\Python37\python.exe
4

Process finished with exit code 0
```

Figure 2-14 output in python

### 2.5.2 Division operator

The division is a Python operation that divides the operand on the left of the operator with the operand on the right hand of the operator. The code below creates two variables of integer type named "x" and' "y" and assigns them values of 4 and 5 respectively. The program then creates a variable name "div" and assigns the result of the division of variables x and y.

**Python code:**

```
x = 9
y = "Alex and John"
print (x)
print (y)
```

Figure 2-15 Division operator script in Python

```
C:\Users\btaze\AppData\Local\Programs\Python\Python37\python.exe
pydev debugger: process 4792 is connecting

Connected to pydev debugger (build 183.5912.18)
9
Alex and John

Process finished with exit code 0
```

Figure 2-16 Display in CMD for division operator

### 2.5.3 Modulus operator

Modulus is a Python operator that divides the operator on the left hand of the operator with that on the right-hand side of the operator and brings the reminder. The Python code below creates two variables "x" and "y" and assigns them integer values. The program code then creates a variable name "mod" and assign it the modulus value when "x" is divided by "y" then prints the value.

**Program code:**

```
1    x = 9
2    y = 5
3    mod = x % y
4    print (mod)
```

Figure 2-17 Demonstration of Modulus Operator

```
C:\Users\btaze\AppData\Local\Programs\Python\Python37\python.exe
4

Process finished with exit code 0
```

Figure 2-18 Display of code execution in CMD

### 2.5.4 Assignment operator

Assignment operator assigns the value on the left-hand side of the operator to the variable on the right-hand side of the operator. The program code below creates two variables "x" and "y" and assigns "x" an integer value of 9 and a "y" is assigned a string name "Alex and John". The program then prints the two variables with the print function.

**Python program:**

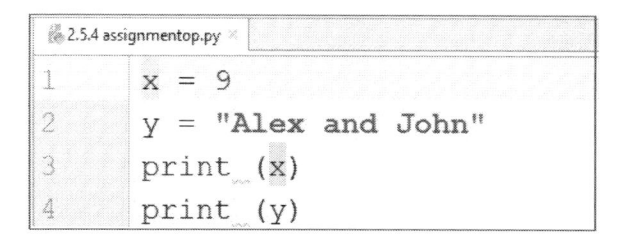

```
1    x = 9
2    y = "Alex and John"
3    print (x)
4    print (y)
```

Figure 2-19 Demonstrating code for assignment operator

```
C:\Users\btaze\AppData\Local\Programs\Python\Python37\python.exe
pydev debugger: process 4792 is connecting

Connected to pydev debugger (build 183.5912.18)
9
Alex and John

Process finished with exit code 0
```

Figure 2-20 Display of code execution in CMD

### 2.5.5 Comparison operators

Comparison operators are used to compare two or more variables. There are seven main comparison operators in Python (Seitz, 2009). These operators include; equal to, not equal to, greater than, less than, less than or equal to, greater than or equal to and not equal. The Python program code below creates three variables "a", "b" and "c" then checks if "a" is equal to "b" then attempts to print "Line 1 - a is equal to b" if equal but prints "Line 1 - a is not equal to b" if found not to be equal. The program then assigns the variables "a" and "b" the integer values of 5 and 20 respectively then checks if "a" is less than or equal to "b". The program then prints "Line 6 - a is either less than or equal to b" if "a" is found to be less than or equal to "b" and prints "Line 6 - a is neither less than nor equal to b" otherwise. Lastly, the program checks if "b is either greater than or equal to b" and prints "Line 7 - b is either greater than or equal to b" else it prints "Line 7 - b is neither greater than nor equal to b".

**Code sample:**

$a = 21$

$b = 10$

$c = 0$

*if ( a == b ):*

  *print ("Line 1 - a is equal to b")*

*else:*

  *print ("Line 1 - a is not equal to b")*

*if ( a != b ):*

  *print ("Line 2 - a is not equal to b")*

*else:*

  *print ("Line 2 - a is equal to b")*

*if ( a < b ):*

  *print ("Line 4 - a is less than b")*

*else:*

　*print ("Line 5 - a is not greater than b")*

*a = 5;*

*b = 20;*

*if ( a <= b ):*

　*print ("Line 6 - a is either less than or equal to  b")*

*else:*

　*print ("Line 6 - a is neither less than nor equal to  b")*

*if ( b >= a ):*

　*print ("Line 7 - b is either greater than  or equal to b")*

*else:*

　*print ("Line 7 - b is neither greater than  nor equal to b")*

```
C:\Users\btaze\AppData\Local\Programs\Python\Python37\python.exe
pydev debugger: process 2536 is connecting

Connected to pydev debugger (build 183.5912.18)
Line 1 - a is not equal to b
Line 2 - a is not equal to b
Line 5 - a is not greater than b
Line 6 - a is either less than or equal to  b
Line 7 - b is either greater than  or equal to b
```

Figure 2-21 output in python

| Operator | Meaning | Example |
|---|---|---|
| = | Equal to | 1=1 |
| < | Less than | 4<5 |
| > | Greater than | 5>4 |
| <= | Less than or equal to | D<5 |
| >= | Greater than or equal to | D>=5 |
| != | Less than or equal to | 4!=5 |

Table 1 Logical Operators

## 2.5.6 Logical operators

Python has three main logical operators. These include; logical AND, logical NOT and logical OR. Logical AND evaluates to True when both operands are True. Logical NOT evaluate to True if any of the operands is True. Logical NOT is used to reverse the logical state of an operand.

| Operator | What it means | What it looks like |
|---|---|---|
| and | True if both are true | x and y |
| or | True if at least one is true | x or y |
| not | True only if false | not x |

Table 2 Logical Operators

To understand how logical operators, work, let's evaluate three expressions:

```
print((5 > 3) and (1 < 4))    # Both original expressions are True
print((5 == 5) or (4 != 4))   # One original expression is True
print (not(4<= 1))            # The original expression is True
```

Figure 2-22 logical operator

```
C:\Users\btaze\AppData\Local\Programs\Python\Python37\python.exe
pydev debugger: process 7980 is connecting

Connected to pydev debugger (build 183.5912.18)
True
True
True
```

Figure 2-23 output in python

## 2.6 Python Strings

Python strings are referred to as a traditional sequence of characters that are either literal constants or some kind of a variable (Helmus & Collis, 2016).). Strings can allow its length to be changed or remain fixed. There are many operations that can be done on strings which include; printing the length, printing a character in any position, removing whitespace from the beginning or the end, or returning the string in lower or upper case. Replace or split operations can also be done on strings. The program code below demonstrates the printing of the second element in the string of words "Hello, World!".

**Code for printing a character in any position:**

#this code prints the character in the second position from the string

```
chara = "Hello, World!"
print(chara[1])
```

Figure 2-24 Script representing a character in Python

```
C:\Users\btaze\AppData\Local\Programs\Python\Python37\python.exe
pydev debugger: process 6660 is connecting

Connected to pydev debugger (build 183.5912.18)
e
```

Figure 2-25 Running code in Python

```
print((5 > 3) and (1 < 4))    # Both original expressions are True
print((5 == 5) or (4 != 4))   # One original expression is True
print (not(4<= 1))            # The original expression is True
```

Figure 2-26 Print Char in position

```
C:\Users\btaze\AppData\Local\Programs\Python\Python37\python.exe
pydev debugger: process 7980 is connecting

Connected to pydev debugger (build 183.5912.18)
True
True
True
```

Figure 2-27 Running code in Python

## 2.6.1 Printing the length of a string

The Python program code below demonstrates a Python function to print the length of the character.

**Code sample:**

#this code returns the actual length of the string

```
chara = "Hello, World!"
print(len(chara))
```

Figure 2-28 Code demonstration of a String in Python

```
C:\Users\btaze\AppData\Local\Programs\Python\Python37\python.exe
pydev debugger: process 12096 is connecting

Connected to pydev debugger (build 183.5912.18)
13
```

Figure 2-29 Display of the code running in CMD

Removing whitespace from the beginning or the end of a string

The program code below demonstrates the Python functions to remove whitespaces at the end of a string.

**Program code:**

#this code removes the whitespaces at the end of the string

```
a = " Hello, World! "
print(a.strip()) # returns "Hello, World!"
```

Figure 2-30 Code demonstration of removing the whitespaces at the end of the string

```
C:\Users\btaze\AppData\Local\Programs\Python\Python37\python.exe
pydev debugger: process 3132 is connecting

Connected to pydev debugger (build 183.5912.18)
Hello, World!
```

Figure 2-31 Display of running code in CMD

Returning the string in lower or upper case

**Program code:**

```
string1= "CHANGING TO LOWER!"
print (string1.lower())
string2 = ("changing to upper")
print (string2.upper())
```

Figure 2-32 Code demonstration of changing the upper case to lower case and vice versa

```
C:\Users\btaze\AppData\Local\Programs\Python\Python37\python.exe
Connected to pydev debugger (build 183.5912.18)
pydev debugger: process 10072 is connecting

changing to lower!
CHANGING TO UPPER
```

Figure 2-33 Display of script running in CMD

Replace or split operations can also be done on strings

**Program code:**

```
string1 = "Hello, World!"
print(string1.replace("H", "J"))
print(string1.replace("e", "A"))
string2 = "Hello, World!"
print(string2.split(",")) # returns ['Hello', ' World!']
```

Figure 2-34 Code demonstration of replacing a character in a string

```
C:\Users\btaze\AppData\Local\Programs\Python\Python37\python.exe
pydev debugger: process 4428 is connecting

Connected to pydev debugger (build 183.5912.18)
Jello, World!
HAllo, World!
['Hello', ' World!']
```

Figure 2-35 Demonstration of the above code in CMD

## 2.7 Data Structures

There are several very useful data structures used in Python Scripting namely Lists, Sets, Tuples and Dictionaries. All these elements of Python programming work together in meeting the needs of different programmers in the programming work. These elements help in creating effective Python programs used in several applications. We will discuss each of these in detail here

## 2.8 Lists

List is the most versatile datatype available in Python which can be written as a list of comma-separated values (items) between square brackets (Bjørndalen, Vinter & Anshus, 2007). Lists are created by separating values that are in square brackets. Lists are Python data structures which are a mutable ordered sequence of elements. Each element in the list has a value called item. They are mainly defined by having values inside brackets.

Example of a List [ Sunday, Monday….]

Lists are used in Python where programmers need to work with many related values. They help in condensing the code by keeping the related data together hence allowing the programmer to perform the same functions and operations on multiple values at once.

Each item in the list corresponds to a given index number. The index is usually an integer value starting at 0.

An example of a list is given as

$$sea\_creatures = ['shark', 'cuttlefish', 'squid', 'mantis\ shrimp', 'anemone'].$$

The first item named "shark" is at index 0 while the second item named "cuttlefish" is at index 1 and so on.

The above example can also be given as

## 2.8.1 Example:

```
sea_creatures = ['shark','cuttlefish','squid','mantis shrimp','anemone']
print(sea_creatures[0])
print(sea_creatures[1])
print(sea_creatures[2])
print(sea_creatures[3])
print(sea_creatures[4])
```

Figure 2-36 Code Demonstration of Lists in Python

```
C:\Users\btaze\AppData\Local\Programs\Python\Python37\python.exe
pydev debugger: process 7928 is connecting
Connected to pydev debugger (build 183.5912.18)

shark
cuttlefish
squid
mantis shrimp
anemone
```

Figure 2-34 Output Lists in Python

Elements in a list have the following characteristics:

- They are accessed via numeric (zero-based) indices.
- They maintain their ordering unless explicitly re-ordered (for example, by sorting the list).
- They can be of any type, and types can be mixed (Edwards, Tilden & Allevato, 2014).

**Sample code for lists in python:**

The code below shows the creation of Python lists using the command prompt. The first line shows the declaration of a list named "list1" and the elements of the list are placed under square brackets separated with commas.

```
list1 = ['physics', 'chemistry', 1997, 2000];
list2 = [1, 2, 3, 4, 5 ];
list3 = ["a", "b", "c", "d"]
print(list1)
print(list2)
print(list3)
list1[0] = "Biology"
print(list1)
```

Figure 2-35 Creating Lists in Python

```
C:\Users\btaze\AppData\Local\Programs\Python\Python37\python.exe
pydev debugger: process 8496 is connecting

Connected to pydev debugger (build 183.5912.18)
['physics', 'chemistry', 1997, 2000]
[1, 2, 3, 4, 5]
['a', 'b', 'c', 'd']
['Biology', 'chemistry', 1997, 2000]
```

Figure 2-36 Output Lists in Python

Figure 2-37 Creating Lists in Python

## 2.9 Sets

Set is a container of an unordered collection of unique and immutable objects (Poolman, 2016).The set data type is, as the name implies, a Python implementation of the sets as they are known from mathematics. A set is a collection which is unordered and unindexed. In Python, sets are written with curly brackets. The data types in Python sets are usually iterable, mutable but cannot have duplicate elements. The main advantage of using sets is that it can be easy to check if some element is available in a set or not.

Python elements are contained in curly brackets which are separated by commas or using the built-in Python function set (). Python sets can have different items of different data types such as float, integer, string or even tuple. Sets also do not have a mutable element.

Python set elements cannot be changed but can only be added or updated. The add () and update () functions are used to perform these operations. Elements/items in a set can, however, be removed from the set using the discard () or remove () functions for sets. The discard () function removes an item from the set and returns no error if such item is not found. The remove () function, on the other hand, is used to removed item from a list and raise an error is such an item is not found.

Items from the set can all be removed using the clear () function.

**Sample python code**

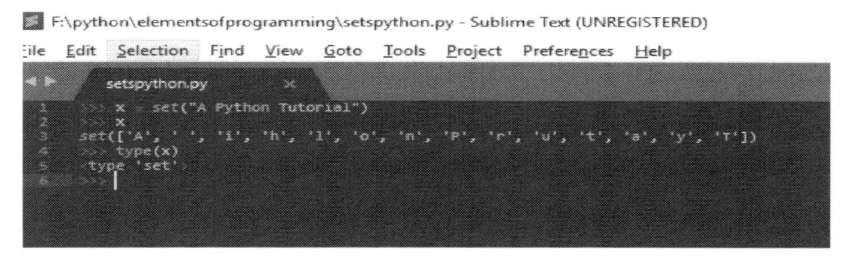

Figure 2-38 Creating sets in Python

```
Python 3.7.0 Shell - C:/Users/btaze/Desktop/Python Scripts/2.9 setspython.py (3.7.0)    —    □    ×
File  Edit  Shell  Debug  Options  Window  Help
Python 3.7.0 (v3.7.0:1bf9cc5093, Jun 27 2018, 04:59:51) [MSC v.1914 64 bit (AMD6
4)] on win32
Type "copyright", "credits" or "license()" for more information.
>>> x = set("A Python Tutorial")
>>> x
{'h', 'l', 'n', ' ', 'u', 't', 'T', 'P', 'r', 'i', 'y', 'o', 'a', 'A'}
>>> type(x)
<class 'set'>
>>>
```

Figure 2-39 Output in Python

The code below creates a set name "my-set" and assigns it the set elements 1, 2 and 3 then prints the set using the print () function of Python.

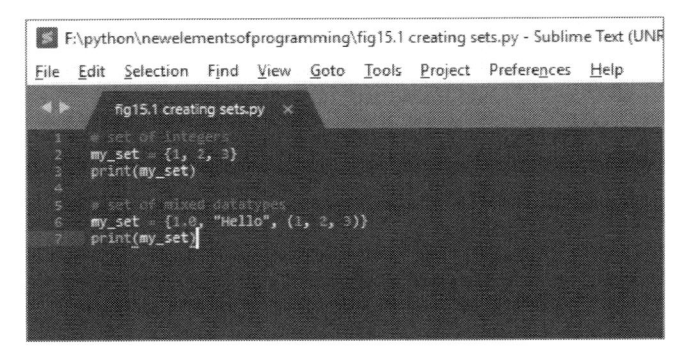

Figure 2-40 Code demonstration of creating sets in Python

### 2.9.1 Changing sets in Python

The code example below creates a set called "my_set" and assigns it the elements 1 and 3. The code then prints the elements of the set using the print () function of Python. The elements can be added to the set using the add () function of the Python language or using the update () function.

```
# initialize my_set
my_set = {1,3}
print(my_set)

# Output: {1, 2, 3}
my_set.add(2)
print(my_set)

# add multiple elements
# Output: {1, 2, 3, 4}
my_set.update([2,3,4])
print(my_set)

# add list and set
# Output: {1, 2, 3, 4, 5, 6, 8}
my_set.update([4,5], {1,6,8})
print(my_set)
```

Figure 2-41 Code demonstration of changing sets in Python

```
C:\Users\btaze\AppData\Local\Programs\Python\Python37\python.exe
Connected to pydev debugger (build 183.5912.18)
pydev debugger: process 6152 is connecting

{1, 3}
{1, 2, 3}
{1, 2, 3, 4}
{1, 2, 3, 4, 5, 6, 8}
```

Figure 2-42 Output of changing sets in Python

### 2.9.2 Removing items from the set

The Python code below creates a set called "my_set" and assigns it elements 1, 3, 4, 5 and 6 the prints the set. The code then removes the element with value 4 using the discard () function of Python language. The code also uses the remove () function of Python to remove element with the value of 6 from and prints the result. The code tries to remove element 2 which is not in the set and hence returns are error.

```
1    # initialize my_set
2    my_set = {1, 3, 4, 5, 6}
3    print(my_set)
4    # discard an element
5    # Output: {1, 3, 5, 6}
6    my_set.discard(4)
7    print(my_set)
8    # remove an element
9    # Output: {1, 3, 5}
10   my_set.remove(6)
11   print(my_set)
12   # discard an element
13   # not present in my_set
14   # Output: {1, 3, 5}
15   my_set.discard(2)
16   print(my_set)
17
```

Figure 2-43 Code demonstration of removing an item from a set

```
C:\Users\btaze\AppData\Local\Programs\Python\Python37\python.exe
{1, 3, 4, 5, 6}
{1, 3, 5, 6}
{1, 3, 5}
{1, 3, 5}
```

Figure 2-44 output removing an item from a set

Windows PowerShell

```
PS F:\python\elementsofprogramming> python
Python 3.6.3 (v3.6.3:2c5fed8, Oct  3 2017, 17:26:49) [MSC v.1900 32 bit (Intel)] on win32
Type "help", "copyright", "credits" or "license" for more information.
>>> x = set("python tutor")
>>> aet (['A','','i','H','L','T'])
Traceback (most recent call last):
  File "<stdin>", line 1, in <module>
NameError: name 'aet' is not defined
>>> Set (['A','','i','H','L','T'])
Traceback (most recent call last):
  File "<stdin>", line 1, in <module>
NameError: name 'Set' is not defined
>>> set (['A','','i','H','L','T'])
{'', 'L', 'i', 'H', 'T', 'A'}
>>> type(x)
<class 'set'>
```

Figure 2-45 Creating Python sets via CMD

## 2.10 Tuples

A tuple is a collection of objects in Python with separations using commas. It can be like lists in terms of repetition, indexing and nested objects (Hammond & Robinson, 2010). In some ways, a tuple is similar to a list in terms of indexing, nested objects and repetition but a tuple is immutable, unlike lists which are mutable. The only difference between a list and a tuple is that lists are mutable while the tuples are immutable.

Python can, therefore, be referred to as a tuple is a sequence of immutable Python objects. Tuples are sequences, just like lists. The differences between tuples and lists are, the tuples cannot be changed unlike lists and tuples use parentheses, whereas lists use square brackets.

### 2.10.1 Creating a Tuple in Python

**Code sample**

2.10.1 Creating an empty tuple.py

```
#An empty tuple
empty_tuple = ()
print (empty_tuple)
```

Figure 2-46 Creating an empty tuple

```
C:\Users\btaze\AppData\Local\Programs\Python\Python37\python.exe
pydev debugger: process 7200 is connecting

Connected to pydev debugger (build 183.5912.18)
()

Process finished with exit code 0
```

Figure 2-47 Output Creating an empty tuple

## 2.10.2 Creating a non-empty tuple
The code below creates a tuple name "tup" and assigns it the elements "python" and "geeks"

**Sample code**

```python
# Creating non-empty tuples

# One way of creation
tup = 'python', 'geeks'
print(tup)

# Another for doing the same
tup = ('python', 'geeks')
print(tup)
```

Figure 2-48 Code for creating a non-empty tuple

```
C:\Users\btaze\AppData\Local\Programs\Python\Python37\python.exe
('python', 'geeks')
('python', 'geeks')

Process finished with exit code 0
```

Figure 2-49 Running the code and output

Sample code below shows that tuples allow repetition, are immutable, can be concatenated and nesting tuples. The code creates a tuple called "tup" and assigns it the values 0, 1, 2 and 3. The code also creates a tuple called "tuple2" and assigns the elements "python" and "geek". The code then concatenates the two tuples as tuple1 + tuple2. On testing the code, it is found out that tuples are immutable.

**Code sample:**

```python
# Code for concatenating 2 tuples

tuple1 = (0, 1, 2, 3)
tuple2 = ('python', 'geek')

# Concatenating above two
print(tuple1 + tuple2)


# Code for creating nested tuples

tuple1 = (0, 1, 2, 3)
tuple2 = ('python', 'geek')
tuple3 = (tuple1, tuple2)
print(tuple3)
```

Figure 2-50 Code snippet for concatenating two tuples

```
C:\Users\btaze\AppData\Local\Programs\Python\Python37\python.exe
(0, 1, 2, 3, 'python', 'geek')
((0, 1, 2, 3), ('python', 'geek'))
('python', 'python', 'python')
[4, 1, 2, 3]

Process finished with exit code 0
```

Figure 2-51 Executing code on CMD

```
#A non-empty tuple
nonemptytuple = ("apple", "banana", "cherry")
print(nonemptytuple)
```

Figure 2-52 Creating a non-empty tuple

```
C:\Users\btaze\AppData\Local\Programs\Python\Python37\python.exe
Connected to pydev debugger (build 183.5912.18)
pydev debugger: process 5964 is connecting

('apple', 'banana', 'cherry')

Process finished with exit code 0
```

Figure 2-53 Output in Python

## 2.11     Differences between Tuples and Lists

The difference between a list and a tuple is that lists are mutable while the tuples are immutable.

Due to this Tuples are simpler, they never change and don't have any of the useful properties found in lists that make working with lists so powerful. Hence if you really don't need what lists have to offer and you just want to create a container for immutable stuff, use tuples instead, since they are simpler and thus, faster.

## 2.12     Dictionaries

A dictionary is an associative array (also known as hashes). Any key of the dictionary is associated (or mapped) to a value (Rivers & Koedinger, 2017). The values of a dictionary can be any Python data type. Each key in a Python dictionary is separated from its value by a colon (:) while the items are separated by a comma. The whole dictionary is then enclosed using curly braces.

Keys within a dictionary are unique and must be from immutable data types such as strings, tuples or numbers. To access dictionary elements, you can use the familiar square brackets along with the key to obtaining its value.

### 2.12.1  Accessing items in a dictionary

The python code below creates a dictionary name "dict" and assigns it the items such as 'Name': 'Zara', 'Age': 7, 'Class': 'First'. The next Python line of code then prints the Zara and 7 since it accesses the elements named "name" and "age" from the tuple.

```
dict = {'Name': 'Zara', 'Age': 7, 'Class': 'First'}
print("dict['Name']:" , dict['Name'])
print("dict['Age']:" , dict['Age'])
print("dict['Class']:" , dict['Class'])
```

Figure 2-54 Code demonstration of accessing an item in dictionary

```
C:\Users\btaze\AppData\Local\Programs\Python\Python37\python.exe
dict['Name']: Zara
dict['Age']: 7
dict['Class']: First

Process finished with exit code 0
```

Fig 2-55 Creating a new dictionary - output

### 2.12.2 Creating and adding values to a dictionary

**Code sample:**

```
#Creating a dictionary

room_num = {'John': 425, 'Liz': 212}
#adding values to a dictionary

room_num['Isaac'] = 345
print (room_num)
```

Figure 2-56 Code snippet of adding a value to dictionary

```
C:\Users\btaze\AppData\Local\Programs\Python\Python37\python.exe
{'John': 425, 'Liz': 212, 'Isaac': 345}

Process finished with exit code 0
```

Figure 2-57 Running program in CMD

### 2.12.3 Counting and looping through Python dictionary

**Sample code:**

```
#Creating a dictionary

room_num = {'John': 425, 'Liz': 212}



#adding values to a dictionary

room_num['Isaac'] = 345
```

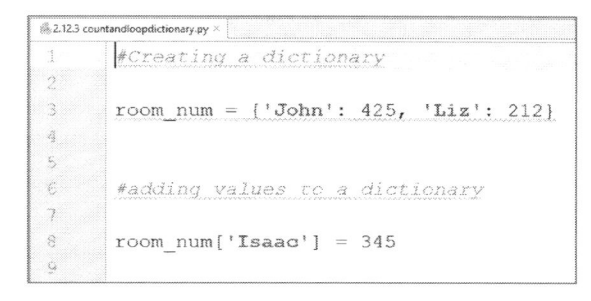

Figure 2-58 Code snippet of counting and looping through Python dictionary

```
C:\Users\btaze\AppData\Local\Programs\Python\Python37\python.exe
{'John': 425, 'Liz': 212, 'Isaac': 345}
John is in room 425
Liz is in room 212
Isaac is in room 345


Process finished with exit code 0
```

Figure 2-59 Running program code in CMD

## 2.13 Difference between a list and a dictionary

List and dictionary are fundamentally different data structures. A list can store a sequence of objects in a certain order such that you can index into the list or iterate over the list. Moreover, List is a mutable type meaning that lists can be modified after they have been created (Antiga, et al, 2008). A python dictionary is an implementation of a hash table and is a key-value store. It is not ordered, and it requires that the keys are a hash table. Also, it is fast for lookups by key (Sieg, et al, 2010).

Elements in a Dictionary have the following characteristics:

- Key values can be of any hash table type (i.e. not a dict) and types can be mixed
- Every entry has a key and a value
- Values can be of any type (including other dict's), and types can be mixed
- Elements are accessed using key values
- Ordering is not guaranteed (Sanner, et al, 2009).
- 

## 2.14 Conclusion

In conclusion, python has many elements that facilitate the programmer's operations (Zelle, 2014). Python has different data types, sets, strings, lists and dictionaries that are important elements in the programming activities of programmers. Lists store sequence of objects in an order and iterate over the list. Lists are mutable, unlike dictionaries which are not mutable.

## 2.15 Summary

In summary, Python programming uses several elements to effectively implement programs useful in several fields. The main elements that this chapter has discussed on include; a variable, strings, sets, lists, dictionaries and several expressions and operators. All these elements of Python programming work together in meeting the needs of different programmers in the programming work. These elements help in creating effective Python programs used in a number of applications.

## 2.16 Assignment Questions

Assignment No. 1

2.1 What is a variable and how variables are declared in python?
2.2 What is an integer and how is it declared in python?
2.3 What is a floating number and how is it declared in python?
2.4 What is a constant?
2.5 How multiplication operator is declared in python?
2.6 How division operator is declared in python?
2.7 What are logical operators?
2.8 What is a string and how is it declared in python?
2.9 How to print the length of a string in python?
2.10 What is a list and how is it defined in python?
2.11 What is a set?
2.12 What is a tuple and how is tuple created in python?
2.13 What is the difference between tuple and list?
2.14 What is a dictionary and how the items are accessed in dictionary?
2.15 What is difference between a list and dictionary?

Assignment No. 2

2.16 Getting Started with your Python IDE. Create a python program file for writing the very first program 'Hello, World".
2.17 Write a pseudocode when run, prints out a tic-tac-toe board. The purpose of this exercise is to make sure you understand how to write programs.
Expected output:

```
1   1
-----------------
1   1
-----------------
1   1
```

2.18 Which of the following are legal python names? If the name is not legal, state the reason.

1. and

2. _and

3. var

4. var1

5. 1var

6. my-name

7. your_name

8. COLOR

**2.19** Write down the type of the values stored in each of the variables below.
1. a = 3.7

2. b = false

3. c = 7

4. d = Alex

5. e = 17

6. f = 'True'

7. g = True

8. h = '17'

**2.20** What is an expression? Give Example
**2.21** Write a Python program to calculate the length of a string.
**2.22** Write the value (True or false) produced by each expression below, using the assigned values of the variables a, b and c. Try doing this without interpreter.

a = False

b = True

c = False

1. b and c

2. b or c

3. not a and b

4. (a and b) or not c

**2.23** Write a Python program which accepts the radius of a circle from the user and compute the area.
Sample Output:
r = 1.1
Area = 3.8013271108436504

**2.24** Write a program that does the following in order:
Asks the user to enter his/her date of birth.

Asks the user to enter his/her last name.

Prints out the user's last name and date of birth, in that order.

**2.25** What does it mean for a program to terminate?

## Assignment No. 3

**2.26** Write a Python function that takes a sequence of numbers and determines if all the numbers are different from each other.

**2.27** Ask the user for a number. Depending on whether the number is even or odd, print out an appropriate message to the user. *Hint: how does an even / odd number react differently when divided by 2?*

**2.28** Take a list, say for example this one:

a = [1, 1, 2, 3, 5, 8, 13, 21, 34, 55, 89]

And write a program that prints out all the elements of the list that are less than 5.

**2.29** Create a program that asks the user for a number and then prints out a list of all the divisors of that number. (If you don't know what a *divisor* is, it is a number that divides evenly into another number. For example, 13 is a divisor of 26 because 26 / 13 has no remainder.)

**2.30** Take two lists, say for example these two:

a = [1, 1, 2, 3, 5, 8, 13, 21, 34, 55, 89]

b = [1, 2, 3, 4, 5, 6, 7, 8, 9, 10, 11, 12, 13]

And write a program that returns a list that contains only the elements that are common between the lists (without duplicates). Make sure your program works on two lists of different sizes.

**2.31** Ask the user for a string and print out whether this string is a palindrome or not. (A palindrome is a string that reads the same forwards and backwards.)

**2.32** Let's say you have a list saved in a variable: a = [1, 4, 9, 16, 25, 36, 49, 64, 81, 100]. Write one line of Python that takes this list 'a' and makes a new list that has only the even elements of this list in it.

**2.33** Write a program that takes a list of numbers (for example, a = [5, 10, 15, 20, 25]) and makes a new list of only the first and last elements of the given list. For practice, write this code inside a function.

**2.34** Write a Python program to sum all the items in a list.

**2.35** Write a Python program to count the number of strings where the string length is 2 or more and the first and last character are same from a given list of strings.
    Sample List: ['abc', 'xyz', 'aba', '1221']
    Expected Result : 2

## Assignment No. 4

**2.36** Write a Python program to get a list, sorted in increasing order by the last element in each tuple from a given list of non-empty tuples.
    Sample List: [(2, 5), (1, 2), (4, 4), (2, 3), (2, 1)]
    Expected Result: [(2, 1), (1, 2), (2, 3), (4, 4), (2, 5)]
**2.37** Write a Python program to remove duplicates from a list.
**2.38** Write a Python program to check a list is empty or not.
**2.39** Write a Python function that takes a list of words and returns the length of the longest one
**2.40** Write a Python program that accepts a comma separated sequence of words as input and prints the unique words in sorted form (alphanumerically).
    Sample Words: red, white, black, red, green, black
    Expected Result: black, green, red, white, red
**2.41** Write a Python program to find the second smallest number in a list.
**2.42** Write a Python program to find a tuple, the smallest second index value from a list of tuples.
**2.43** Write a Python program to create a tuple with different data types.
**2.44** Write a Python program to create a tuple with numbers and print one item.
**2.45** Write a Python program to create an instance of an OrderedDict using a given dictionary. Sort the dictionary during the creation and print the members of the dictionary in reverse order.
Expected Output:
  Angola 244
  Andorra 376
  Algeria 213
  Afghanistan 93
  Albania 355
**in reverse order**:
Albania 355
Afghanistan 93
Algeria 213
Andorra 376
Angola 244

# Chapter 3
# Collection and Sequences

## 3.1 Objectives

The main objective of this chapter is to discuss:

- The concept of Collection and Sequences
- Introduce List, Tuples, Dictionaries, Strings, and Sets.
- Explain the uses of each of the data structures
- Demonstrate with examples the difference between various data structures

## 3.2 Introduction

This chapter focuses on Collections and Sequences which is used to group multiple values together – like a list of numbers, or a dictionary which can be used to store and retrieve key-value pairs. In Python, sequences possess a deterministic ordering and collections. The ordering of things in sets is random. The ordering of values and keys in dictionaries can also be random.

Physically, sets have an arrangement but the sequence can change if you add or remove things. In python, a record, a tuple and string are sequences, all which can be implemented as arrays. Other helpful data structures are discovered at the sets module and feature a deque, a counter plus a default dict.

We will discuss everything in this chapter in detail.

## 3.3 Collections

Collections can be best described as bags of values or containers while sequences are data structures, especially associated with storage and groupings that can be accessed linearly. Most of the sequences are a member of collections. Their relationship between the two when sequences are members of a collection is best described below.

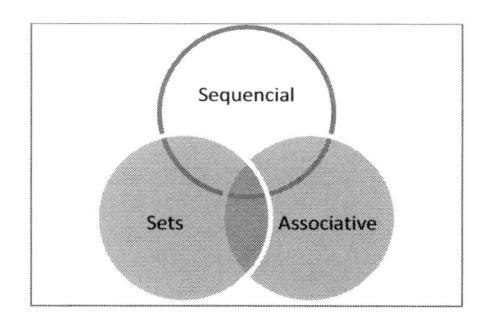

Figure 3-1 Defining Collections

### 3.3.1 Types of Collections

There are several different types of collections in Python. The collection data structure allows storing several objects with or without any guaranteed order. You can add and remove elements from a collection, and you can iterate over a collection. Basically, it's a storage construct that allows you to collect things and perform manipulation on them.

Collection types in Python are grouped into two types

1. **Sequence type** (collections with a concept of order, indexed numerically from 0) and includes string, list, tuple, and a few others. Things always come out of them in the same order they were put in (Tipalty, 2018).
2. **Mapping types** (collections without a concept of order, indexed by keys) which include only one type, dictionary. The ordering of items in sets is arbitrary. (It's not random, and it's technically not unpredictable, but it's good to think of it as both.) The ordering of keys and values in dictionaries is also arbitrary.

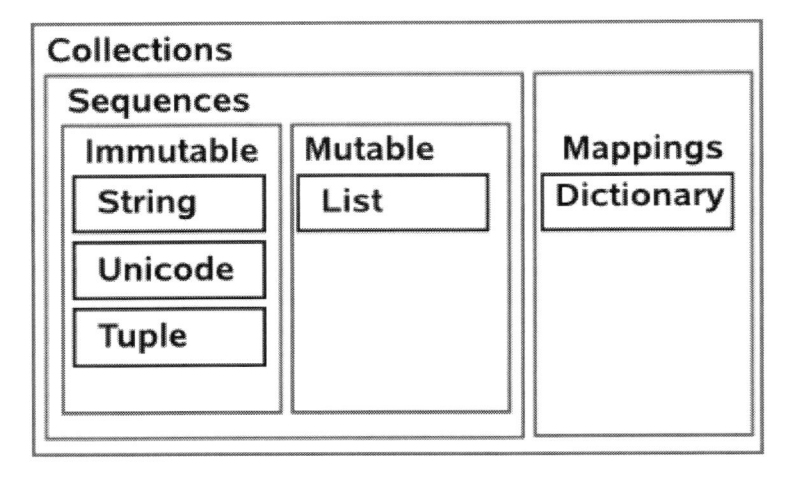

Figure 3-2 Diagram presenting mapping types

Physically, collections have an order - every time you iterate over a set you'll visit its items in the same order - but the order may change if you add or remove items. Basically, if you do anything that depends on a collection having a specific ordering, you'll end up regretting it ( Tipalty, 2018).

A collection is nice because we can put more than one value in them and carry them all around in one convenient package. We have a bunch of values in a single "variable". We do this by having more than one place "in" the variable. We have ways of finding the different places in the variable

The first data structure we are going to review is Sequence.

| Lists | Sets | Dictionaries | Tuples |
|---|---|---|---|
| List=[10,12,15] | Set= {1,23,34} Print(st)->{1,23,24} Set={1,1} Print (set)->{1} | Dict = { "Ram": 26, "mary": 24} | Words= {"spam","eggs"} Or Words= "spam" , "eggs" |
| Access: print (list[0]) | Print(set). Set elements can't be indexed | Print (dict ["ram"]) | Print (words [0]) |
| Can contains duplicate elements | Can't contain duplicate elements. Faster compared to Lists | Can't combine duplicate keys, but can contain duplicate values. | Can't contain duplicate elements. Faster compared to Lists |
| Lists [0] = 100 | Set.add (7) | Dict ["Ram"] = 27 | Words [0]= "care" -> TypeError |
| Mutable | Mutable | Mutable | Immutable- Values Can't be changed once assigned. |
| List = [] | Set= set() | Dict= {} | Words= {} |
| Slicing can be done Print(list [1:2]) -> [12] | Slicing: not done | Slicing: not done | Slicing can also be done on tuples |
| Usage: Use lists if you have a collection of data that doesn't need random access. Use lists when you need a simple, iterable collection that is modified frequently. | Usage: Membership testing and the elimination of duplicate entries. When you need uniqueness for the elements. | Usage: - When you need a logical association b/w key: value pair. - When you need fast lookup for your data, based on a custom key. - When your data is being constantly modified. | Usage: Use tuples when your data cannot change. A tuple is used in combination with a dictionary, e.g. a tuple might represent a key, because its immutable. |

Table 3 Comparison of List, Sets, Dictionary and Tuple

### 3.4 Sequences

One other major data structure in Python are Sequences. It's worth noting that every sequence is a collection, but not every collection is a sequence. Sequences consist of strings, tuples and lists. Sequences have got two main features. The first one is slicing operation. This operation involves obtaining a certain number of items from a list and is described more below. Another operation is the indexing operation. Indexing operation allows a user to fetch a particular item or element in a list. It also gives a chance to perform operations on particular items. We now give several examples on using sequences that demonstrate its usage

#### 3.3.1.1 Example: Sequence Demonstration

Given below is an example that shows cumulative functions in one piece of code like firstly the indexing of objects, then slicing using a list and finally using string.

*fruit = ['apple', 'mango', 'carrot', 'banana']*

*# Indexing or 'Subscription'*

*print(fruit[0])*

*print(fruit[1])*

*print(fruit[2])*

*print(fruit[3])*

*print(fruit[-1])*

*print(fruit[-2])*

*# Slicing using a list*

*print(fruit[1:3])*

*print(fruit[2:])*

*print(fruit[1:-1])*

*print(fruit[:])*

*# Slicing using a string*

*name = 'swaroop'*

*print(name[1:3])*

*print(name[2:])*

*print(name[1:-1])*

*print(name[:])*

*# All of the above operations using List or String will be discussed in detailed now*

```
C:\Users\btaze\AppData\Local\Programs\Python\Python37\python.exe
apple
mango
carrot
banana
banana
carrot
['mango', 'carrot']
['carrot', 'banana']
['mango', 'carrot']
['apple', 'mango', 'carrot', 'banana']
wa
aroop
waroo
swaroop
```

Figure 3-1 Indexing or subscription

### 3.4.1 Lists

Lists are Python's most flexible ordered collection object type. Lists can contain any sort of object: numbers, strings and even other lists. Ordered collections of arbitrary objects (Ramalho, 2015). Lists can contain another list called as 'nested list'. Lists can also be used for negative indexing. The elements used in lists can be changed. This means lists can be mutated unlike tuple or string.

*a = [99, "bottles of beer", ["on", "the", "wall"]]*

*print(a\*3)*

*print(a[0])*

*print(a[-1])*

*print(a[1:])*

*print(len(a))*

*# Item and slice assignment*

*a[0] = 98*

*print(a[0])*

*a[1:2] = ["bottles", "of", "beer"]*

*print(a)*

*# output:- [98, "bottles", "of", "beer", ["on", "the", "wall"]]*

*del a[-1]*

*print(a)*

*# -> [98, "bottles", "of", "beer"]*

*# Variable length, heterogeneous, arbitrary nestable.*

*# A compound data type:*

*[0]*

*[2.3, 4.5]*

*[5, "Hello", "there", 9.8]*

*[]*

```
# Use len() to get the length of a list

names = ['Ben', 'Chen', 'Yaqin']

print(len(names))

# output:- 3

print(names[0])

# 'Ben'

print(names[1])

# 'Chen'

print(names[2])

# 'Yaqin'

print(names[-1])

# 'Yaqin'

print(names[-2])

# 'Chen'

print(names[-3])

# 'Ben'
```

```
Python 3.7.0 Shell                                              —   □   ×
File Edit Shell Debug Options Window Help
Python 3.7.0 (v3.7.0:1bf9cc5093, Jun 27 2018, 04:59:51) [MSC v.1914 64 bit (AMD6
4)] on win32
Type "copyright", "credits" or "license()" for more information.
>>>
 RESTART: C:\Users\btaze\Desktop\Chapter 3 Collection and sequences\3.4.1 List.p
y
[99, 'bottles of beer', ['on', 'the', 'wall'], 99, 'bottles of beer', ['on', 'th
e', 'wall'], 99, 'bottles of beer', ['on', 'the', 'wall']]
99
['on', 'the', 'wall']
['bottles of beer', ['on', 'the', 'wall']]
3
98
[98, 'bottles', 'of', 'beer', ['on', 'the', 'wall']]
[98, 'bottles', 'of', 'beer']
3
Ben
Chen
Yaqin
Yaqin
Chen
Ben
>>> |
```

Figure 3-2 Output in Python

### 3.4.1.1 Example : Demonstration of Lists

The example given below is showing how the lists are created, represented, sliced and length is retrieved.

```
from functools import reduce
def h(x, y):
    if (type(x) == type(y)):
        print(x + y)
    elif (type(x) == type(1)):
        print(str(x) + y)
    else:
        print(x + str(y))

def do_subtract(x1, x2):
    print(x1 - x2)
h(2, 3)
h("2", 3)
reduce(do_subtract, [1, 2, 3, 4])
```

Figure 3-3 Reduce from a lsit

```
C:\Users\btaze\AppData\Local\Programs\Python\Python37\python.exe
5
23
-1
```

Figure 3-4 Output in Python

### 3.4.1.2 Example : Creation of List

The creation of lists is done by placing strings between brackets and separating them with commas. This is done by adding a name just before the brackets. The example is used to show how a list is saved in python 2.7 (Lutz, 2014)
#this is a list that is referenced using the name listItems

*listItems ['mango', 'juice', 'banana', 'tree', 'house', 'toy', 'cow']*

```
listItems = ['mango', 'juice', 'banana', 'tree', 'house', 'toy', 'cow']
print(listItems)
```

Figure 3-5 Create list items

```
C:\Users\btaze\AppData\Local\Programs\Python\Python37\python.exe
pydev debugger: process 4852 is connecting

Connected to pydev debugger (build 183.5912.18)
['mango', 'juice', 'banana', 'tree', 'house', 'toy', 'cow']
```

Figure 3-6 Outout in Python

To retrieve a list, there are two important elements that are used. These elements are the name of the list and the position of the item in the list. It is important to note that the positioning of the items would start from a zero to n-1 supposed n is the total number of items in the list. In this case, the positions are indexed as shown below:

| Item Number | Position Number (n-1) |
|---|---|
| 1 | 0 |
| 2 | 1 |
| 3 | 2 |
| 4 | 3 |
| n | n-1 |

Table 4 Positions of Item numbers

In example one the position of banana will be 2. In a practical example, the following commands will be used to come to recall different addresses of items in the list given in Example 1

| Command | Results |
|---|---|
| listItem [2] | 'banana ' |
| listItem [0] | ' mango' |
| listItem [1] | 'juice ' |
| listItem [4] | 'House ' |

Table 5 Command with results

A data structure that holds an ordered collection of items. I.e. you can store a sequence of items in a list. The list of items should be enclosed in square brackets separated by commas. We can add, remove or search for items in a list.

### 3.4.1.3 Example : How a list is shown

Here is an example that will represent how to display a list by print function.

```
fruit = ['apple', 'mango', 'carrot', 'banana']
print('I have', len(fruit), "fruits to buy")
print('The fruits include:')
for item in fruit:
    print(item)
print('\nI also have to buy rice.')
fruit.append('rice')
print('My shopping list now is', fruit)
fruit.sort()
print('Sorted shopping list is', fruit)
print('The first item I will buy is', fruit[0])
olditem = fruit[0]
del fruit[0]
print('I bought the', olditem)
print('My shopping list now is', fruit)
```

Figure 3-7 Shopping list

```
C:\Users\btaze\AppData\Local\Programs\Python\Python37\python.exe "C:/U
I have 4 fruits to buy
The fruits include:
apple
mango
carrot
banana

I also have to buy rice.
My shopping list now is ['apple', 'mango', 'carrot', 'banana', 'rice']
Sorted shopping list is ['apple', 'banana', 'carrot', 'mango', 'rice']
The first item I will buy is apple
I bought the apple
My shopping list now is ['banana', 'carrot', 'mango', 'rice']
```

Figure 3-8 Output in Python

To call the positions of elements, members or items in the list, we need their position. When using the items position, we can confirm that the positions of the items start from 0 by calling the first item using the zero index.

### 3.4.2 List Slicing

List slicing is a technique in python that helps read a list and return a specific segment of a list. the most important elements in list slicing are the full colons and negative signs. The name of the list is also an element that is used in the construction of a slicing statement. The example below shows how list slicing is done in a single word (cited in VanRossum & Drake, 2010)

#### 3.4.2.1 Example: Slicing of List

Below we present a slicing example that will show up characters and return them after being sliced. It will show positions of characters in list

```
1   x = "samsung"
2   print(x[-1])      # first character from the end
3   # 'g'
4   print(x[-2])      # second character from the end
5   # 'n'
6   print(x[1:3])     # Returns the second to the fourth character
7   # 'am'
8   print(x[2:5])     # returns the third to the fifth character
9   # 'msu'
10  print(x[:5])      # slice from the beginning
11  # 'samsun'
12  print(x[2:])      # slice until the end
13  # 'msung'
14  print(x[-3])
15  # 'u'
```

Figure 3-9 Slicing of List

```
C:\Users\btaze\AppData\Local\Programs\Python\Python37\python.exe
g
n
am
msu
samsu
msung
u
```

Figure 3-10 Output in Python

From the above examples, we can see how slicing of characters is used to come up with constructive results relevant to the situation. When learning about slicing, it is good to also look at the practical use of the skills. In this example, we have learned to find the different positions of the characters in a list. A practical application of this technique is when using password recovery features I.e. in google. You will realize that sometimes the user is shown a phone number in order to be sent some verification code. The user is then shown a few characters of the displayed number and told to complete the rest of the characters. In this case, it helps alit in authentication and security services where all the characters in the data don't have to be shown (VanRossum, 2010).

### 3.4.3 Functions that are used to control and edit the data stored in a list.

Lists have a few functions that are used to control and edit the data stored in a list. These functions are named below.

- **Append()**
  This method gives the chance to add an item or an element to an existing list. It can't be used to add an item to a list that does not exist. If this is done, the function will return an error. The newly added item will be placed at the end of the list as shown in the example below

#### 3.4.3.1 Example : Append a List

Given below is an example that will show how an append function works. It will add new element in the list.

```
fruits = ["mango", "banana", "orange", "avocado", "apple"]
fruits.append ("tomato")
print(fruits)
# ['mango', 'banana', 'orange', 'avocado', 'apple', 'tomato']
# new item has been added to the list.
```

Figure 3-11 Items List

```
C:\Users\btaze\AppData\Local\Programs\Python\Python37\python.exe
['mango', 'banana', 'orange', 'avocado', 'apple', 'tomato']

Process finished with exit code 0
```

Figure 3-12 output on Python

- **Insert()**
  This function works the same as the function append but is more specific to the position at which the new item will appear in the existing list. The main important elements that are used in this function are the item position, the name of the item and the name of the list. The example below shows how the function is used.

### 3.4.3.2 Example: How to insert in a List

Here, is an example to insert an item in the list referring to position. This will show how items are added to specific index.

```python
fruits = ['mango', 'banana', 'orange', 'avocado', 'apple', 'tomato']
fruits.insert(2, 'pears')
print(fruits)
# ['mango', 'banana', 'pears', 'orange', 'avocado', 'apple', 'tomato']
# Considering that the indexing of the element in the list starts from 0
```

Figure 3-13 Item List

```
C:\Users\btaze\AppData\Local\Programs\Python\Python37\python.exe "C:
['mango', 'banana', 'pears', 'orange', 'avocado', 'apple', 'tomato']

Process finished with exit code 0
```

Figure 3-14 Output in Python

**Remove()&pop()**
This is used to delete an item from the list. Its syntax is the same as those of the other functions. When an item appears more than once in the list, the command remove () will only delete the item that appears the first in the list. if the command mentions an item that is not on the list, the functions will return an error which will indicate that the item is not on the list. While using this method, one does not need to specify the position of the item in the list (Sarkar,2016).

### 3.4.3.3 Example : How to remove from a List

Given below is an example that will show how to remove an item from specific position using remove function.

```python
fruits = ['mango', 'banana', 'pears', 'orange', 'avocado', 'apple', 'tomato']
fruits.remove('apple')
print(fruits)
# ['mango', 'banana', 'pears', 'orange', 'avocado', 'tomato']
```

Figure 3-15 code snippet

```
C:\Users\btaze\AppData\Local\Programs\Python\Python37\python.exe
Connected to pydev debugger (build 183.5912.18)
pydev debugger: process 592 is connecting

['mango', 'banana', 'pears', 'orange', 'avocado', 'tomato']
```

Figure 3-16 Output in Python

To remove an item by position, the function pop() is used. When the method pop() is called without specifying the position, the last item is deleted. When this method is used, an item is deleted and the function returns the value equal to the item that was deleted. The function is used as shown below

### 3.4.3.4 Example : How to pop from a List

Given below is an example that will show how to remove an item from specific position using pop function

```
1  fruits = ['mango', 'banana', 'pears', 'orange', 'avocado', 'apple', 'tomato']
2  fruits.pop()
3  # 'tomato'
4  print(fruits)
5  # ['mango', 'banana', 'pears', 'orange', 'avocado', 'apple']
6  fruits.pop(2)
7  # 'pears'
8  print(fruits)
9  # ['mango', 'banana', 'orange', 'avocado', 'apple']
10
```

Figure 3-17 code snippet

```
C:\Users\btaze\AppData\Local\Programs\Python\Python37\python.exe
pydev debugger: process 6800 is connecting

Connected to pydev debugger (build 183.5912.18)
['mango', 'banana', 'pears', 'orange', 'avocado', 'apple']
['mango', 'banana', 'orange', 'avocado', 'apple']

Process finished with exit code 0
```

Figure 3-18 Output in Python

- **Extend()**
  This method is used to add a list to another list. This method is different from append as it deals with joining of two lists. The method joins two lists by adding the second list to the end of the first list as shown in the example below.

### 3.4.3.5 Example: How to Extend a List

Given below is an example that will show how to add a list to another list.

```
fruits = ['mango', 'banana', 'pears', 'orange', 'avocado', 'apple', 'tomato']
fruits.extend(['berries', 'olive', 'crack nuts'])
print(fruits)
# ['mango', 'banana', 'pears', 'orange', 'avocado', 'apple', 'tomato', 'berries', 'olive'
```

Figure 3-19 code snippet

```
C:\Users\btaze\AppData\Local\Programs\Python\Python37\python.exe "C:/Users/btaze/Downloads/Chapter 3
['mango', 'banana', 'pears', 'orange', 'avocado', 'apple', 'tomato', 'berries', 'olive', 'crack nuts']

Process finished with exit code 0
```

Figure 3-20 Output in Python

### 3.4.4 More List Operations

There are some more list operations described below in table. Such as how to append a list to the end, insertion at any specific place, removing of object with certain value and position, returning, sorting and reversing of elements.

| | |
|---|---|
| lst.append(x) | append x to end of lst |
| lst.extend(L) | append list L to end of lst |
| lst.insert(i, x) | insert x at position i |
| lst.remove(x) | remove element with value x |
| lst.pop() | remove last element from lst |
| lst.pop(i) | remove element at position i |
| lst.index(x) | return index of element x |
| lst.count(x) | return count of x in lst |
| lst.sort() | sorts elements of lst |
| lst.reverse() | reverses elements of lst |

Table 6 More list Operations

*lst = []*

*lst.append(3)*

```python
print(lst)
# [3]
lst.extend(["hello", 2, "ab", 10])
print(lst)
# [3, 'hello', 2, 'ab', 10]
lst.insert(2, "world")
print(lst)
# [3, 'hello', 'world', 2, 'ab', 10]
lst.append(2)
print(lst)
# [3, 'hello', 'world', 2, 'ab', 10, 2]
lst.remove(2)
print(lst)
seq = [5, 12, 17, 18, 24, 32]
def myFunc(x):
  if (x < 18):
    return False
  else:
    return True
filtered = filter(myFunc, seq)
for x in filtered:
  print(x)
def myfunc(a, b):
  return a + b
x = map(myfunc, ('2', 2, 'cherry'), ('orange', 4, 'pineapple'))
```

*print(x)*

*#convert the map into a list, for readability:*

*print(list(x))*

```
C:\Users\btaze\AppData\Local\Programs\Python\Python37\python.exe
pydev debugger: process 10640 is connecting

Connected to pydev debugger (build 183.5912.18)
[3]
[3, 'hello', 2, 'ab', 10]
[3, 'hello', 'world', 2, 'ab', 10]
[3, 'hello', 'world', 2, 'ab', 10, 2]
[3, 'hello', 'world', 'ab', 10, 2]
18
24
32
<map object at 0x0000007100A87710>
['2orange', 6, 'cherrypineapple']
```

Figure 3-21 Output in Python

### 3.4.4.1 Reduce(function, sequence)

Reduce is used for performing a function on list. The 'functool' module defines this function. It gives a result of one value which has been created by executing a binary function on the selected number of items.

Firstly, two elements are chosen, and result is gathered. Then same function is applied to the results obtained. This is a continuous process until no element remains in list.

### 3.4.4.1 Example: How to reduce from a List

Given below is an example that will represent how we can reduce from a list
*>>> def h(x, y):*

... *if (type(x) == type(y)):*

... *return x + y*

... *elif (type(x) == type(1)):*

... *return str(x) + y*

... *else:*

... *return x + str(y)*

*>>> h(2, 3)*

5

```
>>> h("2", 3)
```
'23'

```
>>> reduce(h, [2, 3, 4, "ab", "3e", 3, 7, "cde"])
```
'9ab3e37cde'

### 3.4.5 Tuple

A tuple is a list of items enclosed in parenthesis (not brackets like lists)Unlike lists, a tuple is said to be immutable (can't be changed). Can do much the same operations with tuples as with lists, but tuples are more efficient A tuple is data structures that help in the organization of data in python. Since lists do the same organization as a tuple, it can be hard to differentiate between the two. The main difference, however, is that once topless have been created, they are hard to change. The following are the basic elements used by tuples (Sarkar, 2016).

| Operator | Description |
| --- | --- |
| [:] | This is used in slicing |
| * | This is used in repetition |
| + | It is used in concatenation |
| [] | Its known as the index operator |
| In | Indicates membership |
| len | This is more of a function for length |

Table 7 Operators with their descriptions

The difference between tuples and lists is that tuples are immutable while lists aren't. This means that items in the list can be modified while those in a tuple cannot be modified. Definition and calling of tuple related functions are done by calling the elements separated by commas within a pair of **parentheses**.

#### 3.4.4.1 How to use Tuples

After clarification of tuples' basic we will see how we can use tuples with examples.

#### 3.4.4.1.1 Example: The first Tuple Demonstration

Below is an example that will display the items using tuples.

```
zoo = ('dog', 'lion', 'leopard')
print('Number of animals in the zoo is', len(zoo))
new_animals = ('cat', 'bear', 'elephant')
print('Number of new animals in the zoo is', len(new_animals))
print(new_animals) # This function displays all the animals in the new_animals
print(new_animals[2]) # This function displays animals brought from new_ animals
print(new_animals[2][2]) # This function displays the last animal from animals
```

Figure 3-22 code snippet

```
C:\Users\btaze\AppData\Local\Programs\Python\Python37\python.exe
pydev debugger: process 11852 is connecting

Connected to pydev debugger (build 183.5912.18)
Number of animals in the zoo is 3
Number of new animals in the zoo is 3
('cat', 'bear', 'elephant')
elephant
e
```

Figure 3-23 Output in Python

### 3.4.4.1.2  Example : Another example of Tuples

Here is another example of tuples using operators.

```
tup = ("a", "abc", "abcde")
print(tup[0])
# 'a'
print(tup)
print(not tup)
tup = list(tup)
tup[1] = "efg"
tup = tuple(tup)
print(tup)
print (tup[0:])
print(tup[:2])
print(len(tup))
# 3
```

Figure 3-24 code snippet

```
C:\Users\btaze\AppData\Local\Programs\Python\Python37\python.exe
pydev debugger: process 8584 is connecting

Connected to pydev debugger (build 183.5912.18)
a
('a', 'abc', 'abcde')
False
('a', 'efg', 'abcde')
('a', 'efg', 'abcde')
('a', 'efg')
3
```

Figure 3-25 Output in Python

We will take a look at the uses of the operator in detail below.

### 3.4.4.2 Index Operator in Tuple

This is used to find a specific element in a tuple. As previously discussed in lists, tuplets indexing also start with zero going to one in the order. This means that the first items position is 0 and the second is one. The index operator is used to access an element that is found within the tuple.

#### 3.4.4.2.1 Example: Indexing an operator in Tuple

Given example is used to find a specific element in a tuple

```python
tuple1 = (5, 2, 6, 7, 8, "house")
print(tuple1)
# (5, 2, 6, 7, 8, 'house')
print(tuple1[2])
# 6
```

Figure 3-26 code snippet

```
C:\Users\btaze\AppData\Local\Programs\Python\Python37\python.exe
pydev debugger: process 9408 is connecting

Connected to pydev debugger (build 183.5912.18)
(5, 2, 6, 7, 8, 'house')
6
```

Figure 3-27 Output in Python

From the above example, we can complement that the index operator is used to find a specific element within a tuple. If the specified element is not within the tuple, an error message is shown.

#### 3.4.4.2.2 Example : Indexing an operator in Tuple

Not only whole tuple but you can call specific item from tuple by indexing. This is demonstrated in code below

```python
tuple1 = (5, 2, 6, 7, 8, 'house')
print(tuple1)
# (5, 2, 6, 7, 8, 'house')
print(tuple1[7])
```

Figure 3-28 code snippet

```
C:\Users\btaze\AppData\Local\Programs\Python\Python37\python.exe "C:/Users/btaze/Downloads
Traceback (most recent call last):
(5, 2, 6, 7, 8, 'house')
  File "C:/Users/btaze/Downloads/Chapter 3 Collection and sequences - Fixed Scripts/Chapte
    print(tuple1 [7])
IndexError: tuple index out of range

Process finished with exit code 1
```

Figure 3-29 Output in python

### 3.4.4.3 Concatenation Operator

Concatenation is a way to combine strings. The concatenation operators are described by the symbol (+). Python is going to combine two or more strings only. It cannot concatenate string and integer. For concatenating the integer should also be converted to string.

#### 3.4.4.3.1 Example: Concatenation Operator Demonstration

Following example will show how to combine two strings.

```
1   tuple1 = (8, 9, 5, 2, 4)
2   tuple2 = (7, 1, 0, 2, 3)
3   tuple3 = tuple1 + tuple2
4   print(tuple3)
5   # (8, 9, 5, 2, 4, 7, 1, 0, 2, 3)
6
```

Figure 3-30

```
C:\Users\btaze\AppData\Local\Programs\Python\Python37\python.exe
(8, 9, 5, 2, 4, 7, 1, 0, 2, 3)

Process finished with exit code 0
```

Figure 3-31 Output in Python

### 3.4.4.4 Repetition Operator

This operator is used to reprint the tuple as many times as mentioned. It is represented by the symbol (*). The function works within the print function as it can be compiled by the python compilers during execution.

#### 3.4.4.4.1 Example: Demonstration of Repetition Operator

The example will show how a tuple is printed 2 times using *2. It will call as many times as mentioned.

```
tuple1 = (8, 9, 5, 2, 4)
print(tuple1 *2)
# (8, 9, 5, 2, 4, 8, 9, 5, 2, 4)
```

Figure 3-32 code snippet

```
C:\Users\btaze\AppData\Local\Programs\Python\Python37\python.exe
(8, 9, 5, 2, 4, 8, 9, 5, 2, 4)

Process finished with exit code 0
```

Figure 3-33 Output in Python

From the above example, you realize that tuples are not easy to modify, here the modification is done during execution and not compilation as it is impossible then.

### 3.4.4.5 Slicing operation in Tuples

Slicing function is used to obtain part of the tuple. The main elements used in slicing is the index operator and the slicing symbol (:) the example below explains how slicing is done with tuples.

#### 3.4.4.5.1 Example: Demonstration of Slicing Operators

The example below will demonstrate the printing of tuple and obtain its specific part using slicing operator.

*Print() we use for print tuple*

*tuple1 = (5, 2, 6, 7, 8, 'house')*

*print(tuple1)*

*# (5, 2, 6, 7, 8, 'house')*

*print(tuple1[2:4])*

*# (6, 7)*

*# this prints from exactly position 2 to position before 4 that is position 3.*

*print(tuple1 [:4])*

*# (5, 2, 6, 7)*

*#this prints exactly from the first element to the element just before the element in position 4*

*print(tuple1 [-4:])*

*# (6, 7, 8, 'house')*

*# this function extracts the fourth item from the end of the tuple*

*print(tuple1 [:-4])*

*# (5, 2)*

*# This function shows the first item in the tuple to the item just before item at position*

*# 4 from the end. In other words, if the items were to be rearranged from the end to the first, it*

*# would show the items from the position 4 to the end.*

*print(tuple1 [:])*

*# (5, 2, 6, 7, 8, 'house')*

*# This function prints the whole tuple*

```
C:\Users\btaze\AppData\Local\Programs\Python\Python37\python.exe
(5, 2, 6, 7, 8, 'house')
(6, 7)
(5, 2, 6, 7)
(6, 7, 8, 'house')
(5, 2)
(5, 2, 6, 7, 8, 'house')

Process finished with exit code 0
```

Figure 3-34 Output in Python

### 3.4.6  Strings

String are a collection of characters that have meaning. Characters in other terms are simple letters and symbols that are used to construct a string. Character include alphanumeric letters, numbers and white space. In Python, strings are written and enclosed between either single or double quotes. Another type of build in functions we are going to look at is the operation for python strings. The string can be described as a form of text storage and organization that is ordered in order to provide the easy modification. Strings are basically a group of characters (immutable) (Sarkar, 2016).

#### 3.4.6.1  Example : Demonstration of a String

*Eg. 'table' or "table"*

Strings can also be empty. In the example below, we realize that the strings don't have any characters. That is called an empty string. E.g. '' or "".Single- and Double-Quoted strings are the same

*>>> 'Hello World' , "Hello World"*

The reason for including both is that it allows you to embed a quote character of the other inside a string

>>> "knight's" , 'knight"s'

Strings are usually assigned variables and are immutable, once a string variable has been created and declared, it is impossible to change its values unless a new string is created. Strings, however, have a few operators that are available to facilitate its presentation and storage. The operators are explained below (VanRossum, 2010).

### 3.4.6.1 Index Operators in Strings

The index operators are enclosed in the symbol []. This operator is used to access the individual characters in a string. Index operator is necessary for specification and explanation of the character that needs to be operated. Like any programming indexing, the first character in the string is represented by the position 0, while the $n^{th}$ character will be at position n-1. To display a character at a certain position the function print is called followed by an index operator containing the position of the character.

#### 3.4.6.1.1   Example: Demonstration of Index Operators in Strings

Given below is an example that will demonstrate the index operator in string.

```
school = "Computing"
print(school)
# Computing
print(school [0])
# C
print(school [3])
# P
print(school [22])
```

Figure 3-35 code snippet

```
C:\Users\btaze\AppData\Local\Programs\Python\Python37\python.exe
Traceback (most recent call last):
Computing
C
  File "C:/Users/btaze/Downloads/Chapter 3 Collection and sequenc
p
    print(school [22])
IndexError: string index out of range
```

Figure 3-36 Output in Python

#### 3.4.6.1.1   Slicing Operator in Strings

As mentioned earlier, slicing operator is used when a user wants to extract a certain group of characters from a string. There are various ways of manipulating a string using the slicing method.

### 3.4.6.1.1.1    Example: Demonstration of Slicing operators in Strings

The example below shows how slicing operation is applied on strings

*Print() we use for printing the variable and it also print variable at specific index.*

*school = 'Computing It'*

*print(school)*

*# Computing It*

*print(school [2:4])*

*# mp*

*# this prints from exactly position 2 to position before 4 that is position 3.*

*print(school [:4])*

*# Com*

*#this prints exactly from the first element to the element just before the element in position 4*

*print(school [-4:])*

*# g It*

*# this function extracts the fourth item from the end of the string*

*print(school [:-4])*

*# Computing*

*# This function shows the first item in the string to the item just before item at position*

*# 4 from the end. In other words, if the items were to be rearranged from the end to the first, it*

*# would show the items from the position 4 to the end.*

*print(school [:])*

*# Computing It*

*# This function prints the whole string*

```
C:\Users\btaze\AppData\Local\Programs\Python\Python37\python.exe
Computing It
mp
Comp
g It
Computin
Computing It
```

Figure 3-37 Output in Python

**Addition Operation**

This operator allows the user to put together two strings to come up with the third string

**3.4.6.1.2    Example: Demonstration of Addition Operators**

The following example will demonstrate how two strings to come up with the third string.

```
fname ="John"
sname ="Karuma"
print(fname + sname)
# JohnKaruma
fullname = fname + " "+sname
print(fullname)
# John Karuma
```

Figure 3-38 code snippet

```
C:\Users\btaze\AppData\Local\Programs\Python\Python37\python.exe
pydev debugger: process 1952 is connecting

Connected to pydev debugger (build 183.5912.18)
JohnKaruma
John Karuma

Process finished with exit code 0
```

Figure 3-39 Output in Python

**3.4.6.1.2    Repetition operators**

Repetition may seem a bit obscure at first, but it comes in handy in a surprising number of contexts. For example, to print a line of 80 dashes

*>>> print '-' * 80*

**3.4.6.1.3    Strings with secret codes**

In the early days of computers, each manufacturer used their own encoding of numbers for characters (Lutz, 2014). ASCII system (American Standard Code for Information Interchange) uses 127-bit codes. Python supports Unicode (100,000+ characters) The *ord* function returns the numeric (ordinal) code of a single character.

#### 3.4.6.1.3.1 Example:

The *chr* function converts a numeric code to the corresponding character.

```
print(ord("A"))
# 65
print(ord("a"))
# 97
print(chr(97))
# 'a'
print(chr(65))
# 'A'
```

Figure 3-39 code snippet

```
C:\Users\btaze\AppData\Local\Programs\Python\Python37\python.exe
65
97
a
A

Process finished with exit code 0
```

Figure 3-40 Output in Python

### 3.4.6.1.4 Performing string counts

Python wordcount.py Enter a line of text:the clown ran after the car and the car ran into the tent and the tent fell down on the clown and the car

#### 3.4.6.1.4.1 Example: Demonstration of String Counts

Following is an example that will count the strings

```
str = "welcome to our house"

x = str.split()

print(x)

Words = ['ran', 'after', 'the', 'into', 'the', 'car', 'and', 'the', 'car', 'ran',
         'tent', 'and', 'the', 'tent', 'fell', 'down', 'on', 'the', 'clown', 'the',
         'clown', 'and', 'the', 'car']

for line in Words:
    Type = line.split(",")
    y = Type[0]
    print(y)
```

Figure 3-41 code snippet

```
C:\Users\btaze\AppData\Local\Programs\Python\Python37\python.exe
['welcome', 'to', 'our', 'house']
ran
after
the
into
the
car
and
the
car
ran
tent
and
the
tent
fell
down
```

Figure 3-42 Output in Python

### 3.4.6.1.5 String functions

We introduce String Functions which are made with the aim of reusability. The table below shows the String functions and their descriptions. In this case, reusability simply means that a group of codes can be an accessed using a unique key. In other words, a group of codes is given a name that can be called to make them execute. In most cases, String functions can even be assigned expectations so that when they are called a certain element is pursed in the call in order to be used in the execution of the code. The name given to the function or the keyword given to the function is called an identifier. It can be reused in the whole class. These functions have the main aim of reducing repetition of codes.

### 3.4.6.1.6 Function parameters

Function parameters are those values that are necessary for the execution of the code. In other words, they are the digits or characters that are passed when a function is called so as to facilitate the execution of the codes in the function.

### 3.4.6.1.7 Variables (Global and local)

Variable as mostly used with functions. These variables have to be declared before they can be used in a function. After the declaration, the function will consider the values local and will only use them in the function, this means that they cannot be accessed outside the function. That is why they are called local functions. Global variables are declared at the start of the coding. This is because they are going to be used in the whole application.

| String Function | Description |
|---|---|
| Upper() | Changers the whole string to upper case |
| Lower() | Changes the whole string to lower case |
| Isalpha() | This method checks if all the characters in a string contain only alphabets |
| Strip() | It deletes all the trailing and leading spaces in a string |
| Isspace() | This function is used to check whether the characters that have been stored as a string are all spaces |
| Isdigit() | The function is digit checks if all the characters that are in the string are digits |
| Endswith(x) | This function checks whether the string specified ends with the character or string represented by x |
| Startswith(x) | This function returns true or false on a condition that the string specified starts with the character or string x |
| Find(X) | This function checks of a string contain X, if false, the function returns -1 |
| Replace(x, y) | This function finds every x and replaces it with a y |
| Split(x) | This function splits a string to a list with x as the split point |
| Join(x) | This function reverses the split function |

Table 8 String Functions

The example with detail explanation of String Function usage

### 3.4.6.1.7.1   Example: Demonstration of String Functions

This example will demonstrate how to check for different positions of characters in a list. It will demonstrate the function to check for alphabets, space check or digit check.

*We have used different methods .lower(), .upper(), .strip(), .isdigit()*

school = "Computing It"

print(school)

# Computing It

print(school.lower())

# computing it

print(school.upper())

# COMPUTING IT

print(school.strip())

# ComputingIt

print(school.isalpha())

# False

print(school.isdigit())

# False

print(school.isspace())

# False

print(school.startswith("Comp"))

# True

# This method is case sensitive and returns false if the wrong case is indexed

print(school.endswith("It"))

# True

# This method is also case sensitive and returns false if the wrong case is indexed

print(school.split(" "))

# ['Computing', 'It']

# school = ['Computing', 'It']

print(school.join(school))

# computing it

```
C:\Users\btaze\AppData\Local\Programs\Python\Python37\python.exe "C:/Users/btaze/Download
Computing It
computing it
COMPUTING IT
Computing It
False
False
False
True
True
['Computing', 'It']
CComputing ItoComputing ItmComputing ItpComputing ItuComputing IttComputing ItiComputing

Process finished with exit code 0
```

Figure 3-43 Output in Python

From the example shown on string operations, we can see how of characters is used to come up with constructive results relevant to the situation. When learning about slicing, it is good to also look at the practical use of the skills. In this example, we have learned to find the different positions of the characters in a list. A practical application of this technique is when using password recovery features I.e. in google. You will realize that sometimes the user is shown a phone number in order to be sent some verification code. The user is then shown a few characters of the displayed number and told to complete the rest of the characters. In this case, it helps alit in authentication and security services where all the characters in the data don't have to be shown.

## 3.5 Escape sequences

There is a special characteristic that is understood by the compiler as commands other than characters. All these characters are known as the Escape Sequences. The special characters are marked with a backslash'\'.

The backslash( '\') would, therefore, indicate that the character that is going to be printed next is a special one that should initiate some instructions. Below are the examples of special character that are used with strings:

| Escape Sequence | Description |
|---|---|
| \n | Newline. Position the screen cursor to the beginning of the next line. |
| \t | Horizontal tab. Move the screen cursor to the next tab stop. |
| \r | Carriage return. Position the screen cursor to the beginning of the current line; do not advance to the next line. |
| \a | Alert. Sound the system bell (beep) |
| \\ | Backslash. Used to print a backslash character. |
| \" | Double quote. Used to print a double quote character. |

Table 9 Escape Sequences

We cannot specify 'What's your name?' In python 'What\'s your name?' or "What's your name?" is the correct format
Also, we have to indicate the backslash itself using an escape sequence \\.

Other String features Include

**Raw Strings:**
To avoid special processing on a string such as escape sequences. Specify a raw string by prefixing r or R to the string

*e.g., r "Newlines are indicated by \n."*

**Unicode Strings:**
Unicode is a standard used for internationalization. For writing text in our native languages such as Urdu or Arabic, we need to have a Unicode-enabled text editor. To use Unicode strings in Python, we prefix the string with u or U.

E.g. u "This is a Unicode string."
Strings are immutable. Once created, cannot be changed. String literal concatenation. Placing two string literals side by side get concatenated automatically by Python.E.g., 'What\'s ' "your name?" is automatically converted to "What's your name?" .

## Other string Methods

| | |
|---|---|
| s.capitalize() | returns copy of s with first letter capitalized |
| s.lower() | returns copy of s with first letter in lower case |
| s.swapcase() | returns a copy of s in which the character case of each letter has been switched |
| s.title() | returns a copy of s in which all words start with uppercase and all other characters are lower case |
| s.upper() | returns a copy of s converted to uppercase |
| s.isalpha() | returns True if all characters alphabetic |
| s.isalnum() | returns True if all characters are alphanumeric |
| s.isdigit() | returns True if all characters are digits |
| s.islower() | returns True if all characters are lowercase |
| s.isspace() | returns True if s is only whitespace |
| s.istitle() | returns True if s is titlecased |
| s.isupper() | returns True if all cased characters are uppercase |
| s.count(sub [, start[,end]] | returns the number of non-overlapping occurrence of the string sub in s |
| s.startswith(sub [, start[, end]]) | returns True if the indicated part of s starts with the string sub |
| s.find(sub [, start[, end]]) | returns the leftmost index in the indicated portion of the string s of the string sub; returns -1 if sub not found |
| s.index(sub [, start[, end]]) | like find but introduces an IndexError exception if sub not found |
| s.rfind(sub [, start[, end]]) | like find, but finds rightmost occurrence |
| s.rindex(sub [, start[, end]]) | like rfind but can introduce IndexError exception |
| s.expandtabs([tabsize]) | returns a copy of s with tabs replaced by tabsize (default 8) spaces |
| s.lstrip() | returns a copy of s with leading whitespace removed |
| s.replace(old, new[, maxsplit]) | returns a copy of s with old replaced by new a maximum of maxsplit times |
| s.rstrip() | returns a copy of s with trailing whitespace removed |
| s.strip() | strips leading and trailing whitespace |
| s.translate(table [, deletechars]) | returns a copy of s where all characters in deletechars have been removed and all others have been translated using table (uses maketrans function to create translate table) |
| s.split([sep [, maxsplit]]) | return a list of strings between the occurrences of sep (default whitespace) |
| s.join(seq) | return a string formed by concatenating the strings in the sequence seq |

Table 10 String Methods

### 3.5.1 String formatting

String formatting shows that if the string contains a % then the format following the % is replaced by a value specified following the string

#### 3.5.1.1 Example: String Formatting

Given below is an example how % is replaced

```
a = 3
print("the value of a is %03d " % a)
# the value of a is 003
a = 3
b = 4
print("the values of a and b are %d and %d" % (a, b))
```

Figure 3-44 code snippet

```
C:\Users\btaze\AppData\Local\Programs\Python\Python37\python.exe
pydev debugger: process 6800 is connecting

Connected to pydev debugger (build 183.5912.18)
the value of a is 003
the values of a and b are 3 and 4

Process finished with exit code 0
```

Figure 3-45 Output in Python

#### 3.5.1.1 Components of formatting:

a) The beginning is marked by % .
b) Mapping key in parentheses consisting of a name used as an index into a dictionary (optional)
   conversion flags (optional)
c) Minimum field length (optional)
d) Precision is given as a. followed by the field length (optional)
e) Length modifier (optional)

**Conversion type:**

| # | Conversion will use "alternate form (specific meaning depends upon conversion type) |
|---|---|
| 0 | Numeric values are zero padded |
| - | Converted value is left justified |
|   | Space blank before a positive number |
| + | Sign placed before the conversion |

Table 11 Conversion Types

**String Conversion types and Examples**

| | |
|---|---|
| d, I | signed integer |
| U | unsigned integer |
| O | unsigned octal |
| x,X | unsigned hex |
| e, E | floating point exponential format |
| f,F | floating point decimal format |
| g,G | either floating point or decimal format depending upon precision |
| C | Character |
| r, s | String |
| % | results in % being displayed |

Table 12 String Conversion Types

### 3.5.2.1 Example : Demonstrating Conversion types

Following example will show the conversion type in piece of code
>>> *print "%2d" % 23*

*23*

>>> *print "% 2d" % 23*

 *23*

>>> *print "%5.2f" % 23.478692*

*23.48*

>>> *print "%g" % 100299.399009657*

*100299*

>>> *print "%g" % 1002999.399009657*

*1.003e+06*

>>> *print "hello %10s" % "CS 5530"*

*hello    CS 5530*

>>> *print "hello %s" % "CS 5530"*

*hello CS 5530*

>>> *print "hello %-10s" % "CS 5530"*

*hello CS 5530*
*>>> a = 3*

*>>> str = "the value of a is %f" % a*

*>>> str*

*'the value of a is 3.000000'*

*>>> print "the value of a is %03d" % a*

*the value of a is 003*

*>>> print "the value of a is %+03d" % a*

*the value of a is +03*

*>>> print "the name of dad is %(dad)s" % { "dad" : "jay", "mom":"cindy" }*

*the name of dad is jay*

*>>> print "the name of mom is %(mom)10s" % { "dad" : "jay", "mom":"cindy" }*

*the name of mom is      cindy*

*>>> print "the name of mom is %(mom)-10s!" % { "dad" : "jay", "mom":"cindy" }*

*the name of mom is cindy     !*

## 3.6 Mappings

Mappings contain immutable arbitrary objects that are used to store data in python. A passed-in function is applied to every item. All the function call results will be in this list returned. Mapping works exactly how a for loop but, it is faster than for loop. Maps in multiple arguments will send them each in parallel manner as distinctive one.

Dictionaries are its major primary category and discussed in the next section

## 3.7 Dictionaries

Dictionary is built in a way similar to that of contacts in a phone. This means that data and items are searched using the names or the values i.e. the name in the contact is given a value that is a telephone number.

Each name must be different in order to maintain uniqueness i.e. to get the correct information about a person named John in a phone book, there has to be only one name that is saved as John. The best values to use for storage in dictionaries are the immutable lines, this includes the strings. When creating the values, any kind of data can be used. Miutability of the data does not matter very much d = {firstkey : firstvalue, secondkey : secondvalue }.

To differentiate between the key and the value, we use a colon, while to differentiate between two keys, we use a comma.

The dictionary type is Python's name for the associative array. Dictionary literal is a set of braces enclosing a comma-separated list of key-value pairs where key-value pairs are separated by a colon.

### 3.7.1.1 Example: Demonstration of Dictionary

Following example will demonstrate creation of dictionaries and will show its immutable nature

>>> *fam = {"mom":"cindy", "dad":"jay", "oldest": "baron", "middle":"grayson", "youngest": "ethan"}*

>>> *fam["mom"]*

*'cindy'*

*keys must be an immutable type: string, number, tuple*

>>> *dic = {1:"integer", "abc":"string", 3.7:"float", (1, 3):"tuple"}*

>>> *dic[1]*

*'integer'*

>>> *dic["abc"]*

*'string'*

>>> *dic[3.7]*

*'float'*

>>> *dic[(1, 3)]*

```
Python 3.7.0 Shell                                    —   □   ×
File Edit Shell Debug Options Window Help
Python 3.7.0 (v3.7.0:1bf9cc5093, Jun 27 2018, 04:59:51) [MSC v.1914 64 bit (AMD6
4)] on win32
Type "copyright", "credits" or "license()" for more information.
>>> fam = {"mom":"cindy", "dad":"jay", "oldest": "baron",
"middle":"grayson",  "youngest": "ethan"}
>>> fam["mom"]
'cindy'
>>> dic = {1:"integer", "abc":"string", 3.7:"float", (1, 3):"tuple"}
>>> dic[1]
'integer'
>>> dic["abc"]
'string'
>>> dic[3.7]
'float'
>>> dic[(1, 3)]
'tuple'
>>>
```

Figure 3-46 Output in Python

### 3.7.1 Modification of dictionaries

Dictionary elements can be created, accessed, modified or deleted. While a dictionary is created, its elements will contain a key value pair to be accessed. Access it using myDict and key variable. You can also delete some values or delete a complete dictionary using del and clear respectively.

#### 3.7.1.1 Example: Demonstration of modifying a dictionary

Here, is a demonstration to modify the dictionary items. Use dictionary keys to modify the values. Also remove the undesired item from given elements.

>>> *fam = {"mom":"cindy", "dad":"jay", "oldest": "baron",*

*"middle":"grayson", "youngest": "ethan"}*

>>> *fam["mom"]*

*'cindy'*

*keys must be an immutable type: string, number, tuple*

>>> *dic = {1:"integer", "abc":"string", 3.7:"float", (1, 3):"tuple"}*

>>> *dic[1]*

*'integer'*

>>> *dic["abc"]*

*'string'*

>>> *dic[3.7]*

*'float'*

>>> *dic[(1, 3)]*

```
Python 3.7.0 Shell                                      —  □  ×
File Edit Shell Debug Options Window Help
Python 3.7.0 (v3.7.0:1bf9cc5093, Jun 27 2018, 04:59:51) [MSC v.1914 64 bit (AMD6
4)] on win32
Type "copyright", "credits" or "license()" for more information.
>>> fam = {"mom":"cindy", "dad":"jay", "oldest": "baron",
"middle":"grayson",  "youngest": "ethan"}
>>> fam["mom"]
'cindy'
>>> dic = {1:"integer", "abc":"string", 3.7:"float", (1, 3):"tuple"}
>>> dic[1]
'integer'
>>> dic["abc"]
'string'
>>> dic[3.7]
'float'
>>> dic[(1, 3)]
'tuple'
>>>
```

Figure 3-47 Output in Python

### 3.7.1.2 Example: Nested Dictionary

A dictionary within dictionary constitutes nested dictionary. It accumulated multiple dictionaries into one. Each dictionary will have its own value and key. It is quite evident from the example below.

>>> *family = {"mom":"carol", "dad":"mike"}*

>>> *family["momkids"] = {"oldest":"marcia", "middle":"jan", "youngest":"cindy"}*

>>> *family["dadkids"] = {"oldest":"greg", "middle":"peter", "youngest":"bobby"}*

>>> *print family*

*{'dad': 'mike', 'momkids': {'youngest': 'cindy', 'middle': 'jan', 'oldest': 'marcia'}, 'mom': 'carol', 'dadkids': {'youngest': 'bobby', 'middle': 'peter', 'oldest': 'greg'}}*

>>> *family["housekeeper"] = "alice"*

>>> *print family*

*{'dad': 'mike', 'housekeeper': 'alice', 'momkids': {'youngest': 'cindy', 'middle': 'jan', 'oldest': 'marcia'}, 'mom': 'carol', 'dadkids': {'youngest': 'bobby', 'middle': 'peter', 'oldest': 'greg'}}*

```
Python 3.7.0 Shell                                              —    □   ×
File Edit Shell Debug Options Window Help
Python 3.7.0 (v3.7.0:1bf9cc5093, Jun 27 2018, 04:59:51) [MSC v.1914 64 bit (AMD6
4)] on win32
Type "copyright", "credits" or "license()" for more information.
>>> family = {"mom":"carol", "dad":"mike"}
>>> family["momkids"] = {"oldest":"marcia", "middle":"jan", "youngest":"cindy"}
>>> family
{'mom': 'carol', 'dad': 'mike', 'momkids': {'oldest': 'marcia', 'middle': 'jan',
'youngest': 'cindy'}}
>>> family["housekeeper"] = "alice"
>>> family
{'mom': 'carol', 'dad': 'mike', 'momkids': {'oldest': 'marcia', 'middle': 'jan',
'youngest': 'cindy'}, 'housekeeper': 'alice'}
>>>
```

Figure 3-48 Output in Python

### 3.7.1.3 Example:

Dictionaries are lookup tables. They map from a "key" to a "value". This is because dictionaries are convertible and can be mutated.

```
symbol_to_name = {
    "H": "hydrogen",
    "He": "helium",
    "Li": "lithium",
    "C": "carbon",
    "O": "oxygen",
    "N": "nitrogen"
}
print(symbol_to_name["H"])
print(symbol_to_name["He"])
print(symbol_to_name["Li"])
print(symbol_to_name["C"])
print(symbol_to_name["O"])
print(symbol_to_name["N"])
```

Figure 3-49 code snippet

```
C:\Users\btaze\AppData\Local\Programs\Python\Python37\python.exe
pydev debugger: process 6556 is connecting

Connected to pydev debugger (build 183.5912.18)
hydrogen
helium
lithium
carbon
oxygen
nitrogen
```

Figure 3-50 Output in Python

Dictionary Keys are arbitrary values that aren't hashable and can be compared by use of values instead of their preferred object identity. All the values obey the normal string and numeric rules that are usually used. Creation of dictionaries is done by placing a comma-separated in the syntax of the key then the value. e.g. 'name': jack

## 3.7.2 Constructor

Another method of dictionary creation is the use of a constructor. A contractor declares the class dict then accesses it after the declaration. When a constructor is called, a dictionary is created and initialized. We pass the parameters or key value pairs in constructor block for the construction of dictionary.

### 3.7.1.4 Example: Constructor

Following example will give a demo of how the constructors are build. It will also give us a comparison of values in dictionary.

>>> a = dict(one=1, two=2, three=3)

# Declaration and initialization of a dictionary a

>>> b = {'one': 1, 'two': 2, 'three': 3}

# Declaration and initialization of a dictionary b

>>> c = dict(zip(['one', 'two', 'three'], [1, 2, 3]))

# Declaration and initialization of a dictionary c

>>> d = dict([('two', 2), ('one', 1), ('three', 3)])

# Declaration and initialization of a dictionary d

>>> e = dict({'three': 3, 'one': 1, 'two': 2})

# Declaration and initialization of a dictionary e

>>> a == b == c == d == e

True #    This is known as a comparison, it shows how the values of the dictionaries are compared to each other.

```
Python 3.7.0 Shell
File  Edit  Shell  Debug  Options  Window  Help
Python 3.7.0 (v3.7.0:1bf9cc5093, Jun 27 2018, 04:59:51) [MSC v.1914 64 bit (AMD6
4)] on win32
Type "copyright", "credits" or "license()" for more information.
>>> a = dict(one=1, two=2, three=3)
>>> b = {'one': 1, 'two': 2, 'three': 3}
>>> c = dict(zip(['one', 'two', 'three'], [1, 2, 3]))
>>> d = dict([('two', 2), ('one', 1), ('three', 3)])
>>> e = dict({'three': 3, 'one': 1, 'two': 2})
>>> a == b == c == d == e
True
>>>
```

Figure 3-51 code in Python

*Examples describing the use of dictionaries*

Dictionary has a lot of uses since it is mutable. It can be used to access items, adding new pairs, deletion of variables. It can also return shallow variables, new views of items, returning arbitrary value or updating with the value pairs from overwriting. Some of the functions are performed below depicting how to use dictionary.

### 3.7.1.5 Example: How to use dictionaries

Now the use of dictionary is demonstrated by following example

*variable1={ 'Myname' : 'Sam John,*    *'MySiz' : 'Daniella,*

   *'Dad' : 'david',*

   *'Mom' : 'Dammy' }*

\>>>*print "Myname's address is %s" % variable1['Myname']*

*# Adding a new pair*

\>>>*variable1['Guido'] = 'guido@python.org'*

*# Deleting an existing pair*

*del variable1['Spammer']*

\>>>*print "\nThere are %d contacts in the address-\ book\n" % len(variable1)*

\>>>*for name, address in variable1.items():*

\>>>*print 'Contact %s at %s' % (name, address)*

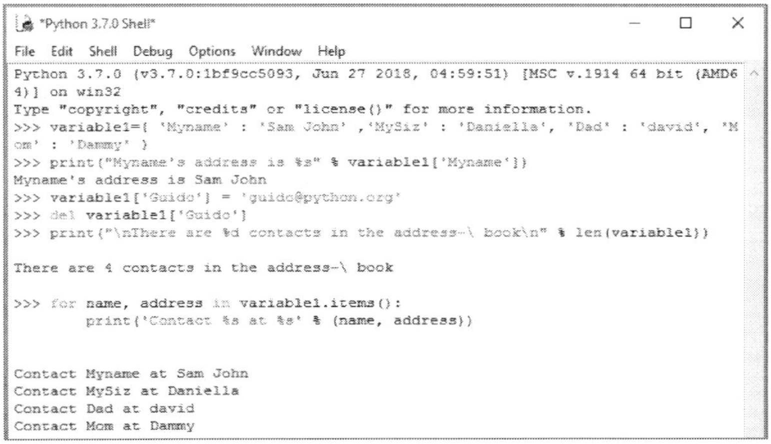

Figure 3-52 Output in Python

### 3.7.3 More on Dictionaries

Let us discuss some more functionalities related to dictionaries:

#### 3.7.3.1 Akin to Java Maps

Like Java Maps

*Hash tables, "associative arrays"*

*elem = {"duck": "eend", "water": "water"}*

```
# Hash tables, "associative arrays"
elem = {"duck": "eend", "water": "water"}
elem["crocodile"] = "water"
print(elem)
```

Figure 3-53 code snippet

```
C:\Users\btaze\AppData\Local\Programs\Python\Python37\python.exe
pydev debugger: process 7336 is connecting

Connected to pydev debugger (build 183.5912.18)
{'duck': 'eend', 'water': 'water', 'crocodile': 'water'}

Process finished with exit code 0
```

Figure 3-54 Output in Python

#### 3.7.3.2 Lookup:

Hash maps allow lookups as shown below.

*elem["duck"] -> "eend"*

*elem["back"] # raises KeyError exception*

```
banana = ("banana", "a yellow fruit")
orange = ("orange", "a orange fruit")
apple = ("apple", "a green fruit")
my_list = [banana, orange, apple]

def lookup():
    word = input("Word to lookup: ")
    print_("\n")
    for fruit in my_list:
        if fruit[0] == word:
            print(fruit[0], ":", fruit[1], "\n")
            return
    print("That word does not exist in the dictionary")
lookup()
```

Figure 3-55 code snippet

```
C:\Users\btaze\AppData\Local\Programs\Python\Python37\python.exe
pydev debugger: process 7944 is connecting

Connected to pydev debugger (build 183.5912.18)
Word to lookup: banana


banana : a yellow fruit
```

Figure 3-56 Output in Python

### 3.7.3.3 Delete, insert, overwrite:

You can even delete, insert or overwrite dictionary.

*del elem["water"] # {"duck": "eend"}*

*elem["back"] = "rug" # {"duck": "eend", "back": "rug"}*

*elem["duck"] = "duik" # {"duck": "duik", "back": "rug"}*

```
elem = {"duck": "eend", "water": "water"}
del elem["water"]  # {"duck": "eend"}
print(elem)
elem["back"] = "rug"  # {"duck": "eend", "back": "rug"}
print(elem)
elem["duck"] = "duik"  # {"duck": "duik", "back": "rug"}
print(elem)
```

Figure 3-57 code snippet

```
C:\Users\btaze\AppData\Local\Programs\Python\Python37\python.exe
Connected to pydev debugger (build 183.5912.18)
pydev debugger: process 5476 is connecting

{'duck': 'eend'}
{'duck': 'eend', 'back': 'rug'}
{'duck': 'duik', 'back': 'rug'}
```

Figure 3-58 Output in Python

### 3.7.3.4 Keys, values, items:

Tree maps show unique keys to values. Consider the code below;

*elem.keys() -> ["duck", "back"]*

*elem.values() -> ["duik", "rug"]*

*elem.items() -> [("duck","duik"), ("back","rug")]*

105

```
3.7.4.4 keys.py
1    elem = {"duck": "eend", "water": "water"}
2    print(elem.keys())
3    print(elem.values())
4    print(elem.items())
5
```

Figure 3-59 code snippet

```
C:\Users\btaze\AppData\Local\Programs\Python\Python37\python.exe
pydev debugger: process 1496 is connecting

Connected to pydev debugger (build 183.5912.18)
dict_keys(['duck', 'water'])
dict_values(['eend', 'water'])
dict_items([('duck', 'eend'), ('water', 'water')])
```

Figure 3-60 Output in Python

### 3.7.3.5 Presence check:

Let us check for the presence of keys by following code.

*elem = {"duck": "eend", "water": "water"}*

*print(elem.has_key("duck"))*

*print(elem.has_key("spam"))*

*# Values of any type; keys almost any*

*{"name":"Guido", "age":43, ("hello","world"):1,*

*42:"yes", "flag": ["red","white","blue"]}*

```
$python main.py
True
False
```

### 3.7.4  Reason for key Immutability:

Immutable elements in python include tuples, strings and numbers, the main reason behind this is because of their first lookout technique not lists or other dictionaries. The only operations that be done to these elements are on values, values can be changed in any way that the programmer wants as long as its within its limits i.e strings remain strings. It is more convenient because the requirements of storage will remain unchanged and fixed. It will ensure safety to reuse strings. The string objects returned will be immutated.

Also, the numbers will remain numbers through the performance. Nothing can convert two into three without any operation.

## 3.8 Sets

Sets are also a mapping object that is hashable and unordered. For this reason, while manipulating sets, the element position or insertion is not recorded. They, therefore, do not support function including slicing, indexing and any other function that is associated with sequencing. The methods applicable to sets are limited. Example of the methods are add() and remove() methods. Sets can also be introduced by a constructor in the syntax

*class set([x]) or*

*class frozenset([x])*

Sets are similar to dictionaries in Python, except that they consist of only keys with no associated values and hence unordered and can't be indexed. Essentially, they are a collection of data with no duplicates. They are very useful when it comes to removing duplicate data from data collections. During this initialization, the function returns a new set and puts the elements x in the set.

| Function | Description |
|---|---|
| **Lens(x)** | This function returns the number of elements in the set x |
| **Y in x** | This function checks if Y is a member of x |
| **Y not in s** | This function checks if Y is not a member of s |
| **Isdisjoint()** | This function returns true if the set has got no common elements |
| **Y is subset(x)** | This function returns true if y is a subset of x |

Table 13 Functions and their demonstration

The set has elements in unordered collection. Testing membership, removal of duplicates and intersection, union, difference on mathematical operations are common uses of sets. However, due to unordered nature they do not support indexing, slicing or any sequential behavior. Sets implication owes to dictionary. As all elements of set are immutable so any mutable element is also converted prior into immutable one. This is done by hash tables or as immutable() method.

There are some other methods like:

Python Set Remove() for removing elements.

Python Set Add() for adding elements.

Python Set Copy() for returning shallow copy.

isdisjoint() to check for disjoint elements.

issubset to check the subset of set.

Symmetric difference update to return the symmetric difference, python enumerate to return enumeration etc.

## 3.9 Summary

In this chapter we have discussed various types of Collections such as Lists, Tuple, Strings, Dictionary and sets. We discussed sequence types and mapping types with the concept of ordering and indexing. Sequence constituted strings, numbers, lists and tuples while dictionary was included in mapping. String, Tuples fall into immutable while lists are in mutable category.

We discussed lists as the most flexible ordered collection and demonstrated it. Creation, slicing, append, insert, pop, extend etc were some of the methods discussed in this chapter. The usage of tuple was also evident from its demonstrations. We discussed some operators with reference to tuples. Then we headed towards strings and showed why they are immutable.

We also dealt with dictionaries, how to create it, access, delete and modify it. Last but not the least we discussed the functionalities of sets.

## 3.10 Conclusion

For organization of data, Python data structures play a most evident role. Objects can be easily manipulated. These data types are user defined having own advantages and disadvantages. Data manipulation and handling becomes quite easy with the usage of different functions and operators. In python there exists several functionalities that make data retrieving quite easy. It can also hold the integrity of data being used. This chapter has demonstrated the usage of various data structures in Python Scripting.

## 3.11 Assignment Questions

Assignment No. 1

**3.1** What are collections and its types?
**3.2** What are sequences?
**3.3** How a list is created using python?
**3.4** What is list slicing technique, give example?
**3.5** How does the append function work in python?
**3.6** How to insert an item in the list?
**3.7** How to extend a list?
**3.8** How tuples are used in python?
**3.9** How concatenation operator is used in python?
**3.10** What are string functions?
**3.11** What is string formatting?
**3.12** How the dictionaries are modified?
**3.13** What is nested dictionary?

Assignment No. 2

**3.14** Write a Python program to generate and print a list except for the first 5 elements, where the values are square of numbers between 1 and 30 (both included).
**3.15** Write a Python program to get the difference between the two lists.
**3.16** Write a Python program to append a list to the second list.
**3.17** Write a Python program to convert a tuple to a string.
**3.18** Write a Python program to remove an item from a tuple.
**3.19** Write a Python program to slice a tuple.
**3.20** Write a Python program to convert a tuple to a dictionary.
**3.21** Write a Python program to reverse a tuple.
**3.22** Write a Python program to convert a list of tuples into a dictionary.
**3.23** Write a Python program to print a tuple with string formatting.
   Sample tuple: (100, 200, 300)
   Output: This is a tuple (100, 200, 300)

# Assignment No. 3

**3.24** Write a Python program to replace last value of tuples in a list.
Sample list: [(10, 20, 40), (40, 50, 60), (70, 80, 90)]
Expected Output: [(10, 20, 100), (40, 50, 100), (70, 80, 100)]

**3.25** Write a Python program to remove an empty tuple(s) from a list of tuples.
Sample data: [(), (), ('',), ('a', 'b'), ('a', 'b', 'c'), ('d')]
Expected output: [('',), ('a', 'b'), ('a', 'b', 'c'),'d']

**3.26** Write a Python program to convert a list of characters into a string.

**3.27** Write a Python program to change the position of every n-th value with the (n+1)th in a list.
Sample list: [0, 1, 2, 3, 4, 5]
Expected Output: [1, 0, 3, 2, 5, 4]

**3.28** Write a Python program to select the odd items of a list.

**3.29** Write a Python program to insert an element before each element of a list.

**3.30** Write a Python program to convert list to list of dictionaries.
Sample lists: ["Black", "Red", "Maroon", "Yellow"], ["#000000", "#FF0000", "#800000", "#FFFF00"]
Expected Output: [{'color_name': 'Black', 'color_code': '#000000'}, {'color_name': 'Red', 'color_code': '#FF0000'}, {'color_name': 'Maroon', 'color_code': '#800000'}, {'color_name': 'Yellow', 'color_code': '#FFFF00'}]

**3.31** Write a Python program to compute the similarity between two lists.
Sample data: ["red", "orange", "green", "blue", "white"], ["black", "yellow", "green", "blue"]
Expected Output:
Color1-Color2: ['white', 'orange', 'red']
Color2-Color1: ['black', 'yellow']

**3.32** Write a Python program to convert a string to a list.

**3.33** Write a Python program to replace the last element in a list with another list.
Sample data: [1, 3, 5, 7, 9, 10], [2, 4, 6, 8]
Expected Output: [1, 3, 5, 7, 9, 2, 4, 6, 8]

# Assignment No. 4

**3.34** Write a Python program to create an array contains six integers. Also print all the members of the array.
Expected Output:
10
20
30
40
50

**3.35** Write a Python program to get the length of an array.
Expected Output e.g.
Length of the array is: 5

**3.36** Write a Python program to insert items into a list in sorted order.
Expected Output:
Original List: [25, 45, 36, 47, 69, 48, 68, 78, 14, 36]
Sorted List:   [14, 25, 36, 36, 45, 47, 48, 68, 69, 78]

**3.37** Write a Python program to create a FIFO queue.
Expected Output:
0 1 2 3
Write a Python program to create a LIFO queue.
Expected Output:
3 2 1 0

**3.38** Write a Python program to count the elements in a list until an element is a tuple

**3.39** A Python program to create a queue and display all the members and size of t t the queue.
  Expected Output:
  Members of the queue:
  0 1 2 3
  Size of the queue:
  4

**3.40** Write a Python program to find the list in a list of lists whose sum of elements   is the highest.
Sample lists: [1,2,3], [4,5,6], [10,11,12], [7,8,9]
Expected Output: [10, 11, 12]

**3.41** Write a Python program to check if all dictionaries in a list are empty or not.
  Sample list : [{},{},{}]
  Return value : True
  Sample list : [{1,2},{},{}]
  Return value : False

**3.42** Write a Python program to shuffle and print a specified list.

# Chapter 4
# Conditional Statements in Python

## 4.1 Objectives

The main objective of this chapter is to discuss:

- To understand basic problem-solving techniques using conditional statements
- To develop algorithms through the process of top down, stepwise refinement.
- To use the if, if/else and if/elif/else structures to select appropriate actions.
- To understand counter-controlled and sentinel-controlled repetition.
- To use augmented assignment symbols and logical operators.
- To use the break and continue program control statements.

## 4.2 Introduction

This chapter discusses the conditional statements which have prevalent use in programming. These conditional statements such as If , If Else give a human like flavour to programming and helps in the decision making. In this same chapter we discuss Boolean expressions. We also have re-visited Variables as these play an important role in program structures.

## 4.3 Variables in python

The following has already been discussed in depth in chapter 2 however since variables are extensively used with conditional statements, we are revisiting this topic.

In Python, one does not have to declare the type of variables such as int word = 2 but can only write word = 2.

The variables are being referred in the program to get the value of it.

The value of the variable can be changed later on.

**Store the value 10 in a variable named foo**
foo = 10

**Store the value of foo+10 in a variable named bar**
bar = foo + 10

```
Word = 2
Word = "nothing"
print(Word)
# Variables in Java
# Int word = 2;
# String word = "nothing";
```

Figure 4-1 code snippet

```
C:\Users\btaze\AppData\Local\Programs\Python\Python37\python.exe
nothing

Process finished with exit code 0
```

Figure 4-2 Output in Python

The language will automatically detect the type of variable as an integer. In Python also, one can write bits of code and see what happens without the need to compile the code as an intermediate stage. It is, therefore, simple and easier to experiment with Python when compared to Java. The main feature with Python is that it is easy to read since it doesn't need much punctuation like most of the programming language.

**Simple Code in Python**

A simple Python Code using variables and operator is written as follows. This will be discussed with several examples in the next sections of this chapter

$X = 1$

$If\ X > 0:$

$Print\ "X\ is\ a\ positive\ integer"$

Python uses whitespace indentation to delimit curly brackets that are used in other programming languages. The white spaces are, therefore, used in nesting the program code to produce the right semantics. The major similarity of Python with Java is that both can handle memory management. They do this through memory allocations and the use of garbage collector when the memory is no longer needed by the program. Python is a suitable programming language for writing program codes for mathematical calculations as it is faster and easy to test. Its program codes are similar in syntax to mathematical expressions used in mathematics literature. Python is available as free software and has versions for different environments and operating systems.

## 4.4 Types, Values, and Expressions

Boolean expressions are expressions in Python programming language that produces are a Boolean value when computed. The value can either be true or false/one or zero. Boolean operations are used to control the flow of a program and in making comparisons. The general expression of a Boolean expression is given below;

```
4.4 Boolean expressions.py
1    checker = bool(2)  # not necessary
2
3    if checker == True:
4        print(checker)
5
```

Figure 4-3 code to return or convert a bool value

113

```
C:\Users\btaze\AppData\Local\Programs\Python\Python37\python.exe
pydev debugger: process 1620 is connecting

Connected to pydev debugger (build 183.5912.18)
True
```

Figure 4-4 Output in Python

## 4.5 Boolean comparisons

In Python programming, the Boolean comparison is used to compare two values and evaluate them down to a single Boolean value that can either be one or zero or rather True or False. Python's Booleans were added with the primary goal of making code clearer (Chan, 2015). This was aimed at evaluating confusion when the final expression of a program returns 1 which made it hard to determine whether it is True or any other value.

Boolean is a subclass of the int class. This can be shown in the expressions below;

```
2  print(x)
3  y = False + 1
4  print(y)
5  z = False * 75
6  print(z)
7  a = True * 75
8  print(a)
9
```

Figure 4-5 Running Code for Boolean comparisons in Python

```
2
1
0
75

Process finished with exit code 0
```

Figure 4-6 Output in Python

The use of Boolean True made it easy to determine the difference in the expression. There are several Boolean operators that can be used to evaluate an expression to either True or False. These expressions include;

*The table below shows Boolean comparison operators*

| Operator | What it means |
|---|---|
| == | Equal to |
| != | Not equal to |
| < | Less than |
| > | Greater than |
| <= | Less than or equal to |
| >= | Greater than or equal to |

Table 14 Boolean Comparison operators

Here is an example of a Boolean comparison in Python programming that uses two integer values.

| + | Addition | x + y |
|---|---|---|
| - | Subtraction | x - y |
| * | Multiplication | x * y |
| / | Division | x / y |
| % | Modulus | x % y |
| ** | Exponentiation | x ** y |
| // | Floor division | x // y |

```
x = 4
y = 7

print ("x == y:", x == y)
print ("x != y:", x != y)
print ("x < y:", x < y)
print ("x > y:", x > y)
print ("x <= y:", x <= y)
print ("x >= y:", x >= y)
```

Figure 4-7 code snippet

```
C:\Users\btaze\AppData\Local\Programs\Python\Python37\python.exe
Connected to pydev debugger (build 183.5912.18)
pydev debugger: process 8772 is connecting

x == y: False
x != y: True
x < y: True
x > y: False
x <= y: True
x >= y: False
```

Figure 4-8 Output in Python

The program asks Python to print out whether the operator evaluates to True or False depending on the outcome of the expression. From the above expression the final output of the program is given below;

```
1    x = 4
2    y = 7
3    print(x != y)
4    # True
5    print(x < y)
6    # True
7    print(x > y)
8    # False
9    print(x <= y)
10   # True
11   print(x >= y)
12   # False
```

Figure 4-9 code snippet

```
C:\Users\btaze\AppData\Local\Programs\Python\Python37\python.exe
pydev debugger: process 756 is connecting

Connected to pydev debugger (build 183.5912.18)
True
True
False
True
False
```

Figure 4-10 Output in Python

The mathematical logic for the above program is given below

```
1    x = 4
2    y = 7
3    print(x == y)
4    # Is 4 (x) equal to 7 (y)? False
5    print(x != y)
6    # Is 4 not equal to 7? True
7    print(x < y)
8    # Is 4 less than 7? True
9    print(x > y)
10   # Is 4 greater than 7? False
11   print(x <= y)
12   # Is 4 less than or equal to 7? True
13   print(not x <= y)
14   # Is 4 not less than or equal to 7? False
```

Figure 4-11 code snippet

```
Connected to pydev debugger (build 183.5912.18)
pydev debugger: process 3392 is connecting

False
True
True
False
True
False

Process finished with exit code 0
```

Figure 4-12 Output in Python

## 4.6 Logical operators

Logical operators are operators that are used to compare two values and the final expression is evaluated down to a Boolean value; True or False. The logical operators in Python include; AND, OR and NOT. These logical operations are given in the table below

| Operator | Meaning | Expression |
|---|---|---|
| AND | The Boolean condition is true of both are True | B1 and B2 |
| OR | The final Boolean condition is True if at least one of the is True | B1 or B2 |
| NOT | It negates the final Boolean condition | not B1 or not B2 |

Table 15 Logical Operators

Logical operations are used to determine whether two expressions evaluate to True or False. An example is in the school system where it can be used to determine the grade of a student and whether the student is registered in the course. On confirming the two cases to be True, the student is assigned a grade in the school system.

Example for logical operations

```
print((9 > 7) and (2 < 4))
# The two expressions are True
print((8 == 8) or (6 != 6))
# One of the expressions is True
print(not (3 <= 1))
```

Figure 4-13 code snippet

```
C:\Users\btaze\AppData\Local\Programs\Python\Python37\python.exe
Connected to pydev debugger (build 183.5912.18)
pydev debugger: process 3208 is connecting

True
True
True
```

Figure 4-14 Output in Python

For AND operator, both expressions must evaluate to True for the final Boolean expression to be True else the final Boolean value will be false. This is to say, for the Boolean expression to evaluate to False then AND operator must have at least one False expression.

For the OR operation, at least one of the two operators must evaluate to True for the final Boolean expression to evaluate to True. That is to say, an OR operation can evaluate to False only if both operations evaluate to False.

Lastly, NOT must have its inner expression be True for the new expression to evaluate to False else if will evaluate to True.

## 4.7 Generating Random Numbers

Python has a standard library that is used to generate random numbers. The library has a suite of functions that perform these requirements. Random numbers are sequences of numbers or symbols whose arrangement cannot be reasonably predicted better than a random chance. A good random number generator must be able to generate the numbers in a uniformly spread manner.

For a given set of random numbers to be considered as random numbers, the numbers must be able to satisfy the numbers must be able to meet the following two conditions; the numbers must be equally probable everywhere and the current value of a random variable has no relation with the previous values.

## 4.8 Properties of a good random number generator

A good arithmetic random number generator should possess the following properties:

The numbers produced should appear in a distributed form but in a uniform manner on [0,1] and should not exhibit any correlation with each other; otherwise random results may be completely invalid.

### *The generator should be fast to avoid the need for a lot of storage.*

It should be possible to reproduce a given stream of random numbers exactly. This makes debugging and verification of the program easier. Also, it may be necessary to use identical random numbers in simulating different systems in order to obtain more precise comparisons.

The generation should be able to produce several separate streams of random numbers. A stream is a sub-segment of the numbers produced by the generator with one stream beginning where the previous stream ends. Different streams can be seen as separate and independent generators provided that the whole stream is not used. The use can dedicate a particular stream to a particular source of randomness in the simulation. E.g. in the single server queuing model, stream one can be used for generating inter-arrival times and stream two for generating service times. Using separate streams for separate purposes facilitates reproducibility and comparability of simulation results.

The generator should be portable i.e. produce the same sequence of random numbers for all standard computers.

Python programming has various ways of generating random numbers. Let's check an example that gives a true reflection of how a random number can be generated in python. The code below shows a random number generator for 10 digits

```
import random
for x in range(10):
    print(random.randint(1, 101))
```

Figure 4-15 code snippet

```
C:\Users\btaze\AppData\Local\Programs\Python\Python37\python.exe
Connected to pydev debugger (build 183.5912.18)
pydev debugger: process 4552 is connecting

50
23
77
10
42
59
44
5
75
30
```

Figure 4-16 Output in Python

The above code is able to print 10 digits within the range of 1 to 50. The first line (import random) is used to call the random number library in python that has the functions for generating the random number.

The second line in the program (for x in range (10) is used to specify the number of digits that will be generated and printed. The statement for x in range (20) is used to generate 20 random numbers.

The last statement (print random.randint(1,51) informs the computer on the range where the random number should be generated from. The statement can be modified to print random.randint(1,101) in order to print random numbers between 1 to 100 by automatically selecting a random number between 1 and 100

*Program code for generating 10 random numbers between 1 and 50 in Python is given below;*

```
# This program will generate 10 random numbers between 1 and 100

# import the random module from python library
import random
for x in range(10):
    print(random.randint(1,51))
```

Figure 4-17 Code demonstration of the random number in Python

```
C:\Users\btaze\AppData\Local\Programs\Python\Python37\python.exe
24
29
34
31
39
38
3
17
32
16
```

Figure 4-18 Screenshot for results by running the above code

## 4.9 Flow Chart, Symbols and usage

Flowcharts in Python or any other programming language is a way of organizing and planning the program code. The aim of the flowchart is to guide the programmer on the format to follow, plan the most appropriate program structure and helps in communicating what the code will be doing. There are many other ways of planning the code but the use of flowcharts looks more appropriate. The general parts or symbols of a flowchart include; the Start/End symbol, Connection symbol, Process symbol, Input/output symbol and the Conditional decision symbol.

| Symbol | Name | Function |
|--------|------|----------|
|  (oval) | Start/end | An oval represents a start or end point |
|  (arrow) | Arrows | A line is a connector that shows relationships between the representative shapes |
|  (parallelogram) | Input/Output | A parallelogram represents input or output |
|  (rectangle) | Process | A rectangle represents a process |
| 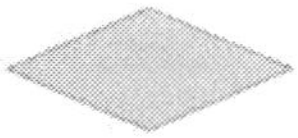 (diamond) | Decision | A diamond indicates a decision |

Figure 4-1 Flowchart symbols

In order to understand the flowchart as a topic, there are several terms that are relevant. Flowcharts involve the terms such as procedure, algorithm and flowchart. Procedure refers to a sequence of well-defined instructions. Each procedure can be done in a finite amount of time. The procedures should get rid of any ambiguity. The algorithm, on the other hand, is a step-by-step procedure followed in solving a given problem. An example is where two numbers are to be compared and the result output. The algorithm involves taking the two integers, comparing the two and displaying the largest. The flowchart is, therefore, the diagram that used to represent this algorithm.

Flowcharts show the structure of the program in a way that humans can understand. Flowchart Python is essentially the Python programming language in visual form. Detailed texts are used when it is not obvious what the program does in order to make it easy for humans to understand. The Ovals show a start point or end point in the code. Arrows show connections between different parts of the code. Rectangles show processes such as calculations (most things the computer does that does not involve an input, output or decision). Parallelograms show inputs and outputs (remember print is normally an input). Diamonds show a decision/conditional (this is normal if, else if/elif, while and for). These symbols are given in the diagram below;

### 4.9.1 Start symbol:

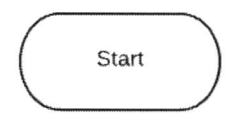

Figure 4-2 Symbol of "Start"

Also known as the "Terminator Symbol," this symbol represents the start points, end points, and potential outcomes of a path. Often contains "Start" or "End" within the shape.

### 4.9.2 Process symbol

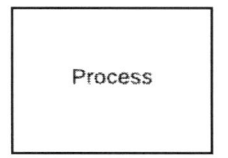

Figure 4-3 Symbol for "Process"

The rectangle is your go-to symbol. It represents any step in the process you're depicting and is the workhorse of the flowchart diagram. Give it a lump of sugar and it will love you forever.

### 4.9.3 Decision symbol

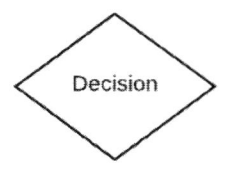

Figure 4-4 Symbol for "Decision"

The diamond symbolizes that a decision needs to be made. If there are only two choices, you can draw arrows directly from the diamond to the next step (example on the left).

In programming, the above symbols can be used in organizing the flow of the program as shown in the diagram below;

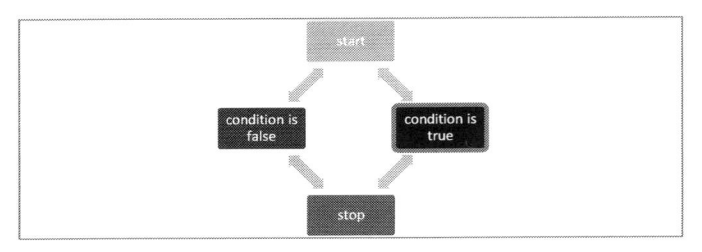

Figure 4-5 Flow chart

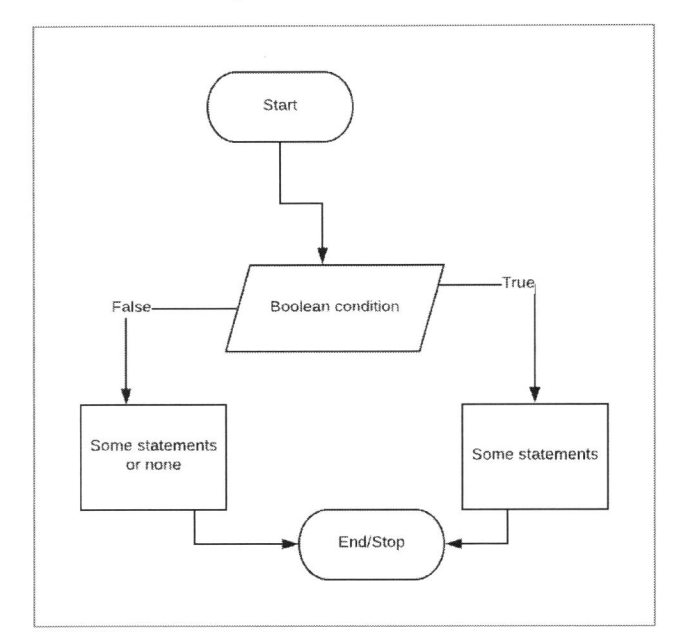

Figure 4-6 Flow chart

## 4.10 Conditional statements in Python

Conditional statements, in python, are program structures or features in the programming language that perform different computations or actions based on the final evaluation of the Boolean condition specified by the programmer. The actions are performed if the final computation of the Boolean condition evaluates to true and fails to perform the action if the final computation of the Boolean program evaluates to false. These statements are also used in alteration of the flow of control in order to achieve the desired outcomes of the program code. The term "conditional statement" has been used in Python since it is an imperative programming language. A conditional is sometimes colloquially referred to as an "if-check," especially when perceived as a simple one and when its specific form is irrelevant or unknown.

There are several conditional statements that are used in Python programming in order to achieve the correct flow of the program and the desired outcome. There are many features that can be exploited in Python that makes the final program project more meaningful. Examples of conditional statements in

Python include; if statements, two-way if statement, nested if and Multi-Way if-elif-else Statements. Other expressions such as for loop and while loop is also part of the many conditional expressions in Python programming which will be discussed in Chapter 5.

Figure 7 and Figure 8 *below shows a general representation of if statement and* **if then else statement respectively**

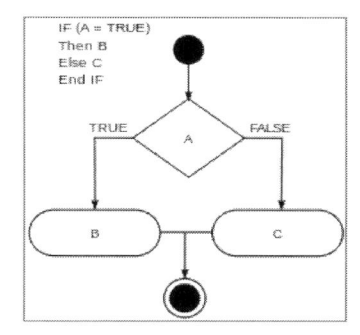

Figure 4-7 General representation of if statement

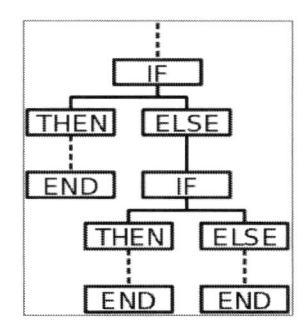

Figure 4-8 General representation of if then else statement

Since python is a major programming language used in the contemporary programming field, there are many areas that need to be exploited. This paper focuses on several areas in Python programming that have made it a powerful programming language. The main features that will be considered in this paper include; Boolean Types, Values, and Expressions, Generating Random Numbers, Introduction to Flow Chart, Symbols and usage, if Statements (Guessing Birthdays), Two-Way if-else Statements, Nested if and Multi-Way if-elif-else Statements, Common Errors in Selection Statements (example one and two), Logical Operators (an Example: Determining Leap Years and Example: Lottery, Conditional Expressions and Operator Precedence and Associativity.

### 4.10.1   IF Statements

If the statement is a conditional statement in programming. If the statement is proved to be True, then a given set to programming statements are executed. If the statement is proved to be false, on the other hand, then another set of programming statements or none of the programming statements are executed.

The general form of an if statement in Python is given below;

**if** BOOLEAN EXPRESSION:

STATEMENTS

An example of a simple if statement is given below;

### 4.10.1 Example:

```
food = 'spam'

if food == 'spam':
    print('Ummmm, my favorite!')
    print('I feel like saying it 100 times...')
    print(100 * (food + '! '))
```

Figure 4-19 code snippet

```
C:\Users\btaze\AppData\Local\Programs\Python\Python37\python.exe "C:/Users/btaze/Downloads
Ummmm, my favorite!
I feel like saying it 100 times...
spam! spam! spam! spam! spam! spam! spam! spam! spam! spam! spam! spam! spam! spam!

Process finished with exit code 0
```

Figure 4-20 Results shown in Python

Boolean expression at the end of the if statement is called a condition. If the condition is true then all the indented statements below the condition are executed. If the condition is false then the indented statements are not executed. The program skips the indented statements are jumps to the next statements.

### 4.10.2 Two-Way if-else Statements

These are programs that use conditional statement if in computation. If the condition is false then another set of statements are executed. If the condition is true then a set of instructions (indented under the condition) are executed.

*An example to demonstrate the above explanation is given below;*

*The diagram below shows what happens when the input is supplied to the above program;*

```
1  x = int(input())
2  if x > 0:
3      print(x)
4  else:
5      print(-x)
```

Input:
1  -150

Output:
1  150
2

Figure 4-21 Code snippet

124

```
Windows PowerShell
PS C:\Users\user> python
Python 3.6.3 (v3.6.3:2c5fed8, Oct  3 2017, 17:26:49) [MSC v.1900 32 bit (Intel)] on win32
Type "help", "copyright", "credits" or "license" for more information.
>>> exit()
PS C:\Users\user> cd .\Downloads\
PS C:\Users\user\Downloads> cd .\python\
PS C:\Users\user\Downloads\python> python ifstate.py
23
23
PS C:\Users\user\Downloads\python> python ifstate.py
-23
23
PS C:\Users\user\Downloads\python>
```

Figure 4-22 Screenshot of output for two way if-else statement

More examples of if else statement

### 4.10.2 Example:

```
4.10.2 ifelsestate.py
var1 = 100
if var1:
   print("1 - Got a true expression value")
   print(var1)
else:
   print ("1 - Got a false expression value")
   print (var1)
```

Figure 4-23 Code demonstration of else statement

```
C:\Users\btaze\AppData\Local\Programs\Python\Python37\python.exe
Connected to pydev debugger (build 183.5912.18)
pydev debugger: process 8316 is connecting

1 - Got a true expression value
100
```

Figure 4-24 working code snippet of the above code

### 4.10.3 Example:

**Program code:**

```
4.10.3 ifelsestate2.py
var2 = 0
if var2:
   print ("Got a true expression value for 2")
   print (var2)
else:
   print ("Got a false expression value for 2")
   print (var2)

print ("Good work!")
```

Figure 4-9 Code snippet

```
C:\Users\btaze\AppData\Local\Programs\Python\Python37\python.exe
Connected to pydev debugger (build 183.5912.18)
pydev debugger: process 8316 is connecting

1 - Got a true expression value
100
```

Figure 4-10 working code snippet

### 4.10.3    Nested if and Multi-Way if-elif-else Statements

The general expression used to represent the nested if and Multi-Way if-elif-else Statements is given by;

**More examples of nested if else statement**

### 4.10.4  Example:

```
if number > 0:
    print("The number is positive")
elif number == 0:
    print("Zero")
else:
    print("The number is negative")
```

Figure 4-11 Code demonstration of if-else statement

```
C:\Users\btaze\AppData\Local\Programs\Python\Python37\python.exe
pydev debugger: process 752 is connecting

Connected to pydev debugger (build 183.5912.18)
The number is positive

Process finished with exit code 0
```

Figure 4-28 otput of the code

### 4.10.5  Example:

```
#checks if number if +ve, -ve or 0
#results are then displayed
num = float(input("Enter a number: "))
if num >= 0:
    if num == 0:
        print("Zero")
    else:
        print("Positive number")
else:
    print("Negative number")
```

Figure 4-29 Code demonstration for nested if-else statement

```
C:\Users\btaze\AppData\Local\Programs\Python\Python37\python.exe
pydev debugger: process 4084 is connecting

Connected to pydev debugger (build 183.5912.18)
Enter a number: -10
Negative number
```

Figure 4-30 Running code/output

The else if statement is used to check for multiple expressions that meet the condition. In the above program, the if statement is checked and if found to be False then the program execution jumps to the else if (elif) statement. If all the conditions under the else if statement is False then the execution is done at the body of the else statement which happens to be the default block to be executed.

### 4.10.4 Common Errors in Selection Statements

Selection statements in programming are programs constructs that's because the control of a program to jump to another specific flow based on the value of evaluation of a given condition. The evaluation statement can either result in True or False (Shaw, 2016). The flow control remains in the default execution format if the condition evaluates to True but jumps the normal execution to other statements if the value of the condition results in False.

There are many errors that are associated with the selection statements in Python programming. These errors include;

#### a. Syntax errors (indentation errors)

A syntax error is a major and the most common error in selection statement in Python programming. This is where the program structure cannot be understood when executing the program code. The major cause of this error is indentation. In Python programming, indentation forms part of the program and helps in determining how the program flows.

The wrong indentation will lead to misinterpretation of the program code or rather a wrong format is read from the code. A wrong program structure causes syntax errors in Python. This can be corrected by using the correct indentation.

### 4.10.6 Example:

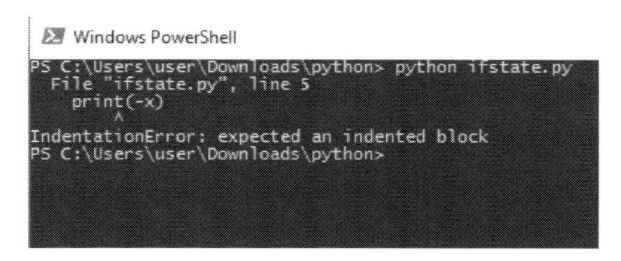

```
Windows PowerShell
PS C:\Users\user\Downloads\python> python ifstate.py
  File "ifstate.py", line 5
    print(-x)
        ^
IndentationError: expected an indented block
PS C:\Users\user\Downloads\python>
```

Figure 4-12 Code snippet for demonstrating common errors in selection statement

#### b. Semantic errors (using "=" instead of "==")

These are miss-interpretational errors found in the code. The code cannot be executed since the semantics do not make sense. The variables do not bring any meaning in the context where they are placed.

## 4.10.7 Example:

```
4.10.7 ifstate.py
x = int(input('Please enter a number: '))
if x == 0:
    print(x)
else:
    print(-x)
```

Figure 3-32 code snippet

```
C:\Users\btaze\AppData\Local\Programs\Python\Python37\python.exe
Please enter a number: 10
-10

Process finished with exit code 0
```

Figure 3-33 Output in python

### c. Typing errors

Typing errors are caused by a programmer when typing the code in Python programming language. Such errors can lead to naming errors when the code is being read. The program execution cannot proceed when such errors are encountered. This error can be corrected by crosschecking the code to identify naming issues and spelling mistakes.

## 4.10.8 Example:

```
Windows PowerShell
PS C:\Users\user\Downloads\python> python
Python 3.6.3 (v3.6.3:2c5fed8, Oct  3 2017, 17:26:49) [MSC v.1900 32 bit (Intel)] on win32
Type "help", "copyright", "credits" or "license" for more information.
>>> exit()
PS C:\Users\user\Downloads\python> python ifstate.py
23
Traceback (most recent call last):
  File "ifstate.py", line 3, in <module>
    print(y)
NameError: name 'y' is not defined
PS C:\Users\user\Downloads\python>
```

Figure 4-13 Running code presenting typing errors

# 4.11 Logical Operators

Logical operators include *AND, OR and NOT.*

| Operator | What it means | What it looks like |
|---|---|---|
| AND | True if both are true | x and y |
| OR | True if at least one is true | x or y |
| NOT | True only if false | not x |

Table 16 Logical Operators

In the case of AND, if both the operands are True then condition becomes True. If any of the operators is false then the condition evaluations to False. For the OR operator, if any of the two operands are non-zero then condition becomes True. If both operators are True then the condition becomes False. For the NOT operator, on the other hand, it reverses the logical state of its operand. If a condition evaluates to True then it becomes False and vice versa.

Python program code to determine if a number of divisible by four

```
# Python program to check if the input number is divisible by four
#getting input from the users
number = int(input("Enter the number"))

if (number % 4) == 0:
    if (number % 100) == 0:
        if (number % 400) == 0:
            print("{0} is divisible by four".format(number))
        else:
            print("{0} is not divisible by four".format(number))
    else:
        print("{0} is divisible by four".format(number))
else:
    print("{0} is not divisible by four".format(number))
```

Figure 4-34 Output screenshot of the above code

```
C:\Users\btaze\AppData\Local\Programs\Python\Python37\python.exe
Enter the number 6
6 is not divisible by four

Process finished with exit code 0
```

Figure 4-35 Display of code running in CMD

# Python program to check if the input number is divisible by four

#getting input from the users

number = int (input ("Enter the number"))

if (number % 4) == 0:

    if (number % 100) == 0:

        if (number % 400) == 0:

        print ("{0} is divisible by four".format(number))

  else:

        print ("{0} is not divisible by four".format(number))

  else:

        print ("{0} is divisible by four".format(number))

  else:

        print ("{0} is not divisible by four".format(number))

### 4.10.9 Example: Three random numbers game

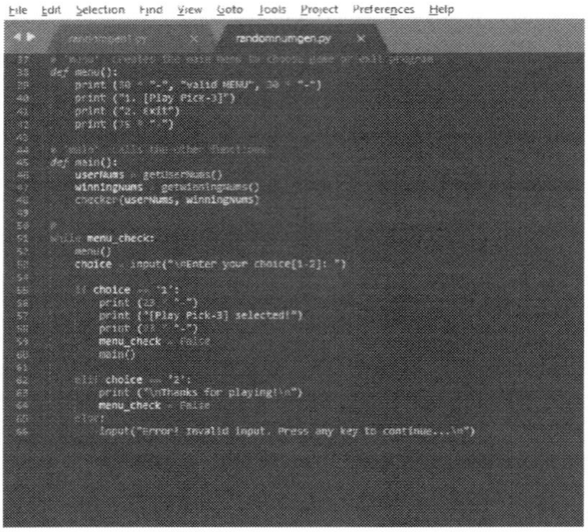

Figure 4-14 Screenshot of the running program

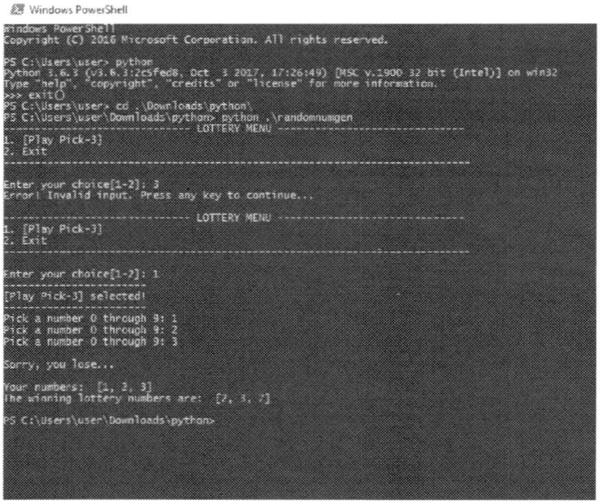

Figure 4-15 Code snippet displaying random number game

*# game for three random winning numbers*

*import random*

*menu_check = True*

*# 'checker', compares userNums and winningNums to see if they have won or lost*

*def checker(userNums, winningNums):*

```
        if userNums == winningNums:
            print ("\nCongratulations! You Win $100!\n")
            print ("Your numbers: ", userNums)
            print ("The winning valid numbers are: ", winningNums, "\n")
        else:
            print ("\nSorry, you lose...\n")
            print ("Your numbers: ", userNums)
            print ("The winning valid numbers are: ", winningNums, "\n")
# 'getUserNums', gets user numbers and puts into a sorted list
def getUserNums():
    userNums = []
    for x in range(3):
        nums = int(input("Pick a number 0 through 9: "))
        if 0 <= nums <= 9:
            userNums.append(nums)
        else:
            input("Error! Invalid input. Press any key to continue...")
            nums = int(input("Pick a number 0 through 9: "))
            userNums.append(nums)
    return sorted(userNums)
# 'getWinningNums', creates a sorted list with random nums ranging from 0-9 with a range of 3 values
def getWinningNums():
    return sorted(random.sample(range(0,10), 3))
# 'menu', creates the main menu to choose game or exit program
```

```
def menu():
    print (30 * "-", "valid MENU", 30 * "-")
    print ("1. [Play Pick-3]")
    print ("2. Exit")
    print (75 * "-")
# 'main', calls the other functions
def main():
    userNums = getUserNums()
    winningNums = getWinningNums()
    checker(userNums, winningNums)
#
while menu_check:
    menu()
    choice = input("\nEnter your choice[1-2]: ")
    if choice == '1':
        print (23 * "-")
        print ("[Play Pick-3] selected!")
        print (23 * "-")
        menu_check = False
        main()
    elif choice == '2':
        print ("\nThanks for playing!\n")
        menu_check = Fals        else:
        input("Error! Invalid input. Press any key to continue...\n")
```

```
---------------------------- valid MENU ----------------------------
1. [Play Pick-3]
2. Exit
--------------------------------------------------------------------

Enter your choice[1-2]: 1
-----------------------
[Play Pick-3] selected!
-----------------------
Pick a number 0 through 9: 0
Pick a number 0 through 9: 1
Pick a number 0 through 9: 2

Sorry, you lose...

Your numbers:  [0, 1, 2]
The winning valid numbers are:  [2, 4, 5]
```

Figure 4-28 Output in python

### 4.11.1 Operator Precedence and Associativity

Operator precedence in computing is a collection of rules that reflect conventions about which procedures to perform first in order to evaluate a given mathematical expression (Olsen, 2017).

| Operator | Description |
|---|---|
| ** | Exponentiation (raise to the power) |
| ~ + - | Complement, unary plus and minus (method names for the last two are +@ and -@) |
| * / % // | Multiply, divide, modulo and floor division |
| + - | Addition and subtraction |
| >> << | Right and left bitwise shift |
| & | Bitwise 'AND'td> |
| ^ \| | Bitwise exclusive `OR' and regular `OR' |
| <= < > >= | Comparison operators |
| <> == != | Equality operators |
| = %= /= //= -= += *= **= | Assignment operators |
| is not | Identity operators |
| in not in | Membership operators |
| not or and | Logical operators |

Table 17 Operators and their description

133

## 4.12 Conclusion

In conclusion, Python is a programming language that resembles Java, however, cleaner and easier to read than Java. Unlike in Java, variables in Python are not declared but the language will automatically detect the type of variable from the inputs of the user. Python's conditional statements are program constructs which are used to change the direction of the flow of program execution. Examples include If Statements, If Else and Nested If Else statements.

These constructs make the program perform different actions based on the Boolean result from the evaluation of the Boolean condition. Different actions are performed if the final computation of the Boolean condition evaluates to True. If the final computation of the Boolean operation results in False then another set of operations are performed or none at all. Conditional statements are, therefore, used in producing the desired outcome in the program execution process.

## 4.13 Summary

In summary, Python has several conditional statements that are used in achieving the desired results and even in alteration of the flow of a program execution. This paper has exploited a number of these conditional statements. The main ones that have been dealt with include; if statements, two-way if statement, nested if and Multi-Way if-elif-else Statements. There are many features that can be exploited in Python that makes the final program project more meaningful and one of these features are conditional statements.

## 4.14 Assignment Questions

Assignment No. 1

**4.1** What are logical operators?
**4.2** How random numbers are generated in python?
**4.3** What are some of the conditional Statements used in programming?
**4.4** What is the difference between if Else and Do While loop?
**4.5** Define nested if with example.
**4.6** What is a multi-way if-else statement?
**4.7** What is a syntax error?
**4.8** What are semantic errors?
**4.9** What are typing errors?
**4.10** What is operator precedence?

Assignment No. 2

**4.11** Write a Python program to find those numbers which are divisible by 7 and multiple of 5, between 1500 and 2700 (both included).
**4.12** Write a Python program to convert temperatures to and from Celsius, Fahrenheit.
[Formula: c/5 = f-32/9 [where c = temperature in Celsius and f = temperature in Fahrenheit]
Expected Output:
60°C is 140 in Fahrenheit
45°F is 7 in Celsius
**4.13** Write a Python program to guess a number between 1 to 9.
Note: User is prompted to enter a guess. If the user guesses wrong then the prompt appears again until the guess is correct, on successful guess, user will get a "Well guessed!" message, and the program will exit.
**4.14** Write a Python program to count the number of even and odd numbers from a series of numbers.
Sample numbers: numbers = (1, 2, 3, 4, 5, 6, 7, 8, 9)
Expected Output:
Number of even numbers: 5
Number of odd numbers: 4
**4.15** Write a Python program that accepts a string and calculate the number of digits and letters.
Sample Data: Python 3.2
Expected Output:
Letters 6
Digits 2
**4.16** Write a Python program to check the validity of password input by users.

- At least 1 letter between [a-z] and 1 letter between [A-Z].
- At least 1 number between [0-9].
- Minimum length 6 characters.
- Maximum length 16 characters

**4.17** Write a Python program to print alphabet pattern 'A'.
Expected Output:
```
  * * *
*       *
*       *
* * * * *
*       *
*       *
*       *
```

**4.18** Write a Python program to check whether an alphabet is a vowel or consonant.
Expected Output:
Input a letter of the alphabet: k
k is a consonant.

**4.19** Write a Python program to convert month name to a number of days.
Expected Output:
List of months: January, February, March, April, May, June, July, August, September, October, November, December
Input the name of Month: February
No. of days: 28/29 days

**4.20** Write a Python program to check a string represent an integer or not.
Input a string: Python
The string is not an integer.

## Assignment No. 3

**4.21** Write a Python program to check a triangle is equilateral, isosceles or scalene.
Note:
An equilateral triangle is a triangle in which all three sides are equal.
A scalene triangle is a triangle that has three unequal sides.
An isosceles triangle is a triangle with (at least) two equal sides.
Expected Output:
        Input lengths of the triangle sides:
        x: 6
        y: 8
        z: 12
Scalene triangle

**4.22** Write a Python program to find the median of three values.

Expected Output:
Input first number: 15
Input second number: 26
Input third number: 29
The median is 26.0

**4.23** Write a Python program to create the multiplication table (from 1 to 10) of a number.
Expected Output:
Input a number: 6
6 x 1 = 6
6 x 2 = 12
6 x 3 = 18
6 x 4 = 24
6 x 5 = 30
6 x 6 = 36
6 x 7 = 42
6 x 8 = 48
6 x 9 = 54
6 x 10 = 60

**4.24** Write a Python program to construct the following pattern, using a nested loop number.
Expected Output:
```
        1
        22
        333
        4444
        55555
        666666
        7777777
        88888888
        999999999
```

**4.25** Write a python program to print the factorial of a given number.

**4.26** Write a python program to check given number is prime or not.

**4.27** Write a python program to print all prime numbers between 0 to 100, and print how many prime numbers are there.

**4.28** Write a Python program which accepts a sequence of comma separated 4 digit binary numbers as its input and print the numbers that are divisible by 5 in a comma separated sequence.
   Sample Data: 0100, 0011, 1010,1001,1100,1001
   Expected Output: 1010

**4.29** Write a python program to print all odd numbers between 1 to 100.

**4.30** Write a Python program to find whether a given number (accept from the user) is even or odd, print out an appropriate message to the user.

## Assignment No. 4

**4.31** Write a Python program to get next day of a given date.
*Expected Output:*
*Input a year: 2019*
*Input a month [1-12]: 08*
*Input a day [1-31]: 23*
*The next date is [yyyy-mm-dd] 2019-8-24*

**4.32** Write a Python program to calculate the sum and average of n integer numbers (input from the user). Input 0 to finish.

**4.33** Write a Python program to get the Fibonacci series between 0 to 50.
Note: The Fibonacci sequence is the series of numbers:
0, 1, 1, 2, 3, 5, 8, 13, 21, ....
Every next number is found by adding up the two numbers before it.
Expected Output: 1 1 2 3 5 8 13 21 34

**4.34** Take 10 integers from keyboard using loop and print their average value.

**4.35** Write a program to print all prime number in between 1 to 100.

**4.36** Write a Python program to create all possible strings by using 'a', 'e', 'i', 'o', 'u'. Use the characters exactly once.

**4.37** Write a Python program which accepts the user's first and last name and print them in reverse order with a space between them.

**4.38** Write a Python program to calculate number of days between two dates.
Sample dates: (2014, 7, 2), (2014, 7, 11)
Expected output : 9 days

**4.39** Write a Python program to test whether a passed letter is a vowel or not.

**4.40** Write a Python program to display your details like name, age, and address in three different lines.

# Chapter 5
# Loops

## 5.1 Objectives

The main objective of this chapter is to :

- Review the basic types of loops in programming languages FOR loop, WHILE loop and DO-WHILE loop
- show how Loops are written in Python
- Comparing the usage of loops in different scenarios

## 5.2 Introduction to Loops

Loops are essential programming ideas that are found in all programming languages. In a computing environment, a loop is a set of instructions or statement that are executed and repeated, until a certain condition is reached. For instance, it involves getting and modifying a set of data. A condition is then checked to determine whether the counter has arrived the given set of instructions. If the requirements are not met, the first instruction is repeated sequentially until a certain condition is arrived. However, if the condition is arrived, the subsequent instruction is then executed (Harold, 2016).
In other words, a loop structure is where "execute this instruction if this condition is reached". The code may either be executed once or multiple times.

In every programming language, there are 3 basic types of loops.

1. FOR loop.
2. WHILE loop.
3. DO-WHILE loop.

For these 3 stated loops, they are mainly comprised of 3 parts: Initialization, Condition, and Increment or Decrement.

### 5.2.1　　FOR Loop

Unlike the while loop, a for loop is used in instances where the user wants to continuously repeat the execution of a given block of code or statements for a known number of times. For instance, a for-loop in Python or C programming language is used to run several blocks of code over a specific number of times until a certain condition is reached. For this reason, it is also known as the counter-controlled loop. Although the other loops such as the while and do-while loop are used for iteration and repetition, the for loop is however considered to be the most useful and flexible (Thomas, 2012).

**For-loop syntax**

For(<initialization>; <condition>; <increment/decrement>) {

    <you may enter code here>
    }
    Execute.
    <?php

```
for(y=1;y<=10;y++){
    echo "value of y is ".y;
    //you may enter code here
}
?>
```

A for-loop contains several variations. For example, the three optional parts contained in it. Therefore, a user may opt to write a for (; ;) which is mainly an infinite loop.
Secondly, for initialization, a user may prefer to put multiple statements:

For (a = b, c = b; a<10; a++)

To wind up, a user may decide to put any expression and neglect having an increment or a decrement in the expression.

For (a = b; a<20; a *2
)

As illustrated above, it is apparent that a for loop is used to determine the number of iterations in advance. For example, by incrementing the counter from 0 to 20 using a for loop, one may traverse an array of 20 elements.

For instance, using a for loop, one may decide to write a program to enable him to determine how many times he would talk to his friend in a given month while calling him once in a week.

### 5.2.1 Example:

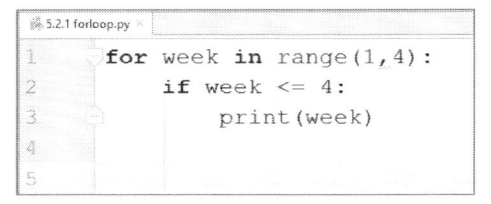

```
for week in range(1,4):
    if week <= 4:
        print(week)
```

Figure 5-1 code snippet

```
Connected to pydev debugger (build 183.5912.18)
1
2
3
```

Figure 5-2 Output in python

### 5.2.2 Example:

An array list in python program

```
Array_names = ['roy', 'kelvin', 'brian', 'sharon']
for index in range (len(Array_names)):
 print('names in the list: ', Array_names[index])
print('Have a nice day!')
```

Figure 5-3 code snippet

```
C:\Users\btaze\AppData\Local\Programs\Python\Python37\python.exe
pydev debugger: process 6120 is connecting

Connected to pydev debugger (build 183.5912.18)
names in the list:   roy
names in the list:   kelvin
names in the list:   brian
names in the list:   sharon
Have a nice day!
```

Figure 5-4 Output in python

### 5.2.2 While loop

This is another very popular kind of a loop structure. The while loop executes a given block of code repeatedly if certain requirements are met or based on a Boolean condition and halts while the condition is false.

**While Loop Syntax**

The general structure of a while loop is:
While (condition)
Block of code {this code is continuously executed as long as the Boolean condition is true}.

Rules when using the while loop
  a. The loop should first appear after the variables have been initialized.
  b. While the loop executes, the user should ensure that the code being used is always updating the variable to avoid an infinite loop.
  c. To continue with the normal execution of the program, the user should ensure that the program at some time return a false condition and continue with the available instructions if any.

### 5.2.3 Example:

For example, a Boolean expression (true) could be z == 10 or while (z !=10)(Z is not equal to 10). It could also be a combination of Boolean legal statements such as (while q ==5 || r ==8). This simply means execute the given set of code while q and r are equal to 5 or 8 respectively.
It is important to note that unlike a for loop, a while loop does not execute or accept an empty condition. In less abstracted terms, a while loop is used in instances where the number of times a loop will execute a certain block of code is unknown (Steve, 2013).
In all scenarios, a while loop will first check the condition then execute the code.

### 5.2.4 Example:

A while loop in python programme.

*Best_mark = 70*

*While (Best_mark <70):*

*Print 'you have failed the test'*

*Best_mark = Best_mark + 1*

*Print ('have a nice day')*

### 5.2.3 Do - While loop:

In the do while loop, the condition is evaluated after executing a set of code in the loop, and then the code runs again to check whether the condition is true.
In the do while loop, the code inside the loop is executed at least once.
If you are well conversant with a for loop, it would then be easier to convert any for loop into a while loop.
A good example of **Do-While** loop is a login prompt. You put some code in a **do-while** that asks for a username, and if it's not valid, ask them again. So, you'd ask for the username in the block of code, then the condition checks if the username is valid, if it's not, it loops and asks again.
Do While Loop Syntax:

*For (initialization; condition; increment or decrement)*

*Block of code;*

*is equal to the while loop:*

*initialization;*

*while (the condition is true)*

*{block of code to be executed}*

The primary objective of the while loop is to ensure that the condition is first met before a certain code is executed.
This is well illustrated while creating a game. The player should attack if the enemy is within range.

**Sample code**

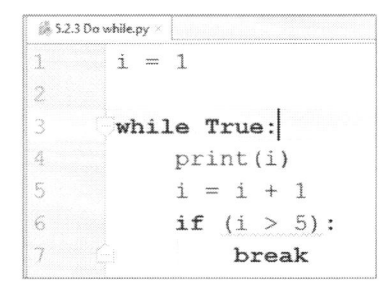

```
i = 1

while True:
    print(i)
    i = i + 1
    if (i > 5):
        break
```

Figure 5-5 code snippet

```
C:\Users\btaze\AppData\Local\Programs\Python\Python37\python.exe
pydev debugger: process 6416 is connecting

Connected to pydev debugger (build 183.5912.18)
1
2
3
4
5
```

Figure 5-6 Output in python

The main objective of a do while loop is to run a given set of code and then check whether a certain condition is reached. Unlike other loops, the do while loop executes a given set of code at least once without checking the condition.

### 5.2.5 Example:

*do {*

*Code block or statements*

*}*

*While (condition);*

```
for x in range(3, 6):
    print(x)        # Prints out 3,4,5
count = 0
while count < 5:
    print(count)
    count += 1      # Prints out 0,1,2,3,4
```

Figure 5-7 code snippet

```
C:\Users\btaze\AppData\Local\Programs\Python\Python37\python.exe
pydev debugger: process 3220 is connecting

Connected to pydev debugger (build 183.5912.18)
3
4
5
0
1
2
3
4
```

Figure 5-8 Output in python

### 5.2.6 Example:

```
Person = 20
Person = int(input("Please enter your id: "))

while Person in range(18,30):
    if Person <= 18:
        print('You are young')
        break
    if Person == 20:
        print('You are very young')
        break
```

Figure 5-9 code snippet

```
C:\Users\btaze\AppData\Local\Programs\Python\Python37\python.exe
Connected to pydev debugger (build 183.5912.18)
pydev debugger: process 4456 is connecting

Please enter your id: 20
You are very young
```

Figure 5-10 output in python

Now we will look at some of the example code to illustrate how the While loop works

### 5.2.7 Example:

We write program that appends some text until the file size becomes 5KB.

*While ( file_size<2K())*

*{*

*Append_some_data()*

*}*

```
import os
print("File size in bytes: ", os.stat("C:/Users/btaze/Downloads/Traffic.txt").st_size )

while os.stat("C:/Users/btaze/Downloads/Traffic.txt").st_size < 76:
    f = open("C:/Users/btaze/Downloads/Traffic.txt", "a")
    f.write("Now the file has one more line!")
    print("file size is less so text is printed on file")
```

Figure 5-11 code snippet

```
C:\Users\btaze\AppData\Local\Programs\Python\Python37\python.exe
pydev debugger: process 3536 is connecting

Connected to pydev debugger (build 183.5912.18)
File size in bytes:   110
```

Figure 5-12 output in python

In this scenario, we cannot use a for a loop since the number of times needed for the program to write some data until the file becomes full is unknown. Further, we cannot use the do-while loop since we are not certain whether the loop should be executed at least once. Or maybe the file was initially 2KB hence there is no need to run the loop.

### 5.2.8 Example:

Imagine that an individual is willing to write his name five times. The instructor, however, instructs him to do the same. Two methods are more likely to be used in this instance.

### 5.2.9 Example Method 1:
*instructor: write your name*
*Him: writes*

*instructor: write your name*
*Him: writes*
*instructor: write your name*
*Him: writes*
*instructor: write your name*
*Him: writes*
*instructor: write your name*
*Him: writes*

**Method 2:**

*Instructor: write your name.*
*Him: writes his name five times.*

From the above two methods, it is apparent that the instructor would prefer the second method. This is because the second method proves to be more efficient and less cumbersome compared to the first method. This method would be achieved by using a while loop.

In this case, you put a condition (which is the number of times) until when an action (write your name) must be repeated.

### 5.2.10 Example:

For example, if the counter variable C holds the number of times the name has to be written (in this case 5 times), the following code should be run.

```
C = 5;
while C>0:
    print('His Name')
    C -= 1
```

Figure 5-13 code snippet

```
C:\Users\btaze\AppData\Local\Programs\Python\Python37\python.exe
pydev debugger: process 7708 is connecting

Connected to pydev debugger (build 183.5912.18)
His Name
His Name
His Name
His Name
His Name
```

Figure 5-14 output in python

The loop is executed at least once. However, if the condition is not satisfied, the loop will not be executed.
In a do while loop, the loop is executed at least once even if the condition is false.

## 5.3 Difference between a FOR loop and a WHILE loop

As illustrated earlier, it is apparent that both the while and for loop structures are used to execute several blocks of code over a given number of times.
A for loop is used in instances where the user knows the number of times that the loop will be executed, but a while loop is used in cases where one does not know the number of times a certain loop is most likely to be executed.

**Scenario 1:**
A for loop is preferred if we have to run a loop 50 times
    *for (int a = 0; a <50; a++).*

**Scenario 2:**

If the user is unsure of the number of times to run a loop, a while loop is most preferred in this case. For example, while (k > 10). In this scenario, the number of times the loop will run is unknown as it will depend on the value of a and the program.
In for loop structure, initialization, increments and decrements conditions appear first, and then the loops come last.

|  | When to use | Template |
|---|---|---|
| **For loop:** | If you know, prior to the start of loop, how many times you want to repeat the loop. | *for (int 1=0; i<max ; i++)*<br>*{*<br>*<statement(s)>}*<br>*}* |
| **While loop:** | If you don't know of a certain number of runs and a set of conditions are to be met. | *<prompt - do it (y/n)?>*<br>*while (<response == 'y'>)*<br>*{*<br>*<statement(s)>*<br>*<prompt - - do it again 'y'>)*<br>*}* |
| **Do While loop:** | If you always need to do the repeated thing at least one time. | *do*<br>*{*<br>*<statement(s)>*<br>*<prompt - do it again (y/n)?>*<br>*} while (<response = ='y'> ;* |

Table 18 Comparison table of Looping structures

In the while loop, the loops appear first and then followed by the condition.
In other words, a for loop is usually used in cases where a piece of code needs to be repeated n number of times. However, a while loop is used when a certain set of conditions are to be met. The loop in a while loop may be executed or repeated forever if some limits are not put in place.
To avoid this inconvenience, a do while loop is used which executes a block of code at least once.

    5.2.11    **Example:**

*do*

*// enter your code here*
*while (this condition is true)*

### 5.3.1 Syntax Comparison
**While loop:**

Form the previous examples; it is clear that a while loop continuously executes a block of code while a particular requirement is true.
The syntax can be written as follows:

*Initialization;*

*While (condition)*

*{*

*Block of code;*

*Increment or decrement counter;*

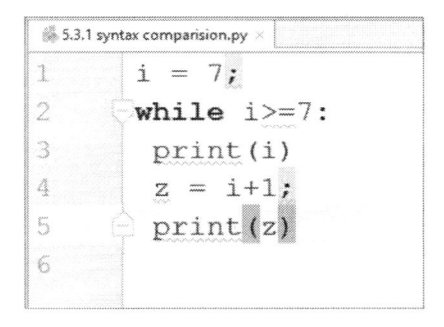

*}*

```
i = 7;
while i>=7:
    print(i)
    z = i+1;
    print(z)
```

Figure 5-15 code snippet

```
8
7
8
7
8
7
8
```

Figure 5-16 output in python

**For loop:**

This loop provides a convenient way to execute a block of statements over a range of values. It is usually referred to as a for a loop because a certain block of code or statement must be executed repeatedly before the condition is satisfied.
The syntax for a for loop is:

*For (initialization; condition; increment or decrement)*

{

// *statements or body*

}

In compiled programming languages, a for loop has better performance compared to the while loop since it combines the three statements in a while loop to a single statement hence reducing the lines of code in a compiler.

The other main difference between the for loop and the while loop is that for a for loop, the condition statement is optional whereas the conditional statement in a while loop is mandatory. For instance, if the condition statement is omitted in a for loop, the code will be executed infinitely while in the while loop, you will be given a compilation or a syntax error.

Occasionally, one may not easily detect much difference between these two loops as they are both entry-controlled loops. However, a while loop is usually regarded as more flexible than a for a loop. This is because, the incremental or decremental statements can be inserted anywhere in the while loop while they are limited in the for loop since the statements are executed after all other statements are executed (Donald, 2010).

### a. Working

In a while loop, the condition is first checked to determine whether it is true. If it is true, the block of codes after the loop is then executed. The condition is then checked again to determine the Boolean expression. If true, the code is repeatedly executed until the condition becomes false.

In the for while loop, the initialization step is first executed only once if it is available. Later, the Boolean expression is evaluated to determine whether it's true and then executes the body of the loop. To finalize, the increment or the decrement is then defined. When all the three statements have been executed, the condition and body executed are executed again until it becomes false(condition).

### b. Usage:

The for loop is used in instances where you know how many times the loop will run or be executed.
The while loop is used in instances where you are unaware of the number of times the loop will run or be executed. However, in some cases, the while loop is similar to the for loop
The do-while loop is used when you want to run or execute a loop at least once.

## 5.3 Comparing "The Do-While loop" with other Looping structures

From the previous section examples related to For Loop and While Loop, it is apparent that all loop statements enable one to execute a block of code or statements multiple times.

The do while loop ensures the code within a loop is executed at least once. Unlike the For and while loops which are the entry-controlled loop, the do while loop is an exit-controlled loop. This is because it checks the condition after executing the loop once. The exit-controlled loop is much less useful and common compared to the entry-controlled loop.

The general syntax for the do-while loop is:

*do*

*// statement*

*While (condition is true or false);*

At the end of the block of the do while loop, the condition is tested instead of at the beginning thus making it possible for the loop to be executed at least once. If the evaluated condition is true, the block will repeatedly be executed until the condition is false. The do while is like the while loop only that the do while loop executes the code only once before evaluating the condition. For instance, the while loop assumes that the code should be executed only if the condition is true. The do while loop assumes that the code should first be executed and then the condition is evaluated. If the condition is true, continue with the execution of the code. For this reason, the do while loop is best used in scenarios where the user wants to execute a block of code once before evaluating the conditions (Denis, 2014).

### 5.4.1    Example:

A do while loop is best applicable where you want to obtain an integer input from the user until a positive digit is entered.
**Syntax:**

*do*

    {

            *User_input()*
            *}*
            *While (user_input<0)*

In this case, the loop should be run at least once because the user should input a number at least once. The code is expected to run until the user has entered a positive digit.
In the while loop, the condition is checked first before running the loop.
From the above code, it means that the while loop will not execute until the code is true while in the do while loop, the code is executed at least once before the condition is evaluated. It would be wise to assume that in the do while loop, the compiler assumes that the user has entered a positive condition hence running the body of the loop.

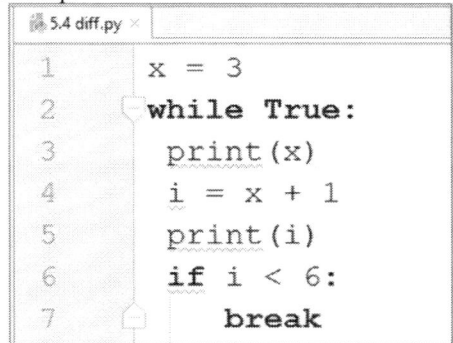

```
1    x = 3
2    while True:
3        print(x)
4        i = x + 1
5        print(i)
6        if i < 6:
7            break
```

Figure 5-17 code snippet

```
pydev debugger: process 3536 is connecting

Connected to pydev debugger (build 183.5912.18)
3
4

Process finished with exit code 0
```

Figure 5-18 output in python

### 5.4.2 Example:

Perhaps you've written a graphical program that runs an animation. When the game ends, you need to show your players the scoreboard. Of course, you need to run the animation loop at least once just to render the scoreboard. So: run your animation in the loop and do the conditional at the end to see if you should stop animating because the game is over.

Whatever u can do with while loop can be done with do-while loop and vice-versa. But it is easy to use "do-while" loop while solving problems related to circular-linked lists.

While and for loops are the only ones you'll need. There are not many uses of the do-while loop.

## 5.4 Difference between the do while loop and the while loop

The do while loop will first run or execute the code before evaluating the condition while the while loop will first evaluate the code then check whether the condition is true.

If you are in a scenario where you want a code to be executed at least once, and then continue to run if the condition is reached, a do while loop is best for your choice.

The condition in a while is checked at the beginning.

*While (this condition is true)*

*{*

*Execute this block of code*

*}*

*Syntax for the do while loop (checks the condition after executing a block of code) is:*

*do {*

*Put some code here (statement)*

*}*

*while (this condition is true).*

```
print('Enter your id:')
x = int(input())

while x<0:
    print(x)
    x= x+1
    if (x > 5):
        break
```

Figure 5-19 code snippet

```
C:\Users\btaze\AppData\Local\Programs\Python\Python37\python.exe
Enter your id:
-1
-1
```

Figure 5-20 output in python

Note that "while loop" is an ENTRY CONTROLLED loop, on the other hand, "do-while loop" is an EXIT CONTROLLED loop.

## 5.5 Conclusion

Loops make scripting tasks easy and help by avoiding to write repetitive code. The execution time of the script decreases as well as the script is easier to read. There are 3 major loops found in scripting, For Loop, While Loop and Do -While Loop.

FOR loop is used whenever, user want to repeat some statements or block of code for a specific time. Do - while body is always executed at least once, whereas while body can be skipped entirely. Consequently, do - while can be always replaced by while, but not vice versa.

As far as you always can use the while or (for), the do-while brings no significant benefit and in fact is used rarely.
You can use it to emphasize the fact that the loop body needs to be executed at least once or to place the loop condition behind the body if it is the place where the condition should naturally occur.
The benefit is usually more on the side of the future human reader (yourself?) rather than the compiler or executable code.
Interestingly, while loop appears to be much more popular than do while loops - I'm not basing this on any official poll, just a few decades of experience. This is slightly surprising since in many cases do while loops seem to be more appropriate. For example, when reading a file until the end, you need to perform a read operation at least once.

## 5.6 Summary

In this chapter we have reviewed 3 kinds of programming loops, studied the general syntax, reviewed the examples and have compared the uses of each of the loop.

## 5.7 Assignment Questions

Assignment No. 1

- **5.1** Explain loops in programming.
- **5.2** What is a FOR loop?
- **5.3** What is a WHILE loop?
- **5.4** What is a DO-WHILE loop? Explain with example.
- **5.5** What is the difference between a FOR and a WHILE loop?
- **5.6** What is the difference between do-while loop and the while loop?
- **5.7** What is the syntax of a FOR loop in python?
- **5.8** What is the syntax of WHILE loop in python?
- **5.9** What is the syntax of DO-WHILE loop in python?

Assignment No. 2

- **5.10** Write a python program to find sum of all natural numbers between 1 to n.
- **5.11** Write a function that takes a list as a parameter and returns the number of items in the list.
- **5.12** Write a function that takes a list of integers as a parameter and returns the max element in the list.
- **5.13** Write a function that takes a list as a parameter and returns the reversed list. Do NOT use the built-in reverse () function.
- **5.14** Write a function that takes a list of integers as a parameter and returns the sum of the list.
- **5.15** Write a python program to print the square of all numbers from 0 to 10.
- **5.16** Write a python program to find the sum of all even numbers from 0 to 10
- **5.17** Write a python program to check given number is prime or not
- **5.18** Write a python program to print all prime numbers between 0 to 100, and print how many prime numbers are there.
- **5.19** Write a program which will find all such numbers which are divisible by 7 but are not a multiple of 5, between 2000 and 3200 (both included).

# Assignment No. 3

**5.20** Write a program that accepts sequence of lines as input and prints the lines after making all characters in the sentence capitalized. Suppose the following input is supplied to the program:
> Hello world
> Practice makes perfect;
> Then the output should be:
> HELLO WORLD
> PRACTICE MAKES PERFECT

**5.21** Write a program, which will find all such numbers between 1000 and 3000 (both included) such that each digit of the number is an even number. The numbers obtained should be printed in a comma-separated sequence on a single line.

**5.22** Define a class with a generator which can iterate the numbers, which are divisible by 7, between a given range 0 and n.

**5.23** Define a function which can print a dictionary where the keys are numbers between 1 and 20 (both included) and the values are square of keys.

**5.24** Write a program which uses a while loop to sum the squares of integers (starting from 1) until the total exceeds 200. Print the final total.

**5.25** Write a program which finds the factorial of a given number. E.g. 3 factorial, or **3!** is equal to **3 x 2 x 1** and **5!** is equal to **5 x 4 x 3 x 2 x 1**, etc. Your program should only contain a single loop.

**5.26** Write a program which sums the integers from 1 to 10 using a for loop (and prints the total at the end).

**5.27** Can you think of a way to write the program in exercise 5.26 without using a loop?

**5.28** Write a program which uses a nested for loop to populate a three-dimensional list representing a calendar: the top-level list should contain a sub-list for each month, and each month should contain four weeks. Each week should be an empty list.

**5.29** Modify your code to make it easier to access a month in the calendar by a human-readable month name, and each week by a name which is numbered starting from 1. Add an event (in the form of a string description) to the second week in July.

# Chapter 6
# Functions in Python Scripting

## 6.1 Objectives

The main objectives of this chapter are to discuss:

- Functions, Constructs and its Uses
- Built-in and User Defined Functions
- Discusses Object Oriented Programming
- Discusses Classes and its usage

## 6.2 Introduction

Python is a general-purpose high-level programming language. Like any other programming language, Python has some codes that are used more than once and hence need not to be rewritten over and over. This chapter discusses how the Python script can be modularized and made repeatable. These repeatable codes are called Functions.

Functions, Object Oriented Programming and Classes are discussed in this chapter that are used extensively in Python Scripts for writing large scripts which can handle many input requests, interrupts and generate kind of actions with changing conditions of the inputs and requirements.

The main objectives of this chapter include; being able to understand why and how programmers divide programs up into sets of cooperating functions, to be able to define new functions in Python and lastly to understand the details of function calls and parameter passing in Python.

### 6.2.1 Functions

Python has some pieces for code that have been organized into a block and can be reused more than once for a single related function. These blocks of codes are the ones referred to as functions of Python. They provide high-levels of reusing program codes and hence enhancing modularity in the program development process. Creating a customized function is easy in Python.

**Code for creating a function**

```
def requiredArg(str,num):
    print(str,num)

requiredArg('Ali',3)
```

Figure 6-1 Code demonstration of creating a function

```
C:\Users\btaze\AppData\Local\Programs\Python\Python37\python.exe
Ali 3

Process finished with exit code 0
```

Figure 6-2 output in python

Functions in Python begin with the key-word def which is then followed by the name of the function and parenthesis. The parenthesis takes all the input parameters and the code block in every function begins with a colon. The return statement is used to exit any function and can be called in any other part of the program.

### 6.2.2 Object-oriented programming

Python is known to be a language. This is because almost everything is in Python is written in terms of objects which are associated with properties and methods.

### 6.2.3 Classes

Classes in Python are like object constructors and is created with the keyword class.

**Code for creating a class in python**

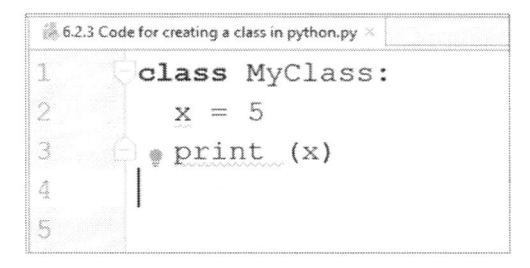

```python
class MyClass:
    x = 5
    print (x)
```

Figure 6-3 Code demonstration of creating a function

```
C:\Users\btaze\AppData\Local\Programs\Python\Python37\python.exe
5
```

Figure 6-4 Code output in python

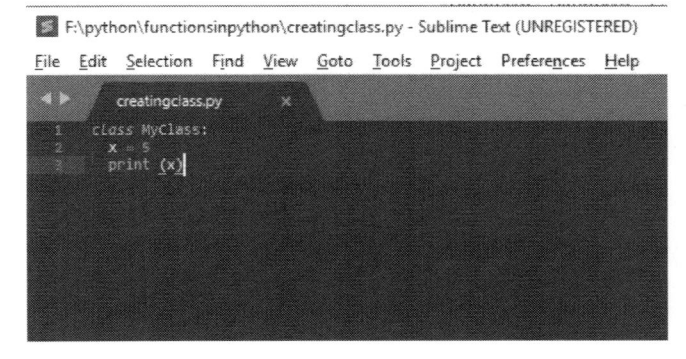

```python
class MyClass:
    x = 5
    print (x)
```

Figure 6-5 Code representing how to create a class in Python

The use of functions and objects in Python programming makes it easy to design a functional code with full functionalities and be easily understandable (Ozer, 2017). Functions increase modularity in program codes and hence make them easy to be reused. This chapter mainly focuses on the programming using Python functions and classes that makes Python termed as an object-oriented programming language.

## 6.3 Program Components in Python

Python language has several components. These components include; numbers, strings, sets, lists, dictionaries, tuples and functions (Rivers & Koedinger, 2017). All these components work together in meeting the specifications of a given program code. Python combines its components in one program hence ensuring that a fully functional program which meets the needs of the users is designed in the process. Same data structures numbers, strings, sets, lists, dictionaries, tuples are used in the Python Scripting.

## 6.4 Python Built-in Functions

Build-in functions refer to those functions that have been prewritten with the Python language and contained in the libraries and headers of the language. They are not declared by a programmer but are rather called to perform a specified function (Olsen, 2017). Python language has several built-in functions that are reused over and over hence making it easy to perform similar functions without necessarily writing the program code from scratch. Examples of some commonly used Python built-in functions include;

- **abs**(*x*)

This function is used to return the absolute value of a number.

- **all**(*iterable*)

This function is used to return the Boolean True is all its elements of the iterable are true.

### 6.4.1 Example:

*def all(iterable):*

  *for element in iterable:*

    *if not element:*

      *return False*

  *return True*

*print(all([6, 7]))*

*# True*

*print(all([6, 7, None]))*

*# False Because this has None*

*print(all([0, 6, 7]))* #

*# False Because this has zero*

*print(all([9, 8, [1, 2]]))*

*# True*

*print(all([9, 8, []]))*

*# False Because it has []*

*print(all([9, 8, [1, 2, []]]))*

*# True*

*print(all([9, 8, {}]))*

*# False Because it has {}*

*print(all([9, 8, {'engine': 'Gcloud'}]))*

*# True*

```
C:\Users\btaze\AppData\Local\Programs\Python\Python37\python.exe
True
False
False
True
False
True
False
True
```

Figure 6-6 output in python

- **any(iterable)**

This function returns true if any element of the iterable is True and returns false if the iterable is empty.

**6.4.2      Example:**

```
def any(iterable):
    for element in iterable:
        if element:
            return True
    return False

print(any([10, "", "one"]))
print(any(("", {})))
print(any([]))
```

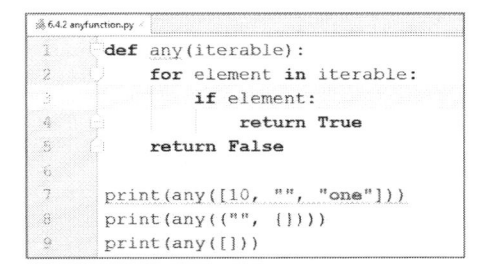

Figure 6-7 Code snippet representing any (iterable)

```
C:\Users\btaze\AppData\Local\Programs\Python\Python37\python.exe
True
False
False
```

Figure 6-8 output in python

- **classmethod**(*function*)

This function returns the class method associated with the function. In this case, the class method receives the class as an implicit first argument.

### 6.4.3    Example:

*# random Person*

*class Person:*

   *def __init__(self, name, age):*

     *self.name = name*

   *self.age = age*

   *@classmethod*

   *def fromBirthYear(cls, name, birthYear):*

     *return cls(name, date.today().year - birthYear)*

   *def display(self):*

     *print(self.name + "'s age is: " + str(self.age))*

*person = Person('Adam', 19)*

*person.display()*

*person1 = Person.fromBirthYear('John', 1985)*

*person1.display()*

```
C:\Users\btaze\AppData\Local\Programs\Python\Python37\python.exe
Adam's age is: 19
John's age is: 34
```

Figure 6-9 Code snippet representing class method() function

- **enumerate**(*sequence, start=0*)

This function returns an enumerated object. The next() method of the iterator returned by enumerate() returns a tuple containing a count (from *start* which defaults to 0) and the values obtained from iterating over *sequence*:

### 6.4.4 Example:

```python
def enumerate(sequence, start=0):
    n = start
    for elem in sequence:
        n += 1
        print(elem, n)

sequence = ['bread', 'milk', 'butter']
enumerate(sequence)
```

Figure 6-10 Code snippet demonstrating enumerate() function

```
C:\Users\btaze\AppData\Local\Programs\Python\Python37\python.exe
pydev debugger: process 8180 is connecting

Connected to pydev debugger (build 183.5912.18)
bread 1
milk 2
butter 3
```

Figure 6-11 output in python

- **reduce**(*function, iterable*[, *initializer*])

This function takes two arguments of iterable elements cumulatively from left to right and reduces the arguments to one value.

### 6.4.5 Example:

```python
from functools import reduce   # only in Python 3

def do_sum(x1, x2): return x1 + x2

print(reduce(do_sum, [1, 2, 3, 4]))
```

Figure 6-12 Code snippet representing reduce() function

```
C:\Users\btaze\AppData\Local\Programs\Python\Python37\python.exe
10
```

Figure 6-23 output in python

159

There are several other functions used in python. The staticmethod () returns the static method of the function, classmethod () is used to convert a method into a class method, chr () returns a character from a given Unicode code, complex () returns a complex number, dict () returns a dictionary array, format () is used to format a specified value, hash () is used to return a hash value of a specified object, open () is use to open a file and return a file object and pow () returns a value of x to the power of y.

**Some other examples of the above functions are given below;**

Program code for pow () function

### 6.4.6  Example:

```
# positive x, positive y (x**y)
print(pow(2, 2))

# negative x, positive y
print(pow(-2, 2))

# positive x, negative y (x**-y)
print(pow(2, -2))

# negative x, negative y
print(pow(-2, -2))
```

Figure 6-14 Code snippet representing pow() function

```
C:\Users\btaze\AppData\Local\Programs\Python\Python37\python.exe
4
4
0.25
0.25
```

Figure 6-35 output in python

Program code for open () function

### 6.4.7  Example:

```
filename = "C://Users/btaze/Desktop/dev.txt"
file = open(filename, "r")
for line in file:
    print(line)
```

Figure 6-16 Code snippet representing open() function

```
C:\Users\btaze\AppData\Local\Programs\Python\Python37\python.exe
devcommunity0@gmail.com

tazeemdon123
```

Figure 6-17 output in python

## 6.5 User Defined Function

Functions in Python Script can either be built-in or declared by the programmer. Built-in Python functions are not declared when used but are only called because they are part of the Python libraries. In the previous section we have discussed several built-in Python functions. Python language allows the programmer to declare functions (Nelli, 2015). These functions are called the user-defined functions and are created by the programmer during the program coding. Python functions are defined with the keyword def followed by the function name and a parenthesis which carries the arguments required by the function.

**The general syntax for defining a Python function**

```
def functionname(x,y):
    print("Sum:-" ,x+y)

functionname(5,6)
```

Figure 6-18 Code snippet demonstrating functionname() function

```
C:\Users\btaze\AppData\Local\Programs\Python\Python37\python.exe
Sum:- 11
```

Figure 6-49 output in python

There are five main rules when defining a function. First, the block of the function must begin with the keyword def and follow by the name of the function and parenthesis. Secondly, any input parameter required by the function should be placed inside these parentheses. Thirdly, the first statement of a function can be an optional statement - the documentation string of the function or *docstring*. The block of code within every function must always start with a colon and is usually indented. Lastly, the function must be closed with the return expression to show where the function exits.

**Program code for a basic example of a function**

### 6.5.1    Example:

```
def printme(str):
    "This prints a passed string into this function"
    print(str)

printme('Ali')
```

Figure 6-20 Code snippet demonstrating printme(str) function

```
C:\Users\btaze\AppData\Local\Programs\Python\Python37\python.exe
pydev debugger: process 5272 is connecting

Connected to pydev debugger (build 183.5912.18)
Ali
```

Figure 6-21 output in python

## 6.6 Calling a Function

Definition of the function only sets the name of the function and specifies the parameters associated with the function (Marin-Sanguino, 2016). Once the function is defined, it can then be called in various locations of the program code where it needs to be applied. This can be done directly from the Python prompt or from another function.

**General format for calling a function**

### 6.6.1 Example:

```
def my_function():
    print("Hello from a function")

my_function()
```

Figure 6-5 Code snippet demonstrating my-function()

```
C:\Users\btaze\AppData\Local\Programs\Python\Python37\python.exe
Connected to pydev debugger (build 183.5912.18)
pydev debugger: process 8032 is connecting

Hello from a function
```

Figure 6-23 output in python

Example of a Program code for calling a function

### 6.6.2 Example:

```
def printme(str):
    print(str)


# Now you can call printme function
printme("I'm first call to user defined function!")
printme("Again second call to the same function")
```

Fifure 6-24 code snippet

```
C:\Users\btaze\AppData\Local\Programs\Python\Python37\python.exe
I'm first call to user defined function!
Again second call to the same function
```

Figure 6-25 output in python

Calling functions in turlle drawing example

### 6.6.3   Example:

*def printme(str):*

  *print(str)*

*# Now you can call printme function*

*printme("I'm first call to user defined function!")*

*printme("Again second call to the same function")*

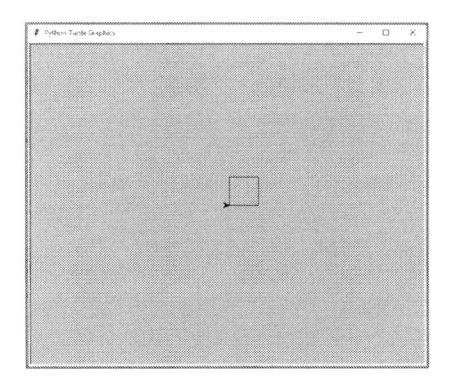

Figure 6-26 Code snippet representing how to call a functio

## 6.7 Functions with/without Return Values
### 6.7.1   Python functions without return values
### 6.7.1   Example:

```
        return None

    def my_func2():
        print("Hello World2")
        return

    def my_func3():
        print("Hello World3")

    my_func1()
    my_func2()
    my_func3()
```

Figure 6-27 code snippet

```
C:\Users\btaze\AppData\Local\Programs\Python\Python37\python.exe
Hello World1
Hello World2
Hello World3
```

Figure 6-28 output in python

### 6.7.2 Python functions without return none
### 6.7.2 Example:

```python
class Person:
    def __init__(self, name):
        self.name = name

    def myfunc(self):
        print("My name is " + self.name)


p1 = Person("Ali")
p1.myfunc()
```

Figure 6-29 code snippet

```
C:\Users\btaze\AppData\Local\Programs\Python\Python37\python.exe
My name is Ali
```

Figure 6-30 output in python

### 6.7.3 Python functions with return values
### 6.7.3 Example:

```python
def find_prisoner_with_knife(prisoners):
    for prisoner in prisoners:
        if "knife" in prisoner:
            return  # no need to check rest of the prisoners nor raise an alert

var = find_prisoner_with_knife('ALi')
```

Figure 6-31 code snippet

```
C:\Users\btaze\AppData\Local\Programs\Python\Python37\python.exe

Process finished with exit code 0
```

Figure 6-32 output in python

## 6.8 Positional and Keyword Arguments

Keyword arguments are one of those Python features that often seems a little odd for folks moving to Python from many other programming languages. It doesn't help that folks learning Python often discover the various features of keyword arguments slowly over time. When teaching Python, I've often wished I had a summary of the various keyword argument-related features that I could link learners too. I hope that this section will accomplish that task.

### 6.8.1 Example:

*import math*

*def quadratic (a, b, c):*

   *r = b \*\* 2 - 4 \* a \* c*

   *print("Quadratic function : (a \* x^2) + b\*x + c")*

   *if r > 0:*

      *num_roots = 2*

      *x1 = (((-b) + math.sqrt(r)) / (2 \* a))*

      *x2 = (((-b) - math.sqrt(r)) / (2 \* a))*

      *print("There are 2 roots: %f and %f" % (x1, x2))*

   *elif r == 0:*

      *num_roots = 1*

      *x = (-b) / 2 \* a*

      *print("There is one root: ", x)*

   *else:*

      *num_roots = 0*

      *print("No roots, discriminant < 0.")*

      *exit()*

*quadratic(5,20,10)*

```
C:\Users\btaze\AppData\Local\Programs\Python\Python37\python.exe
Quadratic function : (a * x^2) + b*x + c
There are 2 roots: -0.585786 and -3.414214
```

Figure 6-33 output in python

## 6.9 Passing Arguments by Reference and by Values

Pass by value means that the caller and the callee have two and independent variables but with the same value. If the callee modifies the value of the argument in the variable, then the effects will not be seen on the caller's side. Pass by reference, on the other hand, means that the caller and the callee use the same variable for the argument. It, therefore, means that any changes on what a function parameter refers to within a function, the change also reflects in the calling function. The caller only has a reference to the memory location of the callee's variable and if the callee changes the value of the variable then effects are seen on the caller's variable. All Python arguments (parameters) have their value passed by reference.

### 6.9.1 Example:

```python
# Function definition is here
def changeme( mylist ):
    "This changes a passed list into this function"
    mylist.append([1,2,3,4]);
    print ("Values inside the function: ", mylist)
    return

# Now you can call changeme function
mylist = [10,20,30];
changeme( mylist );
print ("Values outside the function: ", mylist)
```

Figure 6-34 Code snippet representing the passing arguments by reference and values

```
C:\Users\btaze\AppData\Local\Programs\Python\Python37\python.exe
Values inside the function:   [10, 20, 30, [1, 2, 3, 4]]
Values outside the function:  [10, 20, 30, [1, 2, 3, 4]]
```

Figure 6-35 output in python

## 6.10 Modularizing Code

Modularizing code is the process in which a huge program code is subdivided into sub-programs referred to as modules. A module can be seen as a separate software component but does not work to fulfil all the requirements and hence must be integrated with the rest of the program codes to form a complete program (Havill, 2016). Modules can be used in other applications and functions that use them with other components of the whole system. This allows the codes to be reused by other applications and this also allows many programmers to work on the same task since the whole system can be separated into modules and each programmer assigned a particular module to work on.

Modularizing a code makes it easy to enforce logical boundaries and improve maintainability of the components. These components/modules can be integrated together to form a complete system with interfaces. They are also easy to work on since a programmer doesn't have to be knowledgeable in other modules.

There are several advantages associated with modularizing codes in Python. First, less code has to be written. It also programming allows many programmers to collaborate on the same application and code can be stored across multiple files. Modular codes are also short and simple to understand as well as making it easy to identify and correct errors. A single procedure can be developed for reuse, eliminating the need to retype the code many times as well as allowing the same code can be used in many applications.

## 6.11 Important Functions used in Network Scripting

- **s.bind()**

This function binds address (hostname, port number pair) to socket

- **s.listen()**

This method sets up and start TCP listener.

- **s.accept()**

This passively accept TCP client connection, waiting until connection arrives (blocking).

- **s.connect()**

This method actively initiates TCP server connection.

- **s.recv()**

This method receives TCP message.

- **s.send()**

This method transmits TCP message

- **s.recvfrom()**

This method receives UDP message

- **s.sendto()**

This method transmits UDP message

- **s.close()**

This method closes socket

- **socket.gethostname()**

Returns the hostname

### 6.11.1 Example: Simple client code in Python

```
#!/usr/bin/python            # This is client.py file

import socket                # Import socket module

s = socket.socket()          # Create a socket object
host = socket.gethostname()  # Get local machine name
port = 12345                 # Reserve a port for your service.

s.connect((host, port))
print(s.recv(1024))
s.close()                    # Close the socket when done
```

Figure 6-36 Simple server code in python

Figure 6-37 output in python

## 6.11.2 Example: Simple server code in Python

```python
import socket                      # Import socket module

s = socket.socket()                # Create a socket object
host = socket.gethostname()        # Get local machine name
port = 12345                       # Reserve a port for your service.
s.bind((host, port))               # Bind to the port

s.listen(5)                        # Now wait for client connection.
while True:
    c, addr = s.accept()           # Establish connection with client.
    print('Got connection from', addr)
    c.sendall(b'Thank you for connecting')
    c.close()                      # Close the connection
```

Figure 6-38 Code snippet representing simple server code in Python

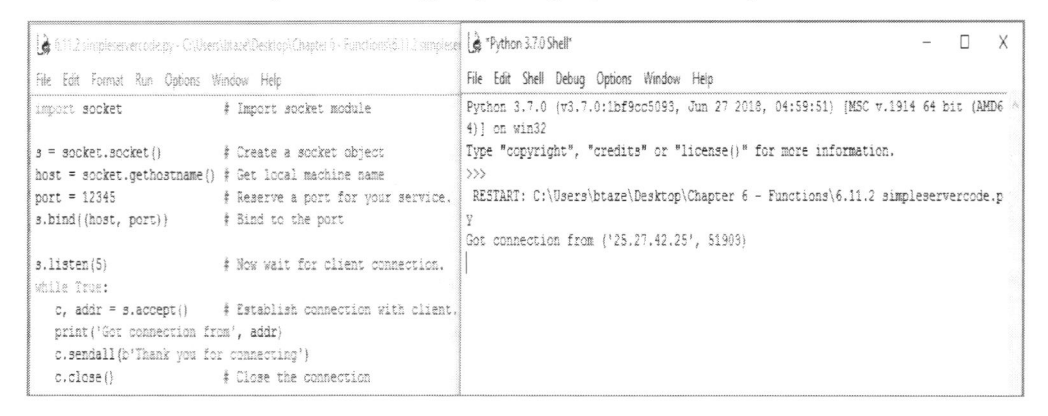

Figure 6-39 output code in Python

## 6.12 Case Study: Converting Decimals to Hexadecimal

There are several Python codes that can be used to convert a decimal number to its equivalent hexadecimal value. The case study below shows a Python code that allows the user to enter a given whole number and the code converts the decimal number to its equivalent hexadecimal number.

The Python code below can do the conversion from decimal to hexadecimal.

168

### 6.12.1 Example:

```
def main():
    result = int(input("Enter a whole, positive, number to be converted to hexadecimal: "))
    hexadecimal = ""
    while result != 0:
        remainder = changeDigit(result % 16)
        hexadecimal = str(remainder) + hexadecimal
        result = int(result / 16)
    print(hexadecimal)

def changeDigit(digit):
    decimal = [10, 11, 12, 13, 14, 15]
    hexadecimal = ["A", "B", "C", "D", "E", "F"]
    for counter in range(7):
        if digit == decimal[counter - 1]:
            digit = hexadecimal[counter - 1]
    return digit
main()
```

Figure 6-40 Code snippet representing the conversion of decimal to hexadecimal

```
C:\Users\btaze\AppData\Local\Programs\Python\Python37\python.exe "
pydev debugger: process 4332 is connecting

Connected to pydev debugger (build 183.5912.18)
Enter a whole, positive, number to be converted to hexadecimal: 10
A
```

Figure 6-41 output in python

The code below is used to reverse the process of the above code (Helmus & Collis, 2016). The code changes the hexadecimal number to a decimal number. It allows the user to enter a number in a hexadecimal format and converts that number to a decimal format.

Python program code to convert hexadecimal to decimal.

### 6.12.2 Example:

```
# Python Program - Convert Hexadecimal to Decimal

print("Enter 'x' for exit.");
hexdec = input("Enter number in Hexadecimal Format: ");
if hexdec == 'x':
    exit();
else:
    dec = int(hexdec, 16);
    print(hexdec,"in Decimal =",str(dec));
```

Figure 6-42 Code snippet of converting decimal into hexadecimal

```
C:\Users\btaze\AppData\Local\Programs\Python\Python37\python.exe
Enter 'x' for exit.
Enter number in Hexadecimal Format: B
B in Decimal = 11
```

Figure 6-43 Output of the code

## 6.13 The Scope of Variables

Python variables can have different scopes depending on their location in the program code and based on the programmer's intentions with the code/variables. A variable can only be accessed depending on where it has been declared. Variables can either be local or global. A local variable is referred to as those that are declared within a function or are arguments passed to the function. Global variables are those variables that are declared at the top of the script and hence become accessible from anywhere in the program including functions.

### 6.13.1 Global variables

There are variables declared at the top of the Python scripts and not within any function. These variables are accessible anywhere in the program and within the functions within the Python program code. The example below shows a variable named "a" that has been created at the top of the script and is accessible from anywhere in the program code.

### 6.13.1 Example:

```
a = 5

def function():
    print(a)

function()

print(a)
```

Figure 6-44 Code snippet demonstrating local variables in Python

```
C:\Users\btaze\AppData\Local\Programs\Python\Python37\python.exe
5
5
```

Figure 6-45 output in Python

### 6.13.2 Local variables

These are variables that are declared within the functions or passed as references to the functions. These variables are only accessible within the functions where they are declared. These variables cannot be used/accessed on other parts of the program code except within the functions. The example below shows two variables named "a" and "b" for which "a" has been declared at the top of the script while "b" has been declared within the function. The variable "b" is, therefore, only accessible within the function "b" and not in any other part of the program.

Program code example for local variable

170

### 6.13.2 Example:

```
a = 5

def function():
    a = 3
    print(a)

function()

print(a)
```

Figure 6-46 Code example representing local variables

```
C:\Users\btaze\AppData\Local\Programs\Python\Python37\python.exe
pydev debugger: process 9092 is connecting

Connected to pydev debugger (build 183.5912.18)
3
5
```

Figure 6-47 Code example representing local variables

## 6.14 Default Arguments

Default arguments are values that are assigned to the arguments when a function is called without any arguments associated with them. Python allows function arguments to have default values; if the function is called without the argument, the argument gets its default value. Default arguments show the values that the function will take if no argument values are indicated. The default arguments are assigned using the assignment operator.

**Program code to show creation of default arguments in Python**

### 6.14.1 Example:

```
def defaultArg(name, foo='Come here!'):
    print(name, foo)
defaultArg('Joe')
```

Figure 6-48 Code snippet demonstrating default arguments

```
C:\Users\btaze\AppData\Local\Programs\Python\Python37\python.exe
Joe Come here!
```

Figure 6-49 Code snippet demonstrating default arguments

Example two for default arguments in Python

## 6.14.2 Example: Example for default arguments in Python

```
def print_id(ph):
  print(hex(id(ph)))
a = 5
print(hex(id(a)))
# 0x84ab460
print_id(a)
# 0x84ab460
def alter_value(ph):
  ph = ph + 1
  return ph
b = alter_value(a)
print(b)
# 6
print(a)
# 5
print(hex(id(a)))
# '0x84ab460'
hex(id(b))
# '0x84ab470'
def alter_value(ph):
  ph.append(1)
  return ph
a = [1,2,3]
```

*b = alter_value(a)*

*print(a)*

*# [1, 2, 3, 1]*

*print(b)*

*# [1, 2, 3, 1]*

*print(hex(id(a)))*

*# '0xb701f72c'*

*print(hex(id(b)))*

*'0xb701f72c'*

```
C:\Users\btaze\AppData\Local\Programs\Python\Python37\python.exe
pydev debugger: process 4216 is connecting

Connected to pydev debugger (build 183.5912.18)
0x7ffa23b7d4a0
0x7ffa23b7d4a0
6
5
0x7ffa23b7d4a0
[1, 2, 3, 1]
[1, 2, 3, 1]
0xbf00410ec8
0xbf00410ec8
```

Figure 6-50 output in python

## 6.15  Returning Multiple Values

In Python Script, it is possible to return many values from a function. There are several ways in which to carry out operations that return multiple values in Python programming. In order to make a function return multiple values of a particular data type, one needs to return the pointer to array of that data types (Gold, 2016). A function can also be made to return many values using the arguments of the function by providing the pointers as arguments. Ways of making a function return multiple values.

### 6.15.1  Using object

When using an object to make a function return multiple values, one can create a class that holes multiple values and then return the object of the class. Code example below shows how objects can be used to make a function return many values.

### 6.15.1 Example: Using object to return multiple values

```python
# A Python program to to return multiple
# values from a method using dictionary

# This function returns a dictionary
def fun():
    d = dict();
    d['str'] = "GeeksforGeeks"
    d['x']   = 20
    return d

# Driver code to test above method
d = fun()
print(d)
```

Figure 6-51 Code snippet demonstrating use of an object

```
C:\Users\btaze\AppData\Local\Programs\Python\Python37\python.exe
{'str': 'GeeksforGeeks', 'x': 20}

Process finished with exit code 0
```

Figure 6-52 output in python

### 6.15.2 Using tuple

Tuple is a list of items in a sequence and separated by commas. Tuples are immutable and are created with or without parenthesis (). Example below shows how tuples are used to return multiple values.

### 6.15.2 Example: Program code demonstrating the use of tuples to return multiple values

```python
# A Python program to to return multiple
# values from a method using class
class Test:
    def __init__(self):
        self.str = "geeksforgeeks"
        self.x = 20

# This function returns an object of Test
def fun():
    return Test()

# Driver code to test above method
t = fun()
print(t.str)
print(t.x)
```

Figure 6-53 Code snippet demonstrating use of a tuple

```
C:\Users\btaze\AppData\Local\Programs\Python\Python37\python.exe
pydev debugger: process 5892 is connecting

Connected to pydev debugger (build 183.5912.18)
geeksforgeeks
20
```

Figure 6-54 output in python

### 6.15.3 Using a list

The list is an array of items. Lists in Python are created using square brackets and are only different from arrays since they contain different data types and are mutable. The example below shows the use of lists to return multiple values.

### 6.15.3 Example: Program code showing the use of lists to return multiple values

```python
# A Python program to to return multiple
# values from a method using list

# This function returns a list
def fun():
    str = "geeksforgeeks"
    x = 20
    return [str, x];

# Driver code to test above method
list = fun()
print(list)
```

Figure 6-55 Code snippet demonstrating use of list

```
C:\Users\btaze\AppData\Local\Programs\Python\Python37\python.exe
['geeksforgeeks', 20]
```

Figure 6-56 outpu in python

### 6.15.4 Using a dictionary

The example below demonstrates how a dictionary in Python can be used to make a function return multiple values.

### 6.15.4 Example:

```
# A Python program to return multiple
# values from a method using a dictionary
# This function returns a dictionary
def fun ():
    d = dict ();
    d['str'] = "GeeksforGeeks"
    d['x'] = 20
    return d
# Driver code to test above method
d = fun ()
print(d)
```

Figure 6-57 code snippet demonstrating dictionary to return multiple vales

```
C:\Users\btaze\AppData\Local\Programs\Python\Python37\python.exe
{'str': 'GeeksforGeeks', 'x': 20}
```

Figure 6-58 output in python

### 6.16 Oriented Programming (and how it is used in Python)

Object-oriented programming is the organization of program codes based on the concept of objects and data rather than logic (Yim, et al, 2018). A program has been viewed as a logical procedure that takes input data, processes it, and produces output data. The date in objects are in the form of fields and are referred to as attributes. The code, on the other hand, is written in form of procedures usually referred to as methods.

### 6.17 Characteristics and features of OOP

OOP is characterized by Encapsulation, Inheritance, Polymorphism and OOP is characterized by Encapsulation, Inheritance, Polymorphism and Abstraction. Polymorphism is the ability to exist in various forms (Zhao, et al, 2017). Encapsulation is capturing data and keeping it safely and securely from outside interfaces. Inheritance is the process by which a class can be derived from a base class. The main features of OOP include; division of programs into entities called objects, emphasis on data, bottom-up design, object communication via functions, and hiding of data from external functions.

Python applies object-oriented programming in several ways. Python is a multi-paradigm programming language. Meaning, it supports different programming approaches where the use of objects is one of the approaches. Python objects have attributes and behaviours as the two major characteristics.

#### 6.17.1 Example: Example of use of class (object blueprint) in Python to show OOP

*class Parrot:*

  *# class attribute*

species = "bird"

   # instance attribute

   def __init__(self, name, age):

      self.name = name

      self.age = age

# instantiate the Parrot class

blu = Parrot("Blu", 10)

woo = Parrot("Woo", 15)

# access the class attributes

print("Blu is a {}".format(blu.__class__.species))

print("Woo is also a {}".format(woo.__class__.species))

# access the instance attributes

print("{} is {} years old".format( blu.name, blu.age))

print("{} is {} years old".format( woo.name, woo.age))

```
C:\Users\btaze\AppData\Local\Programs\Python\Python37\python.exe
pydev debugger: process 9488 is connecting

Connected to pydev debugger (build 183.5912.18)
Blu is a bird
Woo is also a bird
Blu is 10 years old
Woo is 15 years old
```

Figure 6-59 output in python

### 6.18 What Is a Class (in Python)?

Class in a building block (blueprint) of the object. The class is created using the keyword "*class*". A class is a code template for creating objects. The example below shows how a python class is created (Barupal, Fan & Fiehn, 2018). The class may also contain attributes that describe what a class does. The code below shows the class named "snake" with attributes called "name".

### 6.18.1 Example:

```python
class Snake:
    name = "python"
    def __init__(self, new_name):
        self.name = new_name

# instantiate the Parrot class
blue = Snake("Blu")
red = Snake("Woo")

# access the class attributes
print("Blu colour of {}".format(blue.__class__.name))
print("Red colour of {}".format(red.__class__.name))
```

Figure 6-60 Code snippet demonstrating the creation of a class

```
C:\Users\btaze\AppData\Local\Programs\Python\Python37\python.exe
Blu colour of python
Red colour of python
```

Figure 6-61 output in python

### 6.18.1 Making Your Own Classes

The main way of creating Python class is through declaring the class using the class keyword (Adams, 2018). The following examples show the various classes created in the Python programming language.

### 6.18.2 Example:

```python
class Person:
    def __init__(mysillyobject, name, age):
        mysillyobject.name = name
        mysillyobject.age = age

    def myfunc(abc):
        print("I am " + abc.name)

p1 = Person("Omer", 36)
p1.myfunc()
```

Figure 6-62 Code snippet representing the creation of a class

```
C:\Users\btaze\AppData\Local\Programs\Python\Python37\python.exe
pydev debugger: process 9548 is connecting

Connected to pydev debugger (build 183.5912.18)
I am  Omer
```

Figure 6-63 output in python

### 6.18.3  Example:

```
class MyClass:

    def myfunc(abc):
        print("Hello World")

MyClass().myfunc()
```

Figure 6-64 Code snippet representing the creation of a class

```
C:\Users\btaze\AppData\Local\Programs\Python\Python37\python.exe
Connected to pydev debugger (build 183.5912.18)
pydev debugger: process 7632 is connecting

Hello World
```

Figure 6-65 ouput in python

### 6.18.4  Example

*def ChangeHex(n):*

   *if (n < 0):*

      *print(0)*

   *elif (n<=1):*

      *print(n),*

   *else:*

      *ChangeHex( n / 16 )*

      *x =(n%16)*

*if (x < 10):*

   *print(x),*

*if (x == 10):*

   *print("A"),*

*if (x == 11):*

   *print("B"),*

*if (x == 12):*

   *print("C"),*

*if (x == 13):*

   *print("D"),*

*if (x == 14):*

   *print("E"),*

*if (x == 15):*

   *print ("F"),*

*ChangeHex(15)*

```
C:\Users\btaze\AppData\Local\Programs\Python\Python37\python.exe
0.9375
F
```

Figure 6-66 ouput in python

### 6.18.5 Example

```python
def toHex(dec):
    x = (dec % 16)
    digits = "0123456789ABCDEF"
    rest = dec / 16
    if rest == 0:
        return digits[x]
    return toHex(rest) + digits[x]

numbers = [0, 11, 16, 32, 33, 41, 45, 678, 574893]
print(toHex(x) for x in numbers)
print(hex(x) for x in numbers)
```

Figure 6-67 code snippet

```
C:\Users\btaze\AppData\Local\Programs\Python\Python37\python.exe
<generator object <genexpr> at 0x000000AA34357B10>
<generator object <genexpr> at 0x000000AA34357B10>
```

Figure 6-68 ouput in python

## 6.19 Conclusion

This chapter introduces Functions, Classes and Object Oriented Programming. We have discussed how Functions and Classes make the code modular. When the same code that needs to be used over and over is made repeatable using functions, it's a smart technique to make the code readable and manageable.

## 6.20 Summary

In this chapter we have studied how the Functions are used to modularize and shorten and simplify the Python Scripts. We have discussed how the use of classes makes the Python Script termed as Object Oriented programming. There are built-in functions in Python and a programmer can create their own user defined function based on the need. We have discussed Local and Global variables and how multiple values are returned in the script. Using converting Decimal to Hexadecimal program as a case study helps understand how a large script with repeatable code can be made shorter using functions.

## 6.21 Assignment Questions

Assignment No. 1

**6.1** What are functions in python?
**6.2** Write the syntax for creating a function in python?
**6.3** What is object oriented programming; describe some of its features?
**6.4** What is a class? Write the syntax for defining a class in python?
**6.5** What are built-in functions? Give some of the examples of built-in functions used in python?
**6.6** What are user-defined functions?
**6.7** What are keyword arguments in python?
**6.8** What are Global variables?
**6.9** What are Local variables?
**6.10** What are default arguments?

Assignment No. 2

**6.11** Define a function which can compute the sum of two numbers.
**6.12** Define a function that can convert a integer into a string and print it in console.
**6.13** Define a function that can receive two integral numbers in string form and compute their sum and then print it in console.
**6.14** Define a function that can accept two strings as input and concatenate them and then print it in console.
**6.15** Define a function that can accept two strings as input and print the string with maximum length in console.
**6.16** Define a function that can accept an integer number as input and print the "It is an even number" if the number is even, otherwise print "It is an odd number".
**6.17** Define a class named American which has a static method called printNationality.
**6.18** Define a class named American and its subclass NewYorker.
**6.19** Define a class named Circle which can be constructed by a radius. The Circle class has a method which can compute the area.
**6.20** Define a class named Rectangle which can be constructed by a length and width. The Rectangle class has a method which can compute the area.

# Assignment No. 3

**6.21** Write a Python class to convert a roman numeral to an integer.
**6.22** Write a Python class to get all possible unique subsets from a set of distinct integers.
Input: [4, 5, 6]
Output : [[], [6], [5], [5, 6], [4], [4, 6], [4, 5], [4, 5, 6]]
**6.23** Write a Python class to find a pair of elements (indices of the two numbers) from a given array whose sum equals a specific target number.
Input: numbers= [10,20,10,40,50,60,70], target=50
Output: 3, 4
**6.24** Write a Python class to reverse a string word by word.
Input string: 'hello .py'
Expected Output: '.py hello'
**6.25** Write a Python class which has two methods get_String and print_String. get_String accept a string from the user and print_String print the string in upper case.
**6.26** Write a Python class named Circle constructed by a radius and two methods which will compute the area and the perimeter of a circle.
**6.27** Write a Python class to find the three elements that sum to zero from a set of n real numbers.
Input array: [-25, -10, -7, -3, 2, 4, 8, 10]
Output: [[-10, 2, 8], [-7, -3, 10]]
**6.28** Write a Python function to find the Max of three numbers.
**6.29** Write a Python function to sum all the numbers in a list.
Sample List: (8, 2, 3, 0, 7)
Expected Output: 20
**6.30** Write a Python function to multiply all the numbers in a list.
Sample List: (8, 2, 3, -1, 7)
Expected Output: -336

# Assignment No. 4

**6.31** Write a Python program to reverse a string.
Sample String: "1234abcd"
Expected Output: "dcba4321"

**6.32** Write a Python function that accepts a string and calculate the number of upper case letters and lower case letters.
Sample String: 'The quick Brow Fox'
Expected Output:
No. of Upper case characters: 3
No. of Lower case Characters: 12

**6.33** Write a Python function that takes a number as a parameter and check the number is prime or not.

**6.34** Write a Python program to print the even numbers from a given list.
Sample List: [1, 2, 3, 4, 5, 6, 7, 8, 9]
Expected Result: [2, 4, 6, 8]

**6.35** Write a Python function that checks whether a passed string is palindrome or not.
Note: A palindrome is a word, phrase, or sequence that reads the same backward as forward, e.g., madam

**6.36** Write a Python program to access a function inside a function.

**6.37** Write a Python program to detect the number of local variables declared in a function.

**6.38** What is encapsulation?

**6.39** What is inheritance?

**6.40** What is polymorphism?

# Chapter 7
# Errors and Exceptions in Python

## 7.1 Objectives

The main objectives of this chapter are as following:

- Learn deeply about exceptions in Programs
- Discovering the difference between common Programming mistakes called Syntax errors and Disruptive Instructional errors.
- Introducing the concept of Exception Handlers to avoid errors in the execution of programs
- We discuss the various classes of exceptions
- Writing Python Scripts to anticipate errors.
- Writing Python Scripts to mitigate the errors.

## 7.2 Introduction

This chapter deals with errors and exceptions, an unwanted phenomena that can affect the normal execution of program. This chapter will deal with addressing those situations and our focus will be to find out how these unexpected situation or errors can be handled. These exceptions are discovered using block of statements, for example, using Python code try, except or else, called as error handler. We will also investigate some programs that will recover these errors without terminating application. Our main purpose of this chapter remains to detect and resolve the errors.

## 7.3 What are Exceptions?

An exception is usually considered as an event, may not be an error that occurs during program execution and disrupts the normal flow of the instructions of that program (Haraldsson, et al, 2017). Python as a programming language usually raises an exception if the Python scripts encounter such situation. An exception in python is an object that represents an error. Error or exception handling is a way of saving the execution state of a program at the time the error occurred which interrupted by the normal flow of the program execution. Such handlers ensure that the error is corrected and program execution resumes continue afterwards using the data saved before the error occurred.

Exceptions are regarded as instances that do not conform to the general rule by non-programmers. In order to control the impacts of such errors, an exception handler is introduced into the program. The exception handler ensures that the execution of the code does not cause further issues. It also ensures that the severity of the error is contained within the manageable limits. An exception handler is program constructs whose main aim is to handle or automatically deal with errors. Programming languages such as Ruby, PHP, Java, Python and C++ have built-in exception handlers. A common example is when trying to access a file that does not exist or that has been deleted.

## 7.4 Handling Simple Exceptions:

**Try statement with an except clause**

Just like Java, Python also uses the Try statement to deal with errors. The program constructs that have the code with the risk of encountering the error is embedded in the Try block (Haraldsson, et al, 2017). Let's have an example for further explanation.

In this example, the user is supposed to enter an integer using the raw_input (). The string input will be cast into an integer. If the input is not an integer then the code will generate a ValueError.

### 7.4.1 Example:

```python
n = int (input("Please enter a number: "))
print(n)
```

Figure 7-1 code for value error

```
C:\Users\btaze\AppData\Local\Programs\Python\Python37\python.exe
Please enter a number: 23
23
```

Figure 7-2 Output in python

The error handler helps in writing a robust code that read integer from the input

### 7.4.2 Example:

```python
while True:
    try:
        i = input("Please enter an integer: ")
        n = int(i)
        break
    except ValueError:
        print("No valid integer! Please try again ...")
print("Great, you successfully entered an integer!")
```

Figure 7-3 code for read the integer

```
C:\Users\btaze\AppData\Local\Programs\Python\Python37\python.exe
Please enter an integer: 23
Great, you successfully entered an integer!
```

Figure 7-4 output in python

This error handler has been written in form of a loop. The loop breaks only when a valid integer is encountered in the input hence reducing chances of errors.

The final output of the above code will be given as;

```
$ python integer_read.py
```

Please enter an integer: abc

No valid integer! Please try again ...

Please enter an integer: 42.0

No valid integer! Please try again ...

Please enter an integer: 42

Great, you successfully entered an integer!

$

### 7.4.3 Example:

This code tries to read a file from a specified directory. It causes an error is the directory does not exist.

```python
import sys
try:
    f = open('integers.txt')
    s = f.readline()
    i = int(s.strip())
except IOError as e:
    errno, strerror = e.args
    print("I/O error({0}): {1}".format(errno, strerror))
except ValueError:
    print("No valid integer in line.")
except:
    print("Unexpected error:", sys.exc_info()[0])
    raise
```

Figure 7-5 code for priniting the specified directory

```
C:\Users\btaze\AppData\Local\Programs\Python\Python37\python.exe
I/O error(2): No such file or directory
```

Figure 7-6 output for the specified directory

In order to deal with such exception, the exception clause should have many names in the tuple to be tried. This is shown in the next code

### 7.4.4 Example:

```python
try:
    f = open('integers.txt')
    s = f.readline()
    i = int(s.strip())
except (IOError, ValueError):
    print("An I/O error or a ValueError occurred")
except:
    print("An unexpected error occurred")
    raise
```

Figure 7-7 code of exception

```
C:\Users\btaze\AppData\Local\Programs\Python\Python37\python.exe
Connected to pydev debugger (build 183.5912.18)
pydev debugger: process 3564 is connecting

An I/O error or a ValueError occurred
```

Figure 7-8 output in python

### 7.4.5   Example:

The Try statement can also be followed by a finally statement. In this case, the code does not use the except clause (Vitousek, Kent, Siek & Baker, 2014). The final clause must also be executed even if no error occurred in the Try block. The example below explains this;

```python
try:
    x = float (input("Your number: "))
    inverse = 1.0 / x
finally:
    print ("There may or may not have been an exception.")
    print ("The inverse: ", inverse)
```

Figure 7-9 code try statment

```
C:\Users\btaze\AppData\Local\Programs\Python\Python37\python.exe
Your number: 2
There may or may not have been an exception.
The inverse:  0.5
```

Figure 7-10 output in python

The three clauses can also be added in the same program. The Try block can contain the except clause and the final statement. The example below shows the application of the three clauses;

### 7.4.6   Example:

```python
try:
    x = float (input("Your number: "))
    inverse = 1.0 / x
except ValueError:
    print("You should have given either an int or a float")
except ZeroDivisionError:
    print("Infinity")
finally:
    print ("There may or may not have been an exception.")
```

Figure 7-11 code snippet

```
C:\Users\btaze\AppData\Local\Programs\Python\Python37\python.exe
Your number: 40
There may or may not have been an exception.
```

Figure 7-12 output in python

The else clause can also be used as an exception handler. In this case, the statements under the else clause are executed if the Try block doesn't identify any error in the program code. Below is an example of its application;

### 7.4.7 Example:

```python
import sys
file_name = 'integers.txt'
text = []
try:
    fh = open(file_name, 'r')
    text = fh.readlines()
    fh.close()
except IOError:
    print('cannot open', file_name)

if text:
    print(text[100])
```

Figure 7-13 code snippet

```
C:\Users\btaze\AppData\Local\Programs\Python\Python37\python.exe
cannot open integers.txt
```

Figure 7-14 output in python

### 7.4.8 Example:

Let's have another example with code snippets. The statements are placed in the try block and all the error handlers are placed in the except block.

```python
try:
    text = input('Enter something --> ')
except EOFError:
    print('Why did you do an EOF on me?')
except KeyboardInterrupt:
    print('You cancelled the operation.')
else:
    print('You entered {}'.format(text))
```

Figure 7-15 Code snippet demonstrating exception handling

The output of the above code is given as;

```
C:\Users\btaze\AppData\Local\Programs\Python\Python37\python.exe
pydev debugger: process 6148 is connecting

Connected to pydev debugger (build 183.5912.18)
Enter something --> how are you
You entered how are you
```

Figure 7-16 Running output of the program

## 7.5 Classes of Exception:

Exception objects and the hierarchy of classes

General expression of exception handling objects:

```
def try_function():
    try:
        hrs = float(input("Enter Hours: "))
        rate = float(input("Enter Rate: "))
        return hrs * rate
    except:
        print("Values are non numeric")
        quit()

pay = try_function()
print(pay)
```

Figure 7-17  code of the program

```
C:\Users\btaze\AppData\Local\Programs\Python\Python37\python.exe
Enter Hours: 20
Enter Rate: 10
200.0
```

Figure 7-18  Running output of the program

This can also be represented in hierarchy as shown below:

    *try:*

      *doSomething1()*

    *except:*

      *try:*

        *doSomething2()*

      *except:*

        *pass*

    *else:*

      *try:*

        *doSomething3()*

      *except:*

                pass
            else:
                doSomething4()
    else:
        try:
            doSomething2()
        except:
            try:
                doSomething3()
            except:
                pass
            else:
                doSomething4()
else:
    try:
        doSomething3()
    except:
        doSomething4()

```
C:\Users\btaze\AppData\Local\Programs\Python\Python37\python.exe

Process finished with exit code 0
```

Figure 7-19  Running output of the program

### 7.5.1 Example:

Creating user-defined exceptions

```
import sys, traceback

def run_user_code(envdir):
    source = input(">>> ")
    try:
        exec(source in envdir)
    except:
        print("Exception in user code:")
        print('-'*60)
        traceback.print_exc(file=sys.stdout)
        print('-'*60)
envdir = {}
while 1:
    run_user_code(envdir)
```

Figure 7-20 Code snippet demonstrating user-defined exception

```
C:\Users\btaze\AppData\Local\Programs\Python\Python37\python.exe
>>> 2a
Exception in user code:
------------------------------------------------------------
Traceback (most recent call last):
  File "C:/Users/btaze/Downloads/Chapter 7 - Error and Exception
    exec(source in envdir)
TypeError: exec() arg 1 must be a string, bytes or code object
------------------------------------------------------------
```

Figure 7-21 Running output of the program

### 7.5.2 Example:

Built-in Exceptions are exceptions within the Python programming language (Cornu, Seinturier & Monperrus, 2015). These exceptions are used by deriving from the BaseException class.

Basis expression example:

*raise* new_exc *from* **original_exc**

**Error exception class:**

```
class Error(Exception):
    pass
class InputError(Error):
    def __init__(self, expression, message):
        self.expression = expression
        self.message = message
class TransitionError(Error):
    def __init__(self, previous, next, message):
        self.previous = previous
        self.next = next
        self.message = message
```

Figure 7-22 Code snippet representing error exception class

```
C:\Users\btaze\AppData\Local\Programs\Python\Python37\python.exe
pydev debugger: process 7464 is connecting

Connected to pydev debugger (build 183.5912.18)
```

Figure 7-23 Running output of the program

## 7.6 Creating and Raising an Exception Object

### 7.6.1    Example:

```
def demo_no_catch():
    try:
        str = 'Not catch any exception'
        return str
    except:
        print ('Catch exception')
a = demo_no_catch()
print(a)
```

Figure 7-24 Code snippet demonstrating how to create or raise an exception

```
C:\Users\btaze\AppData\Local\Programs\Python\Python37\python.exe
Not catch any exception
```

Figure 7-25  Running output of the program

In this example, the program generates an exception handling object called demo_no_catch. This handler ensures that general exceptions are not caught in program execution.

### 7.7 Creating custom Exception Classes

The general expression of exception in Python

```
class InvalidInputError(Exception):
    def __init__(self, msg):
        self.msg = msg
    def __str__(self):
        return repr(self.msg)

inp = int(input("Enter a number between 1 to 10:"))
try:
    if type(inp) != int or inp not in list(range(1,11)):
        raise InvalidInputError
except InvalidInputError:
    print("Invalid input entered")
```

Figure 7-26  code of the program

```
C:\Users\btaze\AppData\Local\Programs\Python\Python37\python.exe "C:
Enter a number between 1 to 10:12
Traceback (most recent call last):
  File "C:/Users/btaze/Downloads/Chapter 7 - Error and Exception Han
    raise InvalidInputError
TypeError: __init__() missing 1 required positional argument: 'msg'
```

Figure 7-27 Running output of the program

### 7.7.1 Example:

Here is an example of a code to catch the index errors in python

```
try:
    raise ValueError
except IndexError:
    pass
l = [1,2,3]
try:
    l[0]
except IndexError:
    print("an index error!")
```

Figure 7-28 Code snippet to catch the index errors in python

```
C:\Users\btaze\AppData\Local\Programs\Python\Python37\python.exe
Traceback (most recent call last):
  File "C:/Users/btaze/Downloads/Chapter 7 - Error and Exception
    raise ValueError
ValueError
```

Figure 7-29 Running output of the program

### 7.7.2 Example:

Error handling for array item not in a list;

```
class SuperDuperList(list):
    def getindexdefault(self, elem, default):
        try:
            thing_index = self.index(elem)
            return thing_index
        except ValueError:
            return default
```

Figure 7-30 Code snippet to handle the exception when an item is not in the list

```
C:\Users\btaze\AppData\Local\Programs\Python\Python37\python.exe

Process finished with exit code 0
```

Figure 7-31 Running output of the program

### 7.7.3    Example:

Example to try and catch index errors in Python. This is an exception that rises due to wrong indexes used in the program code.

```
7.7.3 indexerrors.py
1   import sys
2   try:
3       my_list = [3,7, 9, 4, 6]
4       print (my_list[2])
5   except IndexError as e:
6       print (e)
7   print (sys.exc_type)
```

Figure 7-32 Code snippet demonstrating the exception that will rise due to wrong indexing in a program

```
C:\Users\btaze\AppData\Local\Programs\Python\Python37\python.exe
9
Traceback (most recent call last):
  File "C:/Users/btaze/Downloads/Chapter 7 - Error and Exception
    print (sys.exc_type)
AttributeError: module 'sys' has no attribute 'exc_type'
```

Figure 7-33 Running output of the program

## 7.8 Accessing Properties of the Raised Exception

Sometimes, you will want to access the details of the original exception *object* and not just handle them based on their *class*. The object will contain, at a minimum, the readable message you see when an exception reaches the interactive prompt, but it may also contain extra information depending on how it was first raised.

### 7.8.1    Example:

```
7.8.1 raisingexcep.py
1   try:
2       age = int(input("Please enter your age: "))
3       if age < 0:
4           raise ValueError("%d is not a valid age. Age must be positive or zero.")
5   except ValueError as err:
6       print("You entered incorrect age input: %s" % err)
7   else:
8       print("I see that you are %d years old." % age)
```

Figure 7-34  code of the program

```
Please enter your age: 23
I see that you are 23 years old.
```

Figure 7-35 Running output of the program

**Raising Exception:**

### 7.8.2    Example:

Raising exceptions using if statement:

```
def quad(a,b,c):
    if a == 0:
        ex= QuadError( "Not Quadratic" )
        ex.coef= ( a, b, c )
        raise ex
    if b*b-4*a*c < 0:
        ex= QuadError( "No Real Roots" )
        ex.coef= ( a, b, c )
        raise ex
    x1= (-b+math.sqrt(b*b-4*a*c))/(2*a)
    x2= (-b-math.sqrt(b*b-4*a*c))/(2*a)
    return (x1,x2)
```

Figure 7-36 Code snippet demonstrating the exception with if statement

### 7.8.3    Example:

Raising exception using try statement block

```
def quadReport (a, b, c):
    try:
        x1, x2 = quad (a, b, c)
        print("Roots are", x1, x2)
    except ex:
        print (ex, ex.coef)
```

Figure 7-37 Code snippet demonstrating exception with try statement

```
C:\Users\btaze\AppData\Local\Programs\Python\Python37\python.exe

Process finished with exit code 0
```

Figure 7-38 Running output of the program

### 7.8.4 Example:

```
1  l = [1,2,3]
2  print(l[2])
3  print(l[1])
4
```

Figure 7-39 code of the program

```
C:\Users\btaze\AppData\Local\Programs\Python\Python37\python.exe
3
2
```

Figure 7-40 Running output of the program

In this example, line one creates an array of three elements (123) with indexes 0, 1 and 2 respectively. Line two tries to access an element in with the name "apples" which does not exist. Accessing index 4 causes index errors since it is beyond the index range of the array (Johansson, 2014). There needs to be a way of handling such errors hence need to create custom exception classes

## 7.9 Implementing Complex Error handling

### 7.9.1 Example:

*Exception1.py*

```
1   grades = [100, 100, 90, 40, 80, 100, 85, 70, 90, 65, 90, 85, 50.5]
2   def grades_sum(scores):
3       total = 0
4       for i in scores:
5           total += i
6       return total
7   print(grades_sum(grades))
8   def grades_average(lst):
9       l = len(grades)
10      a = grades_sum(lst) / l
11      return a
12  print(grades_average(grades))
```

Figure 7-41 Code snippet representing the implementation of complex error handling

```
C:\Users\btaze\AppData\Local\Programs\Python\Python37\python.exe
1045.5
80.42307692307692
```

Figure 7-42 Running output of the program

### 7.9.2 Example:

```
def get_angle(name):
    try:
        angle = float(input("Angle %s: " % name))
        if 0 < angle < 180: return angle
        else: raise ValueError
    except ValueError:
        get_angle(name)

get_angle("A")
```

Figure 7-2 Code snippet of the program stated above

```
C:\Users\btaze\AppData\Local\Programs\Python\Python37\python.exe
Angle A: 0
Angle A: 180
Angle A: 90
```

### 7.9.3 Example:

```
import sys
import math
a= 2
b= 6
c= 4
try:
    x1= (-b+math.sqrt(b*b-4*a*c))/(2*a)
    x2= (-b-math.sqrt(b*b-4*a*c))/(2*a)
    print(x1, x2)
except:
    e,p,t= sys.exc_info()
    print (e,p)
```

Figure 7-3 Code snippet

```
C:\Users\btaze\AppData\Local\Programs\Python\Python37\python.exe
-1.0 -2.0
```

Figure 7-44 Running output of the program

## 7.10 Using traceback if All Else Fails:
### 7.10.1 Example:

Basic read-eval-print loop

```
import sys, traceback

def run_user_code(envdir):
    source = input(">>> ")
    try:
        exec(source in envdir)
    except:
        print("Exception in user code:")
        print('-'*60)
        traceback.print_exc(file=sys.stdout)
        print('-'*60)
envdir = {}
while 1:
    run_user_code(envdir)
```

Figure 7-45 Code snippet demonstrating trace backs

```
C:\Users\btaze\AppData\Local\Programs\Python\Python37\python.exe
>>> 3a
Exception in user code:
------------------------------------------------------------
Traceback (most recent call last):
  File "C:/Users/btaze/Downloads/Chapter 7 - Error and Exception
    exec(source in envdir)
TypeError: exec() arg 1 must be a string, bytes or code object
------------------------------------------------------------
```

Figure 7-46 Running output of the program

### 7.10.2 Example:

Various ways of printing and formatting traceback

*import sys, traceback*

*def lumberjack():*

　*bright_side_of_death()*

*def bright_side_of_death():*

　*return tuple()[0]*

*try:*

　*lumberjack()*

*except IndexError:*

```python
exc_type, exc_value, exc_traceback = sys.exc_info()
print("*** print_tb:")
traceback.print_tb(exc_traceback, limit=1, file=sys.stdout)
print("*** print_exception:")
# exc_type below is ignored on 3.5 and later
traceback.print_exception(exc_type, exc_value, exc_traceback,
                          limit=2, file=sys.stdout)
print("*** print_exc:")
traceback.print_exc(limit=2, file=sys.stdout)
print("*** format_exc, first and last line:")
formatted_lines = traceback.format_exc().splitlines()
print(formatted_lines[0])
print(formatted_lines[-1])
print("*** format_exception:")
# exc_type below is ignored on 3.5 and later
print(repr(traceback.format_exception(exc_type, exc_value,
                                      exc_traceback)))
print("*** extract_tb:")
print(repr(traceback.extract_tb(exc_traceback)))
print("*** format_tb:")
print(repr(traceback.format_tb(exc_traceback)))
print("*** tb_lineno:", exc_traceback.tb_lineno)
```

```
C:\Users\btaze\AppData\Local\Programs\Python\Python37\python.exe "C:/Users/btaze/Downlo
*** print_tb:
  File "C:/Users/btaze/Downloads/Chapter 7 - Error and Exception Handling in Python/Ch
    lumberjack()
*** print_exception:
Traceback (most recent call last):
  File "C:/Users/btaze/Downloads/Chapter 7 - Error and Exception Handling in Python/Ch
    lumberjack()
  File "C:/Users/btaze/Downloads/Chapter 7 - Error and Exception Handling in Python/Ch
    bright_side_of_death()
IndexError: tuple index out of range
*** print_exc:
Traceback (most recent call last):
  File "C:/Users/btaze/Downloads/Chapter 7 - Error and Exception Handling in Python/Ch
    lumberjack()
  File "C:/Users/btaze/Downloads/Chapter 7 - Error and Exception Handling in Python/Ch
    bright_side_of_death()
IndexError: tuple index out of range
```

Figure 7-47 Code snippet demonstrating traceback

### 7.10.3 Example:

```python
import traceback
def another_function():
    lumberstack()
def lumberstack():
    traceback.print_stack()
    print (repr(traceback.extract_stack()))
    print (repr(traceback.format_stack()))


another_function()
lumberstack()
```

Figure 7-48 Code snippet of the code stated above

```
C:\Users\btaze\AppData\Local\Programs\Python\Python37\python.exe "C:/Users/btaze/Downloads
  File "C:/Users/btaze/Downloads/Chapter 7 - Error and Exception Handling in Python/Chapte
[<FrameSummary file C:/Users/btaze/Downloads/Chapter 7 - Error and Exception Handling in P
    another_function()
  File "C:/Users/btaze/Downloads/Chapter 7 - Error and Exception Handling in Python/Chapte
['  File "C:/Users/btaze/Downloads/Chapter 7 - Error and Exception Handling in Python/Chap
    lumberstack()
[<FrameSummary file C:/Users/btaze/Downloads/Chapter 7 - Error and Exception Handling in P
  File "C:/Users/btaze/Downloads/Chapter 7 - Error and Exception Handling in Python/Chapte
    traceback.print_stack()
  File "C:/Users/btaze/Downloads/Chapter 7 - Error and Exception Handling in Python/Chapte
['  File "C:/Users/btaze/Downloads/Chapter 7 - Error and Exception Handling in Python/Chap
    lumberstack()
  File "C:/Users/btaze/Downloads/Chapter 7 - Error and Exception Handling in Python/Chapte
    traceback.print_stack()
```

Figure 7-49 Running output of the program

## 7.11 Exception chaining and Tracebacks
### 7.11.1 Example:
Exception chaining can be done implicitly

```python
def compute(a, b):
    try:
        print(a/b)
    except Exception as exc:
        log(exc)

def log(exc):
    file = open('read.txt')
    print >>file, exc
    file.close()

compute(2,4)
```

Figure 7-50 Code snippet demonstrating exception chaining

```
C:\Users\btaze\AppData\Local\Programs\Python\Python37\python.exe
0.5
```

Figure 7-51 Running output of the program

In the above example, the method that calls the compute (0, 0) causes an error since there is no division by zero in programming, this is a ZeroDivisionError. The exception is captured by the compute () function catches this exception and calls log(exc). Log () also raises an exception since it tries to write into a file that has not been opened for writing.

### 7.11.2 Example:

```python
def main(filename):
    file = open(filename)
    try:
        try:
            compute()
        except Exception as exc: log(file, exc)
        finally:
            file.close()
def compute(): 1/0
def log(file, exc):
    try:
        print >> file, exc
    except:
        display(exc)
def display(exc):
    print(exc)
main('read.txt')
```

Figure 7-52 Code snippet

203

```
C:\Users\btaze\AppData\Local\Programs\Python\Python37\python.exe
division by zero
```

Figure 7-53 Running output of the program

### 7.11.3   Example:

Here is an example to show the traceback attribute in a Python program

```python
def do_logged(file, work):
    try:
        work()
    except Exception as exc:
        write_exception(file, exc)
        raise exc
from traceback import format_tb
def write_exception(file, exc):
    ...
    type = exc.__class__
    message = str(exc)
    lines = format_tb(exc.__traceback__)
    file.write(type,message,lines)

do_logged()
```

Figure 7-54 Code snippet demonstrating exception chaining

```
C:\Users\btaze\AppData\Local\Programs\Python\Python37\python.exe "C:/Users/btaze/Dow
Traceback (most recent call last):
  File "C:/Users/btaze/Downloads/Chapter 7 - Error and Exception Handling in Python,
    do_logged()
TypeError: do_logged() missing 2 required positional arguments: 'file' and 'work'
```

Figure 7-55  Running output of the program

## 7.12   Conclusion

Every programmer would like to have a code that is running and free from errors. It is, however, hard for one to write a complete code without small errors since everyone is prone to errors. In order to get rid of such errors, a programmer needs to write code that takes errors into account. The major challenge with writing code that takes errors into account is that it can be hard for the programmer to predict the errors that will occur in the program execution. Errors are, therefore, an event that occurs during program execution and disrupts the normal flow of program execution and hence producing undesired results.

Error handling is the process of ensuring that any error that occurs in program execution is dealt with before it produces more damage to the expected output. In this case, the code with the expected error is embedded in a block of statements that takes the error into account.

## 7.13 Summary

In summary, error handling is the process in which an expected error is addressed using a block of code that takes the errors into account. There are several ways in which exceptions are handled in Python programming. The use of Try or else statements can be used to handle several exceptions. This paper has mainly focused on the common errors that programmers face in their programming activities and some of the ways in which these errors can be handled. The best programs of this type forestall errors if possible, recover from them when they occur without terminating the application,

The blocks of statements that are used to detect the presence or absence of errors are called error handlers. Error handling refers to the anticipation, detection, and resolution of programming, application, and communications errors. Specialized programs, called error handlers, are available for some applications. The statements ensure that the program execution is redirected into another block is errors are detected in the current block being executed

## 7.14 Assignment Questions

Assignment 1

**7.1** What are exceptions?
**7.2** How exceptions are handled in python? Explain with an example.
**7.3** How custom exception classes are created in python?
**7.4** Write a function to compute 5/0 and use try/except to catch the exceptions.
**7.5** Define a custom exception class which takes a string message as attribute.
**7.6** What are some advantages of exceptions?
**7.7** What is the difference between an exception and error?
**7.8** What happens when exception is thrown by main method?
**7.9** Is the following code valid?

**try**:

   # Do something

**except**:

   # Do something

**finally**:

   # Do something

**7.10** Is the following code valid?

**try**:

   # Do something

**except**:

   # Do something

**else**:

   # Do something

**7.11** Can one block of except statements handle multiple exceptions?
**7.12** What is the output of the following code?
**def** foo():

   **try**:

      **return** 1

> finally:
>
>> return 2

k = foo()

print(k)

**7.13** What is the output of the following?

```
try:
    if '1' != 1:
        raise "someError"
    else:
        print("someError has not occurred")
except "someError":
    print ("someError has occurred")
```

**7.14** What happens when '1' == 1 is executed?

**7.15** What is the output of the following code?

```
def foo():
    try:
        print(1)
    finally:
        print(2)
foo()
```

**7.16** When is the finally block executed?

**7.17** What is the output of the code shown below?

```
x=10
y=8
assert x>y, 'X too small'
```

**7.18** What happens if the file is not found in the code shown below?

```
a=False
while not a:
    try:
```

```
    f_n = input("Enter file name")
    i_f = open(f_n, 'r')
except:
    print("Input file not found")
```

# Chapter 8 Well Known Python Network Libraries

## 8.1 Objectives

**The main objective of this chapter is to:**

- Introduce the concept of Python Libraries
- Discuss main libraries often used in Python Scripting for the Automation of Networks
- Discuss how a library is used with sample codes

## 8.2 Introduction

Python library is a collection of functions and methods that are prewritten for programmers to use without necessarily written their own. Libraries are prewritten code that has been written can only be used by the programmers by calling them in the program body. There are several Python libraries that are available for use by programmers. Example of Python libraries available include; ntplib, diesel, nmap, scapy, netifaces, netaddr, pyopenssl, pygeocoder, pyyaml, requests, feedparser, paramiko, fabric, supervisor, xmlrpclib, SOAPpy, Bottlenose, Construct, Postfix, OpenSSH server, MySQL server and Apache.

These libraries have different applications and they are called to perform distinct activities. When working with data, for instance, the major libraries applicable include; numpy, scipy and pandas will be the major libraries that one must know. These functions are the most efficient and convenient in data transformation as they save time in performing several tricks with data. The program can take much time to write a code that will take $O(n^3)$ time to run. The use of a library eliminates the time that is used in writing the script and the code can be run in runs in $O(n)$. They are very convenient data transformation functions that will save the programmer's time. These libraries can also save time when going for network and web development as they save much time in the development process. This paper mainly focuses on some of these libraries and how they are applied. Python for Network Engineers wouldn't have been possible it if weren't for the networking libraries, below is provided with some well-known third-party network libraries with their download URLs.

We provided a short description of each of the library and the tasks that each can do.

## 8.3 Installing Libraries in Python Environment

Installing any library in Python is very easy. Run the following command

Pip install <name of the library>

### 8.3.1 Example:

*pip install ntplib*

## 8.4 Python Libraries

In this section we will look at some of the most popular Network Libraries available. These libraries are available in Python 2.7

### 8.4.1 NTPLIB

The ntplib library is used to offer a simple interface that is used in querying NPT servers using Python. This can be very useful in networking activities since servers need a correct time to be distributed. The time in network server must be kept in mind by many business owners.

Figure 8-1 Installing NTP Library

The use of this library, therefore, help in synchronizing time in network servers. Time synchronization helps in preventing unauthorized requests from fraudulent individuals. Time synchronization has many advantages in an organizational network. The major advantages being; easy tracking of security breaches, network usage, or problems affecting many components can be nearly impossible if timestamps in logs are inaccurate. Another major advantage is that helps in reduce confusion, especially in shared filesystems since there needs to be consistency in the modification time. This can also be important in billing services and similar fields where time accuracy is critical.

### 8.4.1 Example: NTP library code example

```
>>> import ntplib
>>> from time import ctime
>>> c = ntplib.NTPClient()
>>> response = c.request('europe.pool.ntp.org', version=3)
>>> print(response.offset)
0.5763351917266846
>>> response.version=3
>>> print(ctime(response.tx_time))
Thu Apr 11 16:55:25 2019
>>> print(ntplib.leap_to_text(response.leap))
no warning
>>> response.root_delay\
...
0.0003509521484375
>>>
```

Figure 8-2 Outcome of the script

### 8.4.2 Example: Sample code

Seeking exact time from time central through the shell.

```
>>> ctime(response.tx_time)
'Sun May 17 09:32:48 2009'
```

Figure 8-3 Output of the code

### 8.4.3 Example:

```
import ntplib
import time

NIST = 'nist1-macon.macon.ga.us'
ntp = ntplib.NTPClient()
ntpResponse = ntp.request(NIST)

if (ntpResponse):
    now = time.time()
    diff = now-ntpResponse.tx_time
    print diff;
```

The above program will produce the following output.

```
D:\Python code>python ntp.py
2.01850914955

D:\Python code>
```

Figure 8-4 Code to display the functionality of ntplib

The image above displays the use of shell to request central time which gives out the exact and accurate time there.

### 8.4.2 Diesel 3.0.24

Diesel is a Python library that provides a framework used in writing network applications. This framework ensures that the network applications written are scalable and highly reliable. It mainly applies the greenlet library layered atop asynchronous socket I/O in Python. This enhances the need for achieving the benefits of both the threaded-style and evented-style. These are the linear and the blocking-ish code flow for the threated-style and the no locking and the low overhead per connection for the event-style concurrency paradigms. This design has been mainly inspired by the Erlang which is also the OTP platform.

```
>> F:\python> pip install diesel
Collecting diesel
  Using cached https://files.pythonhosted.org/packages/6f/b3/7fe2d9aa7485ca190176554b328848a6a67f26f9962639b56686021c6d4
1/diesel-3.0.24.zip
Collecting greenlet (from diesel)
  Using cached https://files.pythonhosted.org/packages/ad/37/d22e23ddf0dc21d37b0ddadc9b29b70e5e6f4b411881c77f745e6c09884
1/greenlet-0.4.15-cp36-cp36m-win32.whl
Collecting twiggy (from diesel)
  Using cached https://files.pythonhosted.org/packages/e1/8a/3a5d86365f73540b97b75d835f97f2ab04a74fb338b7522a34c8ccc426e
b/Twiggy-0.4.7.tar.gz
Collecting pyopenssl (from diesel)
  Using cached https://files.pythonhosted.org/packages/96/af/9d29e6bd40823061aea2e0574ccb2fcf72bfd6130ce53d32773ec375458
c/pyOpenSSL-18.0.0-py2.py3-none-any.whl
Collecting flask (from diesel)
  Using cached https://files.pythonhosted.org/packages/7f/e7/08578774ed4536d3242b14dacb4696386634607af824ea997202cd0edb4
b/Flask-1.0.2-py2.py3-none-any.whl
Collecting http-parser>=0.7.12 (from diesel)
  Using cached https://files.pythonhosted.org/packages/07/c4/22e3c76c2313c26dd5f84f1205b916ff38ea951aab0c4544b6e2f5920d6
4/http-parser-0.8.3.tar.gz
Collecting dnspython (from diesel)
  Using cached https://files.pythonhosted.org/packages/a6/72/209e18bdfedfd78c6994e9ec96981624a5ad7738524dd474237268422cb
8/dnspython-1.15.0-py2.py3-none-any.whl
```

Figure 8-5 Installing Diesel Library

The use of diesel provides a clean API. This API can be used to write the network servers or network clients or both. The API also supports the UDP and TCP hence making the process of writing network applications to be a fun. It bundles battle-tested clients for HTTP, DNS, Redis, Riak and MongoDB.

The link below is the active directory of Diesel since it is also an active project.

```
git clone git://github.com/jamwt/diesel.git
```

Figure 8-6 Snippet of code sample for active directory

### 8.4.4 Example: Code describing Diesel library

```python
import diesel

import argparse

class EchoServer(object):
    """this is an echo server using diesel"""
    def handler (self, remote_addr):
        """for running the echo server"""
        host, port - remote_addr[0], remote_addr[1]
        print ("Echo client connected from: %s: %d" %(host, port))
        while True:
            try:
                message = diesel.until_eol()
                your_message = ':' .join(['You said', 'message'])
                diesel.send(your_message)
            except Exception as e:
                print ("Exception:", e)

def main (server_port):
    app =diesel.Application()
    server = EchoServer()
    app.add_service(diesel.Service(server.handler, server_port))
    app.run()

if _name_ == 'main_':
    parser = argparse.ArgumentParser(description='Echo Server example with diesel')
    parser.add.argument('--port', action-"store", dest-"port", type=int, required=True)
    given_args = parser.parse_args()
    port = given_args.port
    main(port)
```

```
ModuleNotFoundError                       Traceback (most recent call last)
<ipython-input-5-58e9967e8f9e> in <module>
----> 1 import diesel
      2 import argparse
      3 class EchoServer(object):
      4     """this is an echo server using diesel"""
      5     def handler (self, remote_addr):

/srv/conda/lib/python3.6/site-packages/diesel/__init__.py in <module>
      1 # vim:ts=4:sw=4:expandtab
----> 2 from logmod import log, levels as loglevels, set_log_level
      3 import events
      4 from core import sleep, Loop, wait, fire, thread, until, Connection, UDPSocket, ConnectionClosed, ClientConnectionClosed, signal
      5 from core import until_eol, send, receive, call, first, fork, fork_child, label, fork_from_thread

ModuleNotFoundError: No module named 'logmod'
```

Figure 8-7 output diesel library

### 8.4.3 Python NMAP

This is a python library that helps programs that uses the NMAP port scanner. It makes it easy to manipulate NMAP scan results and produce perfect results. It is a helpful tool for network engineers who want to automate the scanning of ports and report generation. They can also be used by system admins for automated scanning of ports and in generating reports from the results. This library also supports NMAP script outputs.

```
PS F:\python> pip install nmap
Collecting nmap
  Downloading https://files.pythonhosted.org/packages/f8/6f/6813025bd575ebc771189afaab7c405fdf3f1febaa197525d5aa6fd88ac5/nmap-0.0.1-py3-none-any.whl
Installing collected packages: nmap
Successfully installed nmap-0.0.1
```

Figure 8-8 Installing NMAP Library

### 8.4.5 Example: Code for Python NMAP Library

*# Logic Finder*

*# This script uses the nmap library.*

*# This script creates a function to use nmaps.PortScanner to scan for host.*

*# It scans the host and will print if it is Down or Live.*

*""""*

*def detect(target):*

    *list1=[]*

    *scn = nmap.PortScanner()*

    *scn.scan(hosts=target,arguments='-sP')*

    *if not scn.all_hosts():*

213

```
            print("Down")
    for host in scn.all_hosts():
            print 'Live: ', host
    return(list1)
```

### 8.4.6 Example: Description of NMAP Library

```
# Logic Finder
# This script uses the nmap library.
# This script creates a function to use nmaps.PortScanner to scan for host.
# It scans the host and will print if it is Down or Live.
"""
def detect(target):
    list1=[]
    scn = nmap.PortScanner()
    scn.scan(hosts=target,arguments='-sP')
    if not scn.all_hosts():
        print("Down")
    for host in scn.all_hosts():
        print 'Live: ', host
    return(list1)
```

### 8.4.7 Example: Python NMAP Script

```
"""
# Logic Finder
# This script uses the nmap library.
# nmap.PortScanner is used to scan all the ports.
# It will then specify it to make a list to provide descriptions about the status of the host.
# It will then scan for open ports.
# If there is no host then it will simply end the program.
"""
def real_scan(self, domain):
    try:
```

```
        open_ports = []
        nm = nmap.PortScanner()
        results = nm.scan(domain.ip)
        hosts_list = [(x, nm[x]['status']['state']) for x in nm.all_hosts()]
        for host, status in hosts_list:
            if status == "up":
                protocols = nm[host].all_protocols()
                for protocol in protocols:
                    ports = nm[host][protocol]
                    for port in ports:
                        if ports[port]['state'] == 'open':
                            open_ports.append(port)
        return open_ports
    except:
        return []
```

### 8.4.4 Scapy

This is a Python library that is used in packet manipulation. It mainly consists of Python-based programs and libraries.

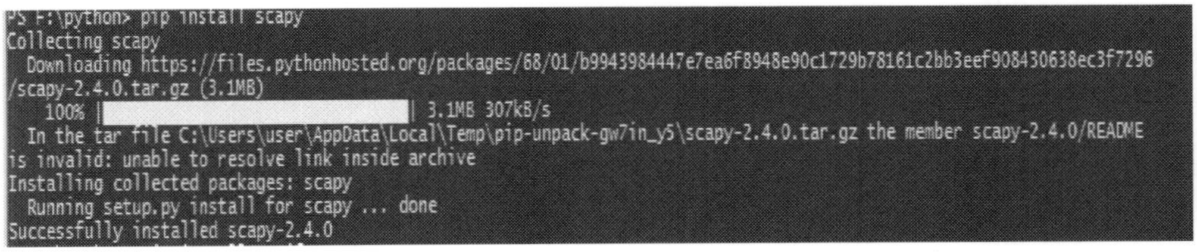

```
PS F:\python> pip install scapy
Collecting scapy
  Downloading https://files.pythonhosted.org/packages/68/01/b9943984447e7ea6f8948e90c1729b78161c2bb3eef908430638ec3f7296
/scapy-2.4.0.tar.gz (3.1MB)
    100% |████████████████████████████████| 3.1MB 307kB/s
  In the tar file C:\Users\user\AppData\Local\Temp\pip-unpack-gw7in_y5\scapy-2.4.0.tar.gz the member scapy-2.4.0/README
is invalid: unable to resolve link inside archive
Installing collected packages: scapy
  Running setup.py install for scapy ... done
Successfully installed scapy-2.4.0
```

Figure 8-9 Installing Scapy Library

The library can decode packets with a varied number of protocols, send the files on a wire, capture the packets, store the packets and read the packets using PCAP files, and even match the network requests against the replies. Scapy allows for fast packet prototyping that uses default but working values.

### 8.4.8 Example: Code for describing use of Scapy Library

```
# LogicFinder
# The script uses the scapy library.
```

# In this example, our layer has three fields. The first one is a 2-byte integer field named mickey and whose default value is 5. The second one is a 1-byte integer field named minnie and whose default value is 3. The difference between a vanilla ByteField and an XByteField is only the fact that the preferred human representation of the field's value is in hexadecimal. The last field is a 4-byte integer field named donald. It is different from a vanilla IntField by the fact that some of the possible values of the field have literate representations. For example, if it is worth 3, the value will be displayed as angry. Moreover, if the "cool" value is assigned to this field, it will understand that it must take the value 2.

"""

*from scapy.all import \**

*class Disney(Packet):*

  *name = "DisneyPacket "*

  *fields_desc=[ ShortField("mickey",5),*

      *XByteField("minnie",3) ,*

      *IntEnumField("donald" , 1 ,*

         *{ 1: "happy", 2: "cool" , 3: "angry" } ) ]*

*d=Disney(mickey=1)*

*ls(d)*

*d.show()*

```
from scapy.all import *
class Disney(Packet):
    name = "DisneyPacket "
    fields_desc=[ ShortField("mickey",5),
                 XByteField("minnie",3) ,
                 IntEnumField("donald" , 1 ,
                 { 1: "happy", 2: "cool" , 3: "angry" } ) ]
d=Disney(mickey=1)
ls(d)
d.show()
mickey    : ShortField              = 1        (5)
minnie    : XByteField              = 3        (3)
donald    : IntEnumField            = 1        (1)
###[ DisneyPacket ]###
  mickey    = 1
  minnie    = 0x3
  donald    = happy
```

Figure:8-10  output scapy lib

## 1.1 Example: Code for Scapy Library

    *#! /usr/bin/env python*

    *from scapy.all import \**

    *ans,unans=sr(IP(dst="192.168.86.130",ttl=5)/ICMP())*

    *ans.nsummary()*

    *unans.nsummary()*

    *p=sr1(IP(dst="192.168.86.130")/ICMP()/"XXXXXX")*

*p.show()*

```
>>> from scapy.all import *
>>> ans,unans = sr(IP(dst="192.168.86.130",ttl=5)/ICMP())
Begin emission:
...Finished sending 1 packets.
Received 3893 packets, got 0 answers, remaining 1 packets
>>> print(ans.nsummary())
None
>>> print(unans.nsummary())
0000 IP / ICMP 172.16.0.73 > 192.168.86.130 echo-request 0
None
>>> p = sr1(IP(dst="192.168.86.130")/ICMP()/"XXXXXX")
Begin emission:
..Finished sending 1 packets.
Received 4047 packets, got 0 answers, remaining 1 packets
```

Figure:8-11 Output scapy Lib

### 8.4.5 Netifaces

This is a Python third party and a portable library. It mainly enumerates network interfaces in local machines. It reduces the problems of interfering with network addresses when making network scripts portable.

```
PS F:\python> pip install netifaces
Collecting netifaces
  Downloading https://files.pythonhosted.org/packages/ec/8c/3c02241344b339d166ce7a8b403cee99fe423a3c200a0bc421be19bcb9af
/netifaces-0.10.7-cp36-cp36m-win32.whl
Installing collected packages: netifaces
Successfully installed netifaces-0.10.7
```

Figure 8-12 Installing Netifaces Python Library

It enumerates interfaces and network addresses.

### 8.4.10 Example: Describing Netifaces Library

    *def ipv4():*

        *""" Get all IPv4 addresses for all interfaces. """*

        *try:*

            *from netifaces import interfaces, ifaddresses, AF_INET*

            *# to not consider loopback addresses (no interest here)*

            *addresses = []*

```
for interface in interfaces():
    config = ifaddresses(interface)
    # AF_INET is not always present
    if AF_INET in config.keys():
        for link in config[AF_INET]:
            # loopback holds a 'peer' instead of a 'broadcast' address
            if 'addr' in link.keys() and 'peer' not in link.keys():
                addresses.append(link['addr'])
    return addresses
except ImportError:
    return []
```

```
>>> import netifaces
>>> netifaces.interfaces()
[u'lo', u'ens160']
>>> netifaces.ifaddresses('en0')
Traceback (most recent call last):
  File "<stdin>", line 1, in <module>
ValueError: You must specify a valid interface name.
>>> netifaces.ifaddresses('lo')
{17: [{'peer': u'00:00:00:00:00:00', 'addr': u'00:00:00:00:00:00'}], 2: [{'peer': u'127.0.0.1', 'netmask': u'255.0.0.0', 'addr': u'127.0.0.1'}], 10: [{'netmask': u'ffff:ffff:ffff:ffff:ffff:ffff:ffff:ffff/128', 'addr': u'::1'}]}
>>> netifaces.ifaddresses('lo')[netifaces.AF_LINK]
[{'peer': u'00:00:00:00:00:00', 'addr': u'00:00:00:00:00:00'}]
>>> netifaces.address_families[18]
u'AF_ASH'
```

Figure: 8-13 Output netifaces script

## 8.4.11 Example: Describing Netifaces Library script

```
"""
# Logic Finder
# This script uses the netifaces library.
# This function will get all the IPv4 addresses for all interfaces.
# loopback holds a 'peer' instead of a 'broadcast' address
# AF_INET is not always present
# to not consider loopback addresses (no interest here)
"""

def ipv4():
```

```python
try:
    from netifaces import interfaces, ifaddresses, AF_INET
    addresses = []
    for interface in interfaces():
        config = ifaddresses(interface)
        if AF_INET in config.keys():
            for link in config[AF_INET]:
                if 'addr' in link.keys() and 'peer' not in link.keys():
                    addresses.append(link['addr'])
    return addresses
except ImportError:
    return []
```

### 8.4.11b Example:

```
"""

Logic Finder


Returns a list of 3-tuples of the form (addr, scope, iface) where
'addr' is the address of scope 'scope' associated to the interface
'ifcace'.
This is the list of all addresses of all interfaces available on
the system.
"""

def in6_getifaddr():
    ret = []
    interfaces = get_if_list()
    for i in interfaces:
        addrs = netifaces.ifaddresses(i)
        if netifaces.AF_INET6 not in addrs:
```

```
            continue
        for a in addrs[netifaces.AF_INET6]:
        addr = a['addr'].split('%')[0]
        scope = scapy.utils6.in6_getscope(addr)
        ret.append((addr, scope, i))
    return ret
```

### 8.4.6 netaddr

This is a library whose main purpose is to represent and manipulate network addresses.

```
PS F:\python> pip install netaddr
Collecting netaddr
  Downloading https://files.pythonhosted.org/packages/ba/97/ce14451a9fd7bdb5a397abf99b24a1a6bb7a1a440b019bebd2e9a0dbec74
/netaddr-0.7.19-py2.py3-none-any.whl (1.6MB)
    100% |████████████████████████████████| 1.6MB 354kB/s
Installing collected packages: netaddr
Successfully installed netaddr-0.7.19
```

Figure 8-14 Installing netaddr Python Library

It provides support for layer 3 addresses such as IPv4 and IPv6 addresses, subnets, masks, prefixes. It is also responsible for classifying, slicing and sorting IP networks. It helps in working with set-based operations over IP addresses, responsible for parsing different notations and formats, generating DNS reverse lookups and subnetting. In the layer 2 address, it is responsible for representing and manipulating MAC addresses and generating IPv6 addresses.

**Code:**

```
# LogicFinder
# The purpose of the program is Get a netaddr.IPNetwork for the given IPv6 address
    :param address: a dict as returned by netifaces.ifaddresses
    :returns netaddr.IPNetwork: None if the address is a link local or loopback
    address
def _get_ipv6_network_from_address(address):
    if address['addr'].startswith('fe80') or address['addr'] == "::1":
        return None
    prefix = address['netmask'].split("/")
```

```
if len(prefix) > 1:

    netmask = prefix[1]

else:

    netmask = address['netmask']

return netaddr.IPNetwork("%s/%s" % (address['addr'],

    netmask))
```

```
from netaddr import *
import pprint
ip = IPAddress('192.0.2.1')
ip.version

4

repr(ip)
ip
IPAddress('192.0.2.1')
```

Figure 8-15 output of netaddr

```
ip = IPNetwork('192.0.2.1')

ip.ip
IPAddress('192.0.2.1')

ip.network, ip.broadcast
(IPAddress('192.0.2.1'), None)

ip.netmask, ip.hostmask
(IPAddress('255.255.255.255'), IPAddress('0.0.0.0'))

ip.size
1

IPAddress('ff00::1').is_multicast()
True
```

Figure 8-16 output netaddr

```
for ip in IPNetwork('192.0.2.0/23'):
    print('%s', ip)

%s 192.0.2.0
%s 192.0.2.1
%s 192.0.2.2
%s 192.0.2.3
%s 192.0.2.4
%s 192.0.2.5
%s 192.0.2.6
%s 192.0.2.7
%s 192.0.2.8
%s 192.0.2.9
%s 192.0.2.10
%s 192.0.2.11
%s 192.0.2.12
%s 192.0.2.13
%s 192.0.2.14
%s 192.0.2.15
%s 192.0.2.16
%s 192.0.2.17
%s 192.0.2.18
```

Figure 8-17 output netaddr

### 8.4.7 pyOpenSSL

This library is a thin wrapper used around the OpenSSL library. It was developed by Python Cryptography Authority. The main function of this library is to support OpenSSL lib. It implements a high-level interface over the OpenSSL library.

Figure 8-18 Installing pyOpenSSL Python Library

### 8.4.12 Example: OpenSSL for creating a client-side SSL

```
def _client(self, sock):
    """
    Create a new client-side SSL L{Connection} object wrapped around
    C{sock}.
    """
    # Now create the client side Connection. Similar boilerplate to the
    # above.
    client_ctx = Context(TLSv1_METHOD)
    client_ctx.set_options(OP_NO_SSLv2 | OP_NO_SSLv3 | OP_SINGLE_DH_USE )
    client_ctx.set_verify(VERIFY_PEER|VERIFY_FAIL_IF_NO_PEER_CERT|VERIFY_CLIENT_ONCE, verify_cb)
    client_store = client_ctx.get_cert_store()
    client_ctx.use_privatekey(load_privatekey(FILETYPE_PEM, client_key_pem))
    client_ctx.use_certificate(load_certificate(FILETYPE_PEM, client_cert_pem))
    client_ctx.check_privatekey()
    client_store.add_cert(load_certificate(FILETYPE_PEM, root_cert_pem))
    client_conn = Connection(client_ctx, sock)
    client_conn.set_connect_state()
    return client_conn
```

Figure 8-19 Code snippet displaying the usuage of OpenSSL Library

### 8.4.12b Example:

"""

*# Logic Finder*

*# This scrip uses thge PyOpenSSL library*

*# Verifies that PyOpenSSL's package-level dependencies have been met.*

```
    # Throws `ImportError` if they are not met.
    # See more below
    """

    def _validate_dependencies_met():
# Method added in `cryptography==1.1`; not available in older versions
        from cryptography.x509.extensions import Extensions
        if getattr(Extensions, "get_extension_for_class", None) is None:
            raise ImportError("'cryptography' module missing required functionality. "
                "Try upgrading to v1.3.4 or newer.")
        # pyOpenSSL 0.14 and above use cryptography for OpenSSL bindings. The _x509
        # attribute is only present on those versions.
        from OpenSSL.crypto import X509
        x509 = X509()
        if getattr(x509, "_x509", None) is None:
            raise ImportError("'pyOpenSSL' module missing required functionality. "
                "Try upgrading to v0.14 or newer.")
        # pyOpenSSL 0.14 and above use cryptography for OpenSSL bindings. The _x509
        # attribute is only present on those versions.
        from OpenSSL.crypto import X509
        x509 = X509()
        if getattr(x509, "_x509", None) is None:
            raise ImportError("'pyOpenSSL' module missing required functionality. "
                "Try upgrading to v0.14 or newer.")
```

### 8.4.12c Example:

```
    """
    # Logic Finder
    # This script uses the PyOpenSSL library
    # Verifies that PyOpenSSL's package-level dependencies have been met.
```

```
# Throws `ImportError` if they are not met.
Simple SSL client, using blocking I/O
"""
from OpenSSL import SSL
import sys, os, select, socket
def verify_cb(conn, cert, errnum, depth, ok):
    # This obviously must be updateds
    print 'Got certificate: %s' % cert.get_subject()
    #don't ever do this in production.
    #this force verifies all certs.
    return 1
if len(sys.argv) < 3:
    print 'Usage: python[2] client.py HOST PORT'
    sys.exit(1)
# Initialize context
ctx = SSL.Context(SSL.SSLv23_METHOD)
#you must choose to verify the peer to get
#the verify callbacks called
ctx.set_verify(SSL.VERIFY_PEER, verify_cb)
# Set up client
sock = SSL.Connection(ctx, socket.socket(socket.AF_INET, socket.SOCK_STREAM))
sock.connect((sys.argv[1], int(sys.argv[2])))
#send a simple http request
sock.send("""GET / HTTP/1.0
Host: www.google.com
""".replace("\n","\r\n"))
while True:
    try:
```

>        buf = sock.recv(4096)
>
>    except SSL.SysCallError:
>
>        break
>
>    if not buf:
>
>        break

### 8.4.8 Pygeocoder

It is used to leverage all public geocoding APIs. These may include Google's Geocoding API and Yahoo's Place Finder. Very useful when one has reached the API limit and when the API in use returns an ambiguous result.

Figure 8-20 Installing Pygeocoder Python Library

### 8.4.13 Example: Description of Pygeocoder Library

> """"
>
> # LogicFinder
>
> # This code uses the geocoder library. Geocoder allows you to simplify extracting information, where each provider does not include python libraries and have different JSON responses between each other. Each provider also has their own JSON schema and Geocoder allows you to simplify the task.
>
> # The coder below imports the library, then creates a variable, and finally printing the latitude and longititude.
>
> """"
>
> from pygeocoder import Geocoder
>
> results = Geocoder.geocode("Tian'anmen, Beijing")
>
> print(results[0].coordinates)

225

>>> *(39.908715, 116.397389)*

*print(results[0])*

>>> *Tiananmen, Dongcheng, Beijing, China, 100051*

```
import geocoder
address = 'Tian'anmen, Beijing'
print(geocoder.google(address).coordinates)
print(address[0])
None
2
```

Figure 8-4 Code snippet to show the use of PyGeocode in a script

### 8.4.14 Example: The PyGeocode for correcting minor spellings

It can also correct minor spelling mistakes and give back a properly formatted address

```
result = Geocoder.geocode('1600 amphiteather parkway, mountain view')
result.valid_address
>>> True
print(result)
>>> 1600 Amphitheatre Pkwy, Mountain View, CA 94043, USA
```

Figure 8-21 Code snippet for correcting minor spellings

### 8.4.15 Example: PyGeocoder library for producing or printing the longitude and latitude

```
from pygeocode import geocoder

address = '1600 Amphitheatre Pkwy, Mountain View, CA'
res = geocoder.geocode_google(address)
print res['lat'], res['lng']
```

Figure 8-22 Code snippet for printing the longitude and latitude

### 8.4.16 Example: Sample code for fetching longitude and latitude

*#!/usr/bin/env python3*

*# Foundations of Python Network Programming, Third Edition*

*# https://github.com/brandon-rhodes/fopnp/blob/m/py3/chapter01/search1.py*

*from pygeocoder import Geocoder*

*if __name__ == '__main__':*

    *address = '207 N. Defiance St, Archbold, OH'*

*print(Geocoder.geocode(address)[0].coordinates)*

**Result:**

$ python3 search1.py (41.521954, -84.306691)

```
import geocoder
address = '207 N. Defiance St, Archbold, OH'
print(geocoder.google(address).coordinates)

None

import geocoder
print(geocoder.ip('me'))
print(g.city)
print(g.country)

<[OK] Ipinfo - Geocode [US]>
None
None
```

Figure 8-23 Code snippet for printing the pygeocoder

### 8.4.9  Pyyaml

It is a data serialization format mainly aimed at human readability and aids users in interacting with scripting languages. It is a YAML parser and emitter in Python.

```
PS F:\python> pip install pyyaml
Collecting pyyaml
  Downloading https://files.pythonhosted.org/packages/fb/51/0c49c6caafe8d9a27ad9b0ca9f91adda5a5072b9efbbe7585fb97a4c71c4
/PyYAML-3.13-cp36-cp36m-win32.whl (188kB)
    100%                                              194kB 670kB/s
Installing collected packages: pyyaml
Successfully installed pyyaml-3.13
```

Figure 8-24 Installing Pyyaml Python Library

### 8.4.17  Example: Description of Pyyaml Python Library

*from yaml import load, dump*

*try:*

  *from yaml import CLoader as Loader, CDumper as Dumper*

*except ImportError:*

  *from yaml import Loader, Dumper*

*# ...*

*data = load(stream, Loader=Loader)*

*# ...*

$output = dump(data, Dumper=Dumper)$

```
import yaml
data = { 'Name': 'John',
         'age' : 20,
         'handles':{'facebook': 'John','email':'john@gmail.com'}
       }
document = """
 a: 1
 b:
   c: 3
   d: 4
"""
print(yaml.dump(data))
print(yaml.dump(data,default_flow_style=True))
print(yaml.load(document))

Name: John
age: 20
handles:
  email: john@gmail.com
  facebook: John

{Name: John, age: 20, handles: {email: john@gmail.com, facebook: John}}

{'a': 1, 'b': {'c': 3, 'd': 4}}
```

Figure 8-25 Code snippet for printing the pyyaml

### 8.4.18 Example: Description of a code using Pyyaml Library

class Hero:

...     def __init__(self, name, hp, sp):

...        self.name = name

...        self.hp = hp

...        self.sp = sp

...     def __repr__(self):

...        return "%s(name=%r, hp=%r, sp=%r)" % (

...           self.__class__.__name__, self.name, self.hp, self.sp)

yaml.load("""

... !!python/object:__main__.Hero

... name: Welthyr Syxgon

... hp: 1200

... sp: 0

... """)

Hero(name='Welthyr Syxgon', hp=1200, sp=0)

### 8.4.19 Example:

```
>>> import yaml
>>> print yaml.load("""
... name: Vorlin Laruknuzum
... sex: Male
... class: Priest
... title: Acolyte
... hp: [32, 71]
... sp: [1, 13]
... gold: 423
... inventory:
... - a Holy Book of Prayers (Words of Wisdom)
... - an Azure Potion of Cure Light Wounds
... - a Silver Wand of Wonder
... """)
{'name': 'Vorlin Laruknuzum', 'gold': 423, 'title': 'Acolyte', 'hp': [:
'sp': [1, 13], 'sex': 'Male', 'inventory': ['a Holy Book of Prayers (Wo
'an Azure Potion of Cure Light Wounds', 'a Siver Wand of Wonder'], 'cl:

>>> print yaml.dump({'name': "The Cloak 'Colluin'", 'depth': 5, 'rarity
... 'weight': 10, 'cost': 50000, 'flags': ['INT', 'WIS', 'SPEED', 'STE/
name: The Cloak 'Colluin'
rarity: 45
flags: [INT, WIS, SPEED, STEALTH]
weight: 10
cost: 50000
depth: 5
```

Figure 8-26 Code snippet for printing the pyyaml

### 8.4.10 Request

This is an HTTP library that is licensed and is written in Python. It is mainly an Apache2 HTTP and designed to interact with human language. It helps in a sense that URLs and POST data are not to be added manually. It allows users to send HTTP/1.1 requests using Python.

```
PS F:\python> pip install requests
Requirement already satisfied: requests in c:\users\user\appdata\local\programs\python\python36-32\lib\site-packages (2.
19.1)
Requirement already satisfied: certifi>=2017.4.17 in c:\users\user\appdata\local\programs\python\python36-32\lib\site-pa
ckages (from requests) (2018.8.24)
Requirement already satisfied: urllib3<1.24,>=1.21.1 in c:\users\user\appdata\local\programs\python\python36-32\lib\site
-packages (from requests) (1.23)
Requirement already satisfied: chardet<3.1.0,>=3.0.2 in c:\users\user\appdata\local\programs\python\python36-32\lib\site
-packages (from requests) (3.0.4)
Requirement already satisfied: idna<2.8,>=2.5 in c:\users\user\appdata\local\programs\python\python36-32\lib\site-packag
es (from requests) (2.7)
PS F:\python> pip install feedparser
```

Figure 8-27 Installing request Python Library

### 8.4.20 Example: Description of script using Request Library

*""""*

*# LogicFinder*

```
# This script uses the request Library.

# This script creates a variable that will request the content you need and this is also
done by using the get requests function.
"""

import requests

r = requests.get('https://github.com/timeline.json')

print r.text

# The Requests library also comes with a built-in JSON decoder,

# just in case you have to deal with JSON data

import requests

r = requests.get('https://github.com/timeline.json')

print r.json
```

```
pip install requests
Requirement already satisfied: requests in /srv/conda/lib/python3.6/site-packages (2.21.0)
Requirement already satisfied: certifi>=2017.4.17 in /srv/conda/lib/python3.6/site-packages (from requests) (2019.3.9)
Requirement already satisfied: urllib3<1.25,>=1.21.1 in /srv/conda/lib/python3.6/site-packages (from requests) (1.24.1)
Requirement already satisfied: idna<2.9,>=2.5 in /srv/conda/lib/python3.6/site-packages (from requests) (2.8)
Requirement already satisfied: chardet<3.1.0,>=3.0.2 in /srv/conda/lib/python3.6/site-packages (from requests) (3.0.4)
Note: you may need to restart the kernel to use updated packages.

import requests
r = requests.get('https://github.com/timeline.json')
print (r.text)

{"message":"Hello there, wayfaring stranger. If you're reading this then you probably didn't see our blog post a couple of year
s back announcing that this API would go away: http://git.io/17AROg Fear not, you should be able to get what you need from the
 shiny new Events API instead.","documentation_url":"https://developer.github.com/v3/activity/events/#list-public-events"}

import requests
r = requests.get('https://github.com/timeline.json')
print (r.json)

<bound method Response.json of <Response [410]>>
```

Figure 8-28 install request

### 8.4.21 Example: Another example of Request Library

```
"""

# LogicFinder

# This script uses the request Library.

# This script creates a variable that will request the content you need and this is also
done by using the get requests function.
"""

import requests

r = requests.get('https://github.com/timeline.json')
```

```
print r.text
# The Requests library also comes with a built-in JSON decoder,
# just in case you have to deal with JSON data
import requests
r = requests.get('https://github.com/timeline.json')
print r.json
```

## 8.4.21b Example:

```
"""
# Logic Finder
# This script uses the request library.
# This is a function that will request information from infoareana.ro
"""

def get_best(url):
    url = 'http://www.infoarena.ro' + url
    source_code = requests.get(url)
    plain_text = source_code.text
    soup = BeautifulSoup(plain_text, "html.parser")
    name = soup.find('span', {'class': 'username'}).find('a')['href'][35:]
    tests = soup.find_all('td', {'class': 'number'})
    max_ms = -1
    for test in tests:
        test = test.string
        if test.endswith('ms'):
            time = int(test.strip('ms'))
            max_ms = max(max_ms, time)
    if name not in d or max_ms < d[name][0]:
        d[name] = (max_ms, url)
```

*print(max_ms, name, url)*

```
r = requests.get('https://api.github.com/user', auth=('user', 'pass'))
r.status_code
200
r.headers['content-type']
'application/json; charset=utf8'
r.encoding
'utf-8'
r.text
u'{"type":"User"...'
r.json()
{u'private_gists': 419, u'total_private_repos': 77, ...}
```

Figure 8-29 Code demonstration of Request Library

## 8.4.22 Example:

```
>>> import yaml

>>> print yaml.load("""
... name: Vorlin Laruknuzum
... sex: Male
... class: Priest
... title: Acolyte
... hp: [32, 71]
... sp: [1, 13]
... gold: 423
... inventory:
... - a Holy Book of Prayers (Words of Wisdom)
... - an Azure Potion of Cure Light Wounds
... - a Silver Wand of Wonder
... """)

{'name': 'Vorlin Laruknuzum', 'gold': 423, 'title': 'Acolyte', 'hp': [:
'sp': [1, 13], 'sex': 'Male', 'inventory': ['a Holy Book of Prayers (Wo
'an Azure Potion of Cure Light Wounds', 'a Siver Wand of Wonder'], 'cl

>>> print yaml.dump({'name': "The Cloak 'Colluin'", 'depth': 5, 'rarity
... 'weight': 10, 'cost': 50000, 'flags': ['INT', 'WIS', 'SPEED', 'STE

name: The Cloak 'Colluin'
rarity: 45
flags: [INT, WIS, SPEED, STEALTH]
weight: 10
cost: 50000
depth: 5
```

Figure 8-30 Code snippet for printing the request

## 8.4.11 Feedparser

This is a Python library that allows the user to parse feeds in all known formats. The major formats that this library can parse include Atom, RSS, and RDF. This library is also able to parse all the known extension modules such as Apple's iTunes and Dublin.

```
PS F:\python> pip install feedparser
Collecting feedparser
  Downloading https://files.pythonhosted.org/packages/91/d8/7d37fec71ff7c9dbcdd80d2b48bcdd86d6af502156fc93846fb0102cb2c4
/feedparser-5.2.1.tar.bz2 (192kB)
    100% |████████████████████████████████| 194kB 618kB/s
Installing collected packages: feedparser
  Running setup.py install for feedparser ... done
Successfully installed feedparser-5.2.1
```

Figure 8-31 Installing feedparser Python Library

## 8.4.23 Example: Description of a code using Feedparser Library:

```
import feedparser

import time

from subprocess import check_output

# ------
# uptime
# ------

uptime = check_output(['uptime'])

print "\n"

print '-----------------------------------------------------------'

print uptime.strip()

print '-----------------------------------------------------------'

print "\n"

# --------------------
# tribune (feedparser)
# --------------------

d = feedparser.parse('http://chicagotribune.feedsportal.com/c/34253/f/622872/index.rss')

# print all posts

count = 1

blockcount = 1

for post in d.entries:

    if count % 5 == 1:

        print "\n" + time.strftime("%a, %b %d %I:%M %p") + ' ((( TRIBUNE - ' + str(blockcount) + ' )))'

        print "----------------------------------------\n"

        blockcount += 1

    print post.title + "\n"

    count += 1
```

```
import feedparser
import time
from subprocess import check_output
# ------
# uptime
# ------
uptime = check_output(['uptime'])
print ('----------------------------------------------------')
print (uptime.strip())
print ('----------------------------------------------------')
# --------------------
# tribune (feedparser)
# --------------------
d = feedparser.parse('http://chicagotribune.feedsportal.com/c/34253/f/622872/index.rss')
# print all posts
count = 1
blockcount = 1
for post in d.entries:
    if count % 5 == 1:
        print ("\n" + time.strftime("%a, %b %d %I:%M %p") + '  ((( TRIBUNE - ' + str(blockcount) + ' )))')
        print ("----------------------------------------------\n")
        blockcount += 1
    print (post.title + "\n")
    count += 1


b'04:35:06 up 2 days, 16:22,  0 users,  load average: 5.13, 6.60, 4.81'
```

Figure 8-32 Code snippet for printing the feedparser

## 8.4.23b Example:

*"""*

*# LogciFinder*

*# This function handles all messages incoming from users*

*"""*

*def handle(msg):*

   *content_type, chat_type, chat_id = telepot.glance(msg)*

   *command_input = msg['text']*

   *if command_input == '/start':*

      *# Check if already registred*

      *if register_user(chat_id):*

         *bot.sendMessage(chat_id, start_msg)*

         *feed = feedparser.parse(feed_url)*

         *# Send all news from older to newest*

         *for entry in reversed(feed.entries):*

            *msg = entry.title + '\n' + entry.link*

            *bot.sendMessage(chat_id, msg)*

   *if command_input == '/stop':*

      *bot.sendMessage(chat_id, stop_msg)*

*remove_user(chat_id)*

```
import feedparser
d = feedparser.parse('http://www.reddit.com/r/python/.rss')
print (d['feed']['title'])
print (d['feed']['link'])
print (d.feed.subtitle)
print (len(d['entries']))
print (d.headers)
```

Python
https://www.reddit.com/r/python/
news about the dynamic, interpreted, interactive, object-oriented, extensible programming language Python
27
{'Content-Type': 'application/atom+xml; charset=UTF-8', 'x-ua-compatible': 'IE=edge', 'x-frame-options': 'SAMEORIGIN', 'x-content-type-options': 'nosniff', 'x-xss-protection': '1; mode=block', 'set-cookie': 'session_tracker=3R8TMBFQU76H9xfveT.0.1556S1196 8475.Z0FBQUFBQmN4bnpnVUltSmVSZ2S1S2gSREFNa3lvTlRvQj1yNkFHSFRuU1RmOG5JSDZkcWSVcUZQbGEyXzVsQnAwNVJFTW1xck41bkw3YVIyWERZOHNkREVJN0 NtMHpTUVZtdUJnemQ4TGZOQXJzb2VDT0xmSS31ETFFvRDR6vNRsMVhPLUdSZ1hoaeM; Domain=reddit.com; Max-Age=7199; Path=/; expires=Mon, 29-Apr -2019 06:26:08 GMT; secure', 'cache-control': 'max-age=0, must-revalidate', 'X-Moose': 'majestic', 'Content-Length': '40208', 'Accept-Ranges': 'bytes', 'Date': 'Mon, 29 Apr 2019 04:26:08 GMT', 'Via': '1.1 varnish', 'Connection': 'close', 'X-Served-By': 'cache-mdw17338-MDW', 'X-Cache': 'MISS', 'X-Cache-Hits': '0', 'X-Timer': 'S1556511968.446843,VS0,VE267', 'Set-Cookie': 'session_tracker=3R8TMBFQU76W9xfveT.0.1556511968475.Z0FBQUFBQmN4bnpnVUltSmVSZ2S1S2gSREFNa3lvTlRvQj1yNkFHSFRuU1RmOG5JSDZkcWSVcUZQbGEyXzV sQnAwNVJFTW1xck41bkw3YVIyWERZOHNkREVJN0NtMHpTUVZtdUJnemQ4TGZOQXJzb2VDT0xmSS31ETFFvRDR6vNRsMVhPLUdSZ1hoaeM; Domain=reddit.com; Ma x-Age=7199; Path=/; expires=Mon, 29-Apr-2019 06:26:08 GMT; secure', 'Strict-Transport-Security': 'max-age=15552000; includeSubD omains; preload', 'Server': 'snooserv'}

Figure 8-33 Script demonstrating the use of Feedparser Library

### 8.4.12 Paramiko

Paramiko is a Python (2.7, 3.4+) implementation of the SSHv2 protocol, providing both client and server functionality. While it leverages a Python C extension for low-level cryptography (Cryptography), Paramiko itself is a pure Python interface around SSH networking concepts.

Figure 8-34 Installing Paramiko Python Library

### 8.4.27 Example: Code describing Paramiko Library

*""""*

*# LogicFinder*

*# This script uses Paramiko Library.*

*# This script uses the if loop and checks for 5 conditions to be met before it can proceed. It checks for the hostname, password, source and destination addresses, and username along with password. If the conditions are not met, then it will print 'args mssing'.*

"""

```python
import sys, paramiko

if len(sys.argv) < 5:
    print "args missing"
    sys.exit(1)

hostname = sys.argv[1]

password = sys.argv[2]

source = sys.argv[3]

dest = sys.argv[4]

username = "root"

port = 22

try:

    t = paramiko.Transport((hostname, port))

    t.connect(username=username, password=password)

    sftp = paramiko.SFTPClient.from_transport(t)

    sftp.get(source, dest)

finally:

    t.close()
```

```
import sys, paramiko
if len(sys.argv) < 5:
    print("args missing")
    sys.exit(1)
hostname = sys.argv[1]
password = sys.argv[2]
source = sys.argv[3]
dest = sys.argv[4]
username = "root"
port = 22
try:
    t = paramiko.Transport((hostname, port))
    t.connect(username=username, password=password)
    sftp = paramiko.SFTPClient.from_transport(t)
    sftp.get(source, dest)
finally:
    t.close()
args missing
An exception has occurred, use %tb to see the full traceback.
SystemExit: 1
```

Figure 8-35 Code snippet for printing the paramiko

### 8.4.27b Example:

```
"""
# LogicFinder
# This script uses the paramiko library
# This script will attempt to access a host without a password.
# If granted the user will gain entry via SSH with paramiko successfully.
"""
def _try_passwordless_paramiko(server, keyfile):
    """Try passwordless login with paramiko."""
    if paramiko is None:
        msg = "Paramiko unavaliable, "
        if sys.platform == 'win32':
            msg += "Paramiko is required for ssh tunneled connections on Windows."
        else:
            msg += "use OpenSSH."
        raise ImportError(msg)
    username, server, port = _split_server(server)
    client = paramiko.SSHClient()
    client.load_system_host_keys()
    client.set_missing_host_key_policy(paramiko.WarningPolicy())
    try:
        client.connect(server, port, username=username, key_filename=keyfile,
            look_for_keys=True)
    except paramiko.AuthenticationException:
        return False
    else:
        client.close()
        return True
```

```
#!/usr/bin/env python

import sys, paramiko

if len(sys.argv) < 5:
    print "args missing"
    sys.exit(1)

hostname = sys.argv[1]
password = sys.argv[2]
source = sys.argv[3]
dest = sys.argv[4]

username = "root"
port = 22

try:
    t = paramiko.Transport((hostname, port))
    t.connect(username=username, password=password)
    sftp = paramiko.SFTPClient.from_transport(t)
    sftp.get(source, dest)

finally:
    t.close()
```

Figure 8-36 Code snippet for printing the paramiko

### 8.4.13 Fabric

The fabric is a Python library (i.e. a tool to build *on*) used for interacting with SSH and computer systems [easily] to automate a wide range of tasks, varying from application deployment to general system administration.

```
PS F:\python> pip install fabric
Collecting fabric
  Downloading https://files.pythonhosted.org/packages/d9/e4/e6fa248c94ee5d45def54b609fcf70f39d0b7f7050f2d4405c5f156b5516/fabric-2.4.0-py2.py3-none-any.whl
    100% |████████████████████████████████| 61kB 225kB/s
Requirement already satisfied: cryptography>=1.1 in c:\users\user\appdata\local\programs\python\python36-32\lib\site-packages (from fabric) (2.3.1)
Requirement already satisfied: paramiko>=2.4 in c:\users\user\appdata\local\programs\python\python36-32\lib\site-packages (from fabric) (2.4.1)
Collecting invoke<2.0,>=1.1 (from fabric)
  Downloading https://files.pythonhosted.org/packages/be/9f/8508712c9cad73ac0c8eeb2c3e51c9ef65136653dda2b512bde64109f023/invoke-1.2.0-py3-none-any.whl (20
    100% |████████████████████████████████| 215kB 376kB/s
Requirement already satisfied: idna>=2.1 in c:\users\user\appdata\local\programs\python\python36-32\lib\site-packages (from cryptography>=1.1->fabric) (2.
Requirement already satisfied: six>=1.4.1 in c:\users\user\appdata\local\programs\python\python36-32\lib\site-packages (from cryptography>=1.1->fabric) (1
Requirement already satisfied: asn1crypto>=0.21.0 in c:\users\user\appdata\local\programs\python\python36-32\lib\site-packages (from cryptography>=1.1->fa
Requirement already satisfied: cffi!=1.11.3,>=1.7 in c:\users\user\appdata\local\programs\python\python36-32\lib\site-packages (from cryptography>=1.1->fa
Requirement already satisfied: bcrypt>=3.1.3 in c:\users\user\appdata\local\programs\python\python36-32\lib\site-packages (from paramiko>=2.4->fabric) (3.
Requirement already satisfied: pyasn1>=0.1.7 in c:\users\user\appdata\local\programs\python\python36-32\lib\site-packages (from paramiko>=2.4->fabric) (0.
Requirement already satisfied: pynacl>=1.0.1 in c:\users\user\appdata\local\programs\python\python36-32\lib\site-packages (from paramiko>=2.4->fabric) (1.
Requirement already satisfied: pycparser in c:\users\user\appdata\local\programs\python\python36-32\lib\site-packages (from cffi!=1.11.3,>=1.7->cryptograp
Installing collected packages: invoke, fabric
Successfully installed fabric-2.4.0 invoke-1.2.0
```

Figure 8-37 Installing Fabric Python Library

### 8.4.28 Example: Function to check disk space

```
"""

# LogicFinder

# The script uses the fabric.api library to connect to a host via SSH.

"""

from fabric.api import run
```

```
def host_type():
    run('uname -s')
def diskspace():
    run('df')
```

> **Note**
> You are not reading the most recent version of this documentation. 1.12.1 is the latest version available.

### 8.4.28b Example:

```
"""
# Logic Finder
# This function uses the fabric library
# Setup servers for deployment.
# This does not setup services or push to S3. Run deploy() next.
"""
def setup():
    require('settings', provided_by=['production', 'staging'])
    require('branch', provided_by=['stable', 'master', 'branch'])

    if not app_config.DEPLOY_TO_SERVERS:
        logger.error('You must set DEPLOY_TO_SERVERS = True in your app_config.py before setting up the servers.')
        return
    create_directories()
    create_virtualenv()
    clone_repo()
    checkout_latest()
    install_requirements()
    setup_logs()
    generate_secret_key()
```

```
>>> from fabric import Connection
>>> result = Connection('web1.example.com').run('uname -s', hide=True)
Traceback (most recent call last):
  File "<stdin>", line 1, in <module>
  File "<decorator-gen-3>", line 2, in run
  File "/usr/local/lib/python2.7/dist-packages/fabric/connection.py", line 29, i
n opens
    self.open()
  File "/usr/local/lib/python2.7/dist-packages/fabric/connection.py", line 615,
in open
    self.client.connect(**kwargs)
  File "/usr/local/lib/python2.7/dist-packages/paramiko/client.py", line 334, in
 connect
    to_try = list(self._families_and_addresses(hostname, port))
  File "/usr/local/lib/python2.7/dist-packages/paramiko/client.py", line 204, in
 families_and_addresses
    hostname, port, socket.AF_UNSPEC, socket.SOCK_STREAM
socket.gaierror: [Errno -2] Name or service not known
>>> msg = "Ran {0.command!r} on {0.connection.host}, got stdout:\n{0.stdout}"
Traceback (most recent call last):
  File "<stdin>", line 1, in <module>
NameError: name 'msg' is not defined
>>> msg = "Ran {0.command!r} on {0.connection.host}, got stdout:\n{0.stdout}"
>>> print(msg.format(result))
```

Figure 8-37 fabric import question

## 8.4.14 Supervisor

The supervisor is a client/server system that allows its users to monitor and control several processes on UNIX-like operating systems. It shares some of the same goals of programs like launched, daemontools, and run it. Unlike some of these programs, it is not meant to be run as a substitute for init as "process id 1". Instead, it is meant to be used to control processes related to a project or a customer and is meant to start like any other program at boot time.

## 8.4.29 Example: Configuration code

[program:alexad]

; Set full path to celery program if using virtualenv

command=sh /usr/local/src/gonzo/supervisorctl/alexad.sh

directory=/usr/local/src/gonzo/services/alexa

log_stdout=true        ; if true, log program stdout (default true)

log_stderr=true        ; if true, log program stderr (default false)

stderr_logfile=/usr/local/src/gonzo/log/alexad.err

logfile=/usr/local/src/gonzo/log/alexad.log

autostart=true

autorestart=true

startsecs=1

; Need to wait for currently executing tasks to finish at shutdown.

; Increase this if you have very long running tasks.

stopwaitsecs = 600

; When resorting to send SIGKILL to the program to terminate it

; send SIGKILL to its whole process group instead,

; taking care of its children as well.

killasgroup=true

; Set Celery priority higher than default (999)

### 8.4.30 Example: Sample code of Inet_http_server

```
[inet_http_server]
port = 127.0.0.1:9001
username = user
password = 123
```

Figure 8-37 sample Code

### 8.4.31 Example: Shows server coding

[unix_http_server]

file = /tmp/supervisor.sock

chmod = 0777

chown= nobody:nogroup

username = user

password = 123

### 8.4.32 Example: Shows user coding

[inet_http_server]

port = 127.0.0.1:9001

username = user

password = 123

### 8.4.15 Xmlrpclib

This is a remote procedure call to method that takes into use XML that is passed via HTTP(S) as a transport. It enables client to call methods with restrictions on a remote server and structured data for get back. XML-RPC is the simplest XML-based protocol for exchanging information between computers across a network.

- It supports writing XML-RPC client code (Bhushan et al 2009).
- It always handles all the details in translating between XML on the wire and comfortable python objects

### 8.4.33 Example: The below script was written for the ubuntu VM which acts like a server

```python
#!/usr/bin/python

import SimpleXMLRPCServer

def add(a,b):
    return a+b

def main():
    print "This is a server!"
    server = SimpleXMLRPCServer.SimpleXMLRPCServer(("0.0.0.0", 8000))
    server.register_function(add)
    print "Press CTRL+C to end..."
    server.serve_forever()

if __name__ == "__main__":
    main()
```

Figure 8-38 Code snippet for the ubuntu VM which acts like a server

### 8.4.34 Example: Scripts that were written for the ubuntu client machine

It used the xmlrpclib and this enabled the exchange of information across the network which is good for trouble shooting

```python
#!/usr/bin/python

import xmlrpclib

def main():
    print "This is a client!"

    client = xmlrpclib.ServerProxy("http://localhost:8000")
    print client.add(10,20)

if __name__ == "__main__":
    main()
```

Figure 8-39 Code snippet to enable the exchange of information across network

```
karel@karel-Ideapad-Z570:~$ ./client.py
This is a client!
30
karel@karel-Ideapad-Z570:~$
```

Figure 8-40 Output display

Figure 8-41 Output display of the command

### 8.4.35 Example: Code for description of xmlrpclib

*import xmlrpclib*

*XMLRPC_SERVER_URL = "http://www.python.org/cgi-bin/moinmoin/?action=xmlrpc"*

*pythoninfo = xmlrpclib.ServerProxy( XMLRPC_SERVER_URL )*

*allpages = pythoninfo.getAllPages() # this is the XML-RPC call*

*print ", ".join( allpages*

```
In [16]: import xmlrpc.client
         import pprint
         client = xmlrpc.client.ServerProxy('https://pypi.org/pypi')
         client.package_releases('roundup')
         pprint.pprint(client.release_urls('roundup', '1.6.0'))

[{'comment_text': '',
  'digests': {'md5': '54d587da7c3d9c83f13d04674cacdc2a',
              'sha256': '1814c74b40c4a6287e0a97b810f6adc6a3312168201eaa0badd1dd8c216b1bcb'},
  'downloads': -1,
  'filename': 'roundup-1.6.0.tar.gz',
  'has_sig': True,
  'md5_digest': '54d587da7c3d9c83f13d04674cacdc2a',
  'packagetype': 'sdist',
  'path': 'f0/07/6f4e2164ed82dfff873ee55181f782926bcb4a29f6a83fe4f8b9cbf5489c/roundup-1.6.0.tar.gz',
  'python_version': 'source',
  'sha256_digest': '1814c74b40c4a6287e0a97b810f6adc6a3312168201eaa0badd1dd8c216b1bcb',
  'size': 2893499,
  'upload_time': '2018-07-13T11:30:36.405653Z',
  'url': 'https://files.pythonhosted.org/packages/f0/07/6f4e2164ed82dfff873ee55181f782926bcb4a29f6a83fe4f8b9cbf5489c/roundup-1.6.0.tar.gz'}]
```

Figure 8-42 Code snippet for printing the paramiko

### 8.4.16 Construct

The construct is a python library for the construction and deconstruction of data structures in a declarative fashion. In this context, construction, or building, refers to the process of converting (serializing) a programmatic object into a binary representation. Deconstruction, or parsing, refers to the opposite process of converting (deserializing) binary data into a programmatic object. Being declarative means that user code defines the data structure, instead of the convention of writing procedural code to accomplish the goal. The construct can work seamlessly with a bit- and byte-level data granularity and various byte-ordering.

Figure 8-5 Installing Construct Python Library

### 8.4.36 Example: Code for describing Construct Library

"""

# LogicFinder

# Contextlib provide utilities for common task involving the 'with' statement.

# The contextmanager function is a decorator that can be used to define a factory function for 'with' statement contect managers, without needing to create a class or seperate __enter__() and __exit__ methods.

# The script uses a def function to define custom_open which opens and closes a file.

# The with statement then uses the custom_open function that will automatically close the file which would allow the program to run properly.

"""

from contextlib import contextmanager

@contextmanager

def custom_open(filename):

  f = open(filename)

  try:

    yield f

  finally:

    f.close()

with custom_open('file') as f:

  contents = f.read()

```
>>> from contextlib import contextmanager
>>> @contextmanager
... def tag(name):
...     print("<%s>" % name)
...     yield
...     print("</%s>" % name)
...
>>> with tag("h1"):
...     print("foo")
...
<h1>
foo
</h1>
```

Figure 8-44 Code snippet for the construct

### 8.4.37 Example: Sample code to parse capture for TCP/ OIP frames into frames

```
tcpip_stack = layer2ethernet
pkt = tcpip_stack.parse("...raw captured packet...")
raw_data = tcpip_stack.build(pkt)
```

Figure 8-45 Code to capture frames

### 8.4.38 Example: Sample Code

```
>>> format = Struct(
...     "signature" / Const(b"BMP"),
...     "width" / Int8ub,
...     "height" / Int8ub,
...     "pixels" / Array(this.width * this.height, Byte),
... )
>>> format.build(dict(width=3,height=2,pixels=[7,8,9,11,12,13]))
b'BMP\x03\x02\x07\x08\t\x0b\x0c\r'
>>> format.parse(b'BMP\x03\x02\x07\x08\t\x0b\x0c\r')
Container(signature=b'BMP')(width=3)(height=2)(pixels=[7, 8, 9, 11, 12, 13])
```

A `Sequence` is a collection of ordered fields, and differs from `Array` and `GreedyRange` in that those two are homogenous:

```
>>> format = Sequence(PascalString(Byte, "utf8"), GreedyRange(Byte))
>>> format.build([u"lalaland", [255,1,2]])
b'\nlalaland\xff\x01\x02'
>>> format.parse(b"\x004361789432197")
['', [52, 51, 54, 49, 55, 56, 57, 52, 51, 50, 49, 57, 55]]
```

Figure 8-66 Code for Construct Library

### 8.4.17 Pandas

This is a python package that is designed to do work with labeled and relational data intuitive and simple (Radeta et al., 2018). It is a perfect tool for wrangling data. Panda is designed for easy and quick data aggregation, manipulation and visualization (Radeta et al., 2018). It is consisting of two types that is series one dimensional and data frames which is two dimensional. Panda enables you to;

- Convert data structures to data frame objects.
- Handle the missing data and represent it as NaNs (Radeta et al., 2018).
- Delete and add columns from data frame easily.
- Do the powerful grouping by functionality.

### 8.4.39 Example: Shows how you can a data frame by passing numpy array with a date time index and labelled column.

*In [6]: dates = pd.date_range('20130101', periods=6)*

*In [7]: dates*

*Out[7]:*

*DatetimeIndex(['2013-01-01', '2013-01-02', '2013-01-03', '2013-01-04',*

    *'2013-01-05', '2013-01-06'],*

    *dtype='datetime64[ns]', freq='D')*

*In [8]: df = pd.DataFrame(np.random.randn(6,4), index=dates, columns=list('ABCD'))*

*In [9]: df*

*Out[9]:*

          *A    B    C    D*

*2013-01-01  0.469112 -0.282863 -1.509059 -1.135632*

*2013-01-02  1.212112 -0.173215  0.119209 -1.044236*

*2013-01-03 -0.861849 -2.104569 -0.494929  1.071804*

*2013-01-04  0.721555 -0.706771 -1.039575  0.271860*

*2013-01-05 -0.424972  0.567020  0.276232 -1.087401*

*2013-01-06 -0.673690  0.113648 -1.478427  0.524988*

```
import pandas as pd
import numpy as np
import matplotlib.pyplot as plt
dates = pd.date_range('20130101',periods=6)
dates
DatetimeIndex(['2013-01-01', '2013-01-02', '2013-01-03', '2013-01-04',
               '2013-01-05', '2013-01-06'],
              dtype='datetime64[ns]', freq='D')
df = pd.DataFrame(np.random.randn(6,4),index=dates,columns=list('ABCD'))
df
                   A         B         C         D
2013-01-01   0.150395  0.708408  0.206437 -1.334892
2013-01-02  -1.156714  1.052422  0.231562  0.139136
2013-01-03  -1.041434  2.051013 -1.449596 -1.046680
2013-01-04  -0.581375  1.890658  1.256623 -0.255946
2013-01-05  -0.033571  0.339220  1.408194  0.273776
2013-01-06  -0.381567 -1.190543 -1.469129 -0.786397
```

Figure 8-47 Code snippet for printing the pandas

### 8.4.40 Example: Shows how to create data frame by passing a dict of objects that can be converted to series like

In [10]: df2 = pd.DataFrame({ 'A' : 1.,

.....:             'B' : pd.Timestamp('20130102'),

.....:             'C' : pd.Series(1,index=list(range(4)),dtype='float32'),

.....:             'D' : np.array([3] * 4,dtype='int32'),

.....:             'E' : pd.Categorical(["test","train","test","train"]),

.....:             'F' : 'foo' })

.....:

In [11]: df2

Out[11]:

```
     A       B    C  D     E    F
0  1.0 2013-01-02 1.0 3  test  foo
1  1.0 2013-01-02 1.0 3 train  foo
2  1.0 2013-01-02 1.0 3  test  foo
3  1.0 2013-01-02 1.0 3 train  foo
```

```
import pandas as pd
import numpy as np
import matplotlib.pyplot as plt
df2 = pd.DataFrame({ 'A' : 1.,
'B' : pd.Timestamp('20130102'),
'C' : pd.Series(1,index=list(range(4)),dtype='float32'),
'D' : np.array([3] * 4,dtype='int32'),
'E' : pd.Categorical(["test","train","test","train"]),
'F' : 'foo' })
df2
     A       B    C  D     E    F
0  1.0 2013-01-02 1.0 3  test  foo
1  1.0 2013-01-02 1.0 3 train  foo
2  1.0 2013-01-02 1.0 3  test  foo
3  1.0 2013-01-02 1.0 3 train  foo
```

Figure 8-48 Code snippet for printing the pandas

### 8.4.18 Matplotib

Another python library package that is tailored for just generating simple and powerful visualization (Lescisin and Mahmoud 2016). It is a top-notch software piece that makes python a cognizant competitor to such scientific tools as Mathematica or metlab when used together with numpy, scipy and pandas. This library is quite low meaning that you will be required to write more codes so that you can reach the advanced levels of visualization. In metplotib almost everything is customizable (Lescisin and Mahmoud 2016). This will require more efforts than when using high level tools but the effort is always worth a shot. Despite that with little efforts you can be able to come up with;

- Plots including line plots, scatter plot, stem plots, quiver plots, contour plots among others (Lescisin and Mahmoud 2016).
- Charts including bar charts and histograms, pie charts, and spectrograms.
- Also, it facilitates creation of label grids, legends and grids.

### 8.4.41 Example: Shows coding for a line plot

>>> import matplotlib.pyplot as plt

>>> import numpy as np

>>> a = np.linspace(0, 10, 100)

>>> b = np.exp(-a)

>>> plt.plot(a, b)

>>> plt.show()

```
import matplotlib.pyplot as plt
import numpy as np
a = np.linspace(0, 10, 100)
b = np.exp(-a)
plt.plot(a, b)
plt.show()
```

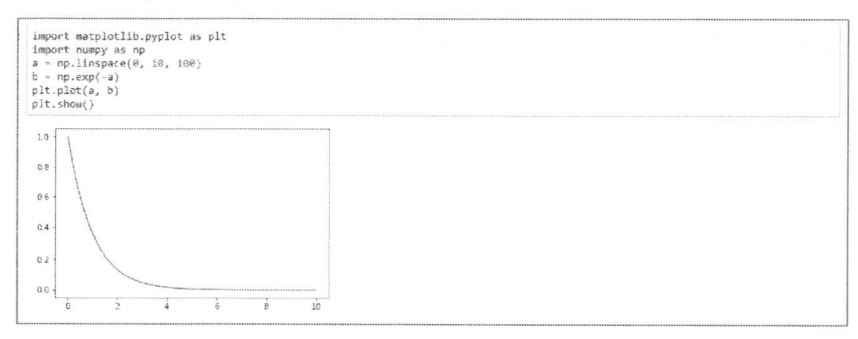

Figure 8-49 Code snippet for printing the matplotib

### 8.4.42 Example: Shows coding for a histogram

>>> import matplotlib.pyplot as plt

>>> from numpy.random import normal,rand

>>> x = normal(size=200)

>>> plt.hist(x, bins=30)

>>> plt.show()

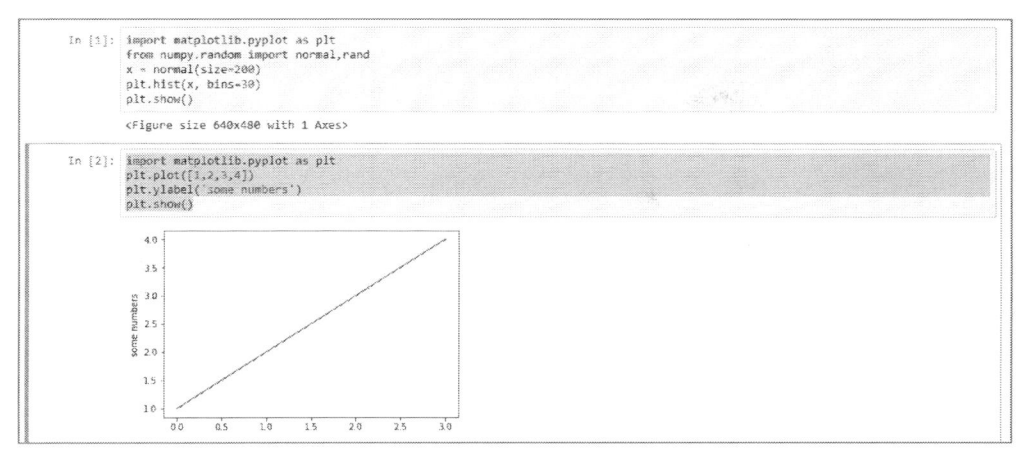

Figure 8-50 Code snippet for printing the pandas

### 8.4.19 SOAPpy

SOAPpy is a simple python library that fully supports dynamic interaction between the server and the client (Lescisin and Mahmoud 2016). This library includes SOAP parser on sax.ml, SOAP builder, SOAP proxy for RPC client code and SOAP server which is a framework for server code. SOAPpy has the following features.

- It handles faults and all SOAP 1.0 types.
- Allows specification of SOAP action and namespace specification.
- Has homogenous typed arrays and it can also support multiple schemas.
- It has SSL clients and SSL server that can be used on python when combined with OpenSSL support (Radeta et al., 2018).
- It has WSDL server and WSDL client support.

### 8.5 Conclusion

In summary, Python library is a collection of functions and methods that are prewritten for programmers to use without necessarily written their own. Libraries are prewritten code that has been written can only be used by the programmers by calling them in the program body. There are several Python libraries that are available for use by programmers.

### 8.6 Summary

This chapter discusses the python libraries in terms of definition function and examples, some of the libraries discussed are Ntplib which is responsible for time synchronization, Contract responsible for declaring and parsing binary data; Xmlrpclib for describing method results and calls, Paramiko which gives functionality to both server and customer, Supervisor that control as well as monitoring of processes among others. It is therefore important to conclude that python library methods are key in automation of networks.

## 8.7 Assignment Questions

Assignment 1

**8.1** How libraries are installed in python environment?
**8.2** What is the use of NTPLIB library?
**8.3** What is python NMAP library used for?
**8.4** What is the use of Scapy library?
**8.5** Describe Netifaces library?
**8.6** Explain netaddr library?
**8.7** What is pyOpenSSL library?
**8.8** What is Pyyaml?
**8.9** What is Feedparser library?
**8.10** Describe Fabric python library?

Assignment 2

**Exploring Python Libraries:**

**XML with xmltodict**

Start an interactive Python interpreter. Example below:

# ipython

Python 3.6.5 (default, Apr 10 2018, 17:08:37)

Type 'copyright', 'credits' or 'license' for more information

IPython 6.5.0 -- An enhanced Interactive Python. Type '?' for help.

In [1]:

Import the xmltodict library:

import xmltodict

Open the sample xml file and read it into variable:

with open("xml_example.xml") as f:
    xml_example = f.read()

Print the raw XML data

print(xml_example)

Parse the XML into a Python (Ordered) dictionary

xml_dict = xmltodict.parse(xml_example)

Pretty Print the Python Dictionary Object

from pprint import pprint

pprint(xml_dict)

Save the interface name into a variable using XML nodes as keys

int_name = xml_dict["interface"]["name"]

Print the interface name

print(int_name)

Change the IP address of the interface

xml_dict["interface"]["ipv4"]["address"]["ip"] = "192.168.0.2"

Check that the IP address has been changed in the dictionary

pprint(xml_dict)

Revert to the XML string version of the dictionary

print(xmltodict.unparse(xml_dict))

After you've completed exploring, exit the interpreter.

exit()

## YAML with PyYAML

Start an interactive Python interpreter. Example below:

# ipython

Python 3.6.5 (default, Apr 10 2018, 17:08:37)

Type 'copyright', 'credits' or 'license' for more information

IPython 6.5.0 -- An enhanced Interactive Python. Type '?' for help.

In [1]:

Import the yamltodict library

```python
import yaml
```

Open the sample yaml file and read it into variable

```python
with open("yaml_example.yaml") as f:
    yaml_example = f.read()
```

Print the raw yaml data

```python
print(yaml_example)
```

Parse the yaml into a Python dictionary

```python
yaml_dict = yaml.load(yaml_example)
```

Pretty Print the Python Dictionary Object

```python
from pprint import pprint
pprint(yaml_dict)
```

Save the interface name into a variable

```python
int_name = yaml_dict["interface"]["name"]
```

Print the interface name

```python
print(int_name)
```

Change the IP address of the interface

```python
yaml_dict["interface"]["ipv4"]["address"][0]["ip"] = "192.168.0.2"
```

Check that the IP address has been changed in the dictionary

```python
pprint(yaml_dict)
```

Revert to the yaml string version of the dictionary

```python
print(yaml.dump(yaml_dict, default_flow_style=False))
```

After you've completed exploring, exit the interpreter.

```python
exit()
```

## CSV with csv

Start an interactive Python interpreter. Example below:

```
# ipython
```

Python 3.6.5 (default, Apr 10 2018, 17:08:37)

Type 'copyright', 'credits' or 'license' for more information

IPython 6.5.0 -- An enhanced Interactive Python. Type '?' for help.

In [1]:

Import the csv library

```
import csv
```

Open the sample csv file and print it to screen

```
with open("csv_example.csv") as f:
    print(f.read())
```

Open the sample csv file, and create a csv.reader object

```
with open("csv_example.csv") as f:
    csv_python = csv.reader(f)
    # Loop over each row in csv and leverage the data in code
    for row in csv_python:
        print("{device} is in {location} " \
            "and has IP {ip}.".format(
                device = row[0],
                location = row[2],
                ip = row[1]
            )
        )
```

Create a new tuple for additional router.

```
router4 = ("router4", "10.4.0.1", "Chicago")
```

Add new router to CSV file.

```
with open("csv_example.csv", "a") as f:
    csv_writer = csv.writer(f)
```

```
csv_writer.writerow(router4)
```

Re-read and print out the CSV content.

```
with open("csv_example.csv") as f:
    print(f.read())
```

After you've completed exploring, exit the interpreter.

```
exit()
```

## YANG with pyang

Print the YANG module in a simple text tree

```
pyang -f tree ietf-interfaces.yang
```

Print only part of the tree

```
pyang -f tree --tree-path=/interfaces/interface \
  ietf-interfaces.yang
```

Print an example XML skeleton (NETCONF)

```
pyang -f sample-xml-skeleton ietf-interfaces.yang
```

Create an HTTP/JS view of the YANG Model (no output expected in the CLI)

```
pyang -f jstree -o ietf-interfaces.html \
  ietf-interfaces.yang
```

Control the "nested depth" in trees

```
pyang -f tree --tree-depth=2 ietf-ip.yang
```

Display a full module.

```
pyang -f tree \
  ietf-ip.yang
```

Include deviation models in the processing

```
pyang -f tree \
  --deviation-module=cisco-xe-ietf-ip-deviation.yang \
  ietf-ip.yang
```

# Chapter 9
# Practice Programs and Scripts Network Automation

## 9.1 Objectives:

The main objective of this chapter is to discuss and show more involving Python Script to achieve Network Automation

- Client communication with server
- Generating IP Address IDCR
- Creation of API
- Interaction with HTTP as client
- Finding IP Address
- Pinging the server
- check OS status
- Finding interface on machine
- creation of packet sniffers to ret ARP requests
- creating firewall to block websites

### 9.3.1 Interacting with HTTP Services as a Client

We can interact with HTTP service as a client too. It includes a short code as given below:

**Script:**

```
>>> import urllib
>>> import urllib.request
>>> from pprint import pprint
>>>
>>> goog_url = 'http://insight.dev.schoolwires.com/HelpAssets/C2Assets/C2Files/C2ImportCalEventSample.csv'
>>>
>>> def dowload(csv_url):
...     response = urllib.request.urlopen(csv_url)
...     csv = response.read()
...     cvs_str = str(csv)
...     lines = cvs_str.split("\\n")
...     for l in lines:
...         print (l +"\n")
...
>>> dowload(goog_url)
b'Start Date ,Start Time,End Date,End Time,Event Title ,All Day Event,No End Time,Event Description,Contact ,Contact Email ,Contact Phone,Location,Category,Mandatory,Registration,Maximum,Last Date To Register\r

9/5/2011,3:00:00 PM,9/5/2011,,Social Studies Dept. Meeting,N,Y,Department meeting,Chris Gallagher,cgallagher@schoolwires.com,814-555-5179,High School,2,N,N,25,9/2/2011\r

9/5/2011,6:00:00 PM,9/5/2011,8:00:00 PM,Curriculum Meeting,N,N,Curriculum Meeting,Chris Gallagher,cgallagher@schoolwires.com,814-555-5179,High School,2,N,N,25,9/2/2011\r
```

Figure 9-1 Output of interacting with HTTP Services as a client

The above program lets you download file from web and print to console.

**Interacting with rest API**

- For this you need to go to https://openweathermap.org/ to get key for API.
- Sign up and get unique key.
- Click API tab and on the topic current weather data, click on API data.
- Copy the link :

*api.openweathermap.org/data/2.5/weather?q={city name}*

- Change to the city whose weather you wish to know. (as done below)
- Copy the below link to browser:

*api.openweathermap.org/data/2.5/weather?q=London*

- Using your key and the above link:

The output is as below:

```
>>> import requests
>>> from pprint import pprint
>>> response = requests.get("http://api.openweathermap.org/data/2.5/weather?q=Karachi&appid=cd8d1141f567bb356a373d8ea8e8d315&units=metric")
>>> weather = response.json()
>>> pprint(weather)
{'base': 'stations',
 'clouds': {'all': 40},
 'cod': 200,
 'coord': {'lat': 24.87, 'lon': 67.03},
 'dt': 1557397500,
 'id': 1174872,
 'main': {'humidity': 49,
          'pressure': 1005,
          'temp': 32,
          'temp_max': 32,
          'temp_min': 32},
 'name': 'Karachi',
 'sys': {'country': 'PK',
         'id': 7576,
         'message': 0.0056,
         'sunrise': 1557363085,
         'sunset': 1557410718,
         'type': 1},
 'visibility': 6000,
 'weather': [{'description': 'scattered clouds',
              'icon': '03d',
              'id': 802,
              'main': 'Clouds'}],
```

Figure 9-2 Output of interaction with rest API

Copy the last link to use in python script.
http://api.openweathermap.org/data/2.5/weather?q=Paris&appid=cd8d1141f567bb356a373d8ea8e8d315&units=metric

**Script:**

To interact with API:

*import requests*

*from pprint import pprint*

*response = requests.get("http://api.openweathermap.org/data/2.5/weather?q=Paris&appid=cd8d1141f567bb356a373d8ea8e8d315&units=metric")*

*weather = response.json()*

*pprint(weather)*

**Output:**

```
>>> import requests
>>> from pprint import pprint
>>> city="Boston"
>>> response = requests.get("http://api.openweathermap.org/data/2.5/weather?q="+city+"&appid=cd8d1141f567bb356a373d8ea8e8d315&units=metric")
>>> weather = response.json()
>>> pprint(weather)
{'base': 'stations',
 'clouds': {'all': 20},
 'cod': 200,
 'coord': {'lat': 42.36, 'lon': -71.06},
 'dt': 1557399995,
 'id': 4930956,
 'main': {'humidity': 45,
          'pressure': 1029,
          'temp': 6.88,
          'temp_max': 10.56,
          'temp_min': 3},
 'name': 'Boston',
 'sys': {'country': 'US',
         'id': 3486,
         'message': 0.0092,
         'sunrise': 1557394178,
         'sunset': 1557445906,
         'type': 1},
 'visibility': 16093,
 'weather': [{'description': 'few clouds',
              'icon': '02d',
              'id': 801,
```

Figure 9-3 Output to interact with rest API

You can test weather for other cities as well by the code given below.

**Script:**

*import requests*

*from pprint import pprint*

*city="Seattle"*

*response = requests.get("http://api.openweathermap.org/data/2.5/weather?q="+city+"&appid=cd8d1141f567bb356a373d8ea8e8d315&units=metric")*

*weather = response.json()*

*pprint(weather)*

```
city="Seattle"
response = requests.get("http://api.openweathermap.org/data/2.5/weather?q="+city+"&appid=cd8d1141f567bb356a373d8ea8e8d315&units=metric")
weather = response.json()
pprint(weather)

{u'base': u'stations',
 u'clouds': {u'all': 40},
 u'cod': 200,
 u'coord': {u'lat': 47.6, u'lon': -122.33},
 u'dt': 1530136680,
 u'id': 5809844,
 u'main': {u'humidity': 52,
           u'pressure': 1017,
           u'temp': 18.88,
           u'temp_max': 19,
           u'temp_min': 18},
 u'name': u'Seattle',
 u'sys': {u'country': u'US',
          u'id': 2949,
          u'message': 0.0056,
          u'sunrise': 1530101645,
          u'sunset': 1530159061,
          u'type': 1},
 u'visibility': 16093,
 u'weather': [{u'description': u'scattered clouds',
               u'icon': u'03d',
               u'id': 802,
               u'main': u'Clouds'}],
 u'wind': {u'deg': 290, u'speed': 2.1}}

print("The weather for",weather['name'])
print(weather['main']['temp'])
print(weather['weather'][0]['description'])

('The weather for', u'Seattle')
18.88
scattered clouds
```

Figure 9-4 Output of testing weather

## 9.2 Introduction

This chapter introduces some practice Python Scripts for Network Automation. It will be really helpful in giving you an idea about the communication techniques with server. We will generate servers and will give you an idea about pinging the servers sequentially. The programs will be designed to deal with the attacks on server.

Similarly, some advanced topics related to network communication will be described in detail.

## 9.3 Network Automation Scripts and Programs

This section includes 11 scripts to get you started with Network Automation. Most of the implementations involve Network Libraries that are already available. Some of these libraries we will discuss in detail in Chapter 10.

### 9.3.1 Setting up a Simple HTTP Server

Given below is a short code that will create a simple HTTP file server.

**Script:**

*import SimpleHTTPServer*
*import SocketServer*
*PORT = 8000*
*Handler = SimpleHTTPServer.SimpleHTTPRequestHandler*
*httpd = SocketServer.TCPServer(("", PORT), Handler)*
*print "Serving at port", PORT*
*httpd.serve_forever()*

https for pointing out portal handle. Server address " "

```
C:\Users\btaze>python -m http.server
Serving HTTP on 0.0.0.0 port 8000 (http://0.0.0.0:8000/) ...
127.0.0.1 - - [09/May/2019 15:45:23] "GET / HTTP/1.1" 200 -
127.0.0.1 - - [09/May/2019 15:45:24] code 404, message File not found
127.0.0.1 - - [09/May/2019 15:45:24] "GET /favicon.ico HTTP/1.1" 404 -
```

Figure 9-5 Output of setting up a simple HTTP server

**On browser:**

Type: localhost:8000

Represents all files in d drive which is shared on Ip and port 8000.

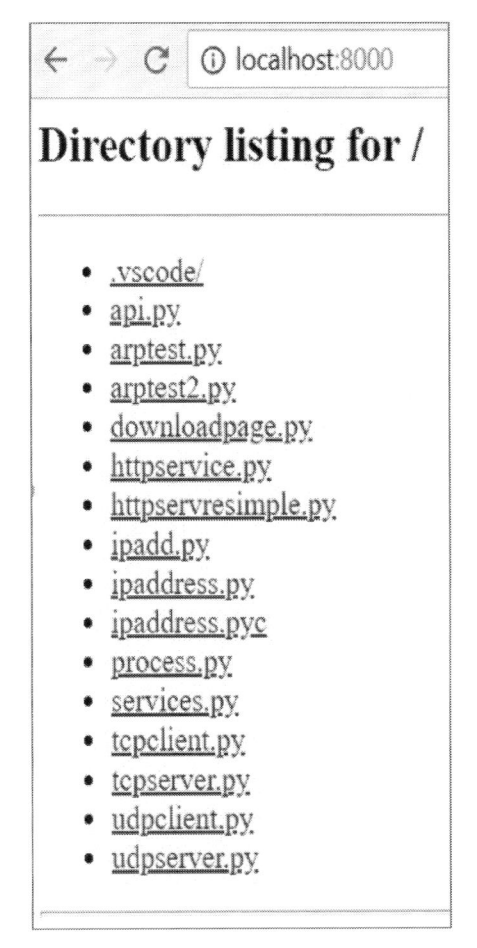

Figure 9-6 Representation of all files in a drive

### 9.3.2 Creating a TCP Server and TCP Client

TCP Server and TCP Client can be created with the following piece of code.

**Script:**

The script below is for server who is listening to the messages from client and replying accordingly.

**Output:**

Import socket

```
server = socket.socket(socket.AF_INET, socket.SOCK_STREAM)
ip = socket.gethostbyname(socket.gethostname())
port = 1234
address= (ip,port)
server.bind(address)
server.listen(1)
#no of connections = no of clients that can connect server at one time
print "Started listening on",ip,":",port
client,addr = server.accept()
print "Got a connection",addr[0],":",addr[1]
while True:
    data = client.recv(1024)
    print "received",data,"from client"
    print " processing data"
    if(data=="Hello server"):
        client.send("Hello client")
        print "     Processinf done. \n Reply sent"
    elif(data=="disconnect"):
        client.send("Goodbye")
        client.close()
        break
    else:
        client.send("Invalid data")
        print "   Processing done Invalid data. \n Reply sent"
Started listening on 10.1.10.96 : 1234
Got a connection 10.1.10.96 : 49553
received jkdfsij from client
 processing data
  Processing done Invalid data.
 Reply sent
received dpfirieojg from client
 processing data
  Processing done Invalid data.
 Reply sent
received Hello server from client
 processing data
     Processinf done.
 Reply sent
received disconnect from client
 processing data
```

Figure 9-7 output in python

**Script :**

This is program for client communicating with the server.

The last error occurs as goodbye message from client will close the connection between the two.

*#TCP client*

*import socket*

*client=socket.socket()*

*client.connect(('10.1.10.96',1234))*

def communicate(data):

   client.send(data)

   print client.recv(1024)

   return

communicate("dpfirieojg")

communicate("Hello server")

communicate("disconnect")

communicate("jfeof")

**Output:**

```
import socket
client=socket.socket()
client.connect(('10.1.10.96',1234))
def communicate(data):
    client.send(data)
    print client.recv(1024)
    return
communicate("dpfirieojg")
Invalid data
communicate("Hello server")
Hello client
communicate("disconnect")
Goodbye
communicate("jfeof")
------------------------------------------------------------
error                                   Traceback (most recent call last)
<ipython-input-10-d2079d067d71> in <module>()
----> 1 communicate("jfeof")

<ipython-input-6-a124acef4f48> in communicate(data)
      1 def communicate(data):
      2     client.send(data)
----> 3     print client.recv(1024)
      4     return
```

Figure 9-7 Output of client code

### 9.3.3 Creating a UDP Server and UDP Client

Similar to UCP connection, UDP Server and Client can be created as follows:

**Script:**

The above program is for server receiving messages from client with UDP connection.

**Output:**

```
import socket

server = socket.socket(socket.AF_INET, socket.SOCK_DGRAM)
# socket object created, AF_INET for ipv4 address. SOCK_DRAM for UDP.
#ip = socket.gethostbyname(socket.gethostname())
port = 5002
address= ("localhost",port)
server.bind(address)
while True:
    print server.recv(1024)


Hello
Hello server
Hello server
```

Figure 9-8 Output of creating a UDP server and UDP client

**Script:**

The program is run on client sending messages to server.

*#UDP client*

```
import socket

import socket
s = socket.socket(socket.AF_INET, socket.SOCK_DGRAM)
# socket object created, AF_INET for ipv4 address. SOCK_DRAM for UDP.
data="Hello server"
s.sendto(data, ("localhost", 5002))
print "sent: " +data

sent: Hello server
```

Figure 9-9 Output of creating a UDP client

### 9.3.4 Generating a Range of IP Addresses from a CIDR

You have a CIDR network address such as "123.45.67.64/27" and you want to generate a range of all the IP addresses that it represents (e.g., "123.45.67.64", "123.45.67.65",..., "123.45.67.95").

You can do it by the following code. The Ip address module can be used to perform such calculations.

**Script:**

```
import ipaddress
net = ipaddress.ip_network(u'123.45.67.64/27')
net
IPv4Network(u'123.45.67.64/27')
for a in net:
    print (a)
```

Figure 9-10 Code of generating a range of IP addresses from a CIDR

```
>>> import ipaddress
>>> net = ipaddress.ip_network(u'123.45.67.64/27')
>>> net
IPv4Network('123.45.67.64/27')
>>> for a in net:
...     print (a)
...
123.45.67.64
123.45.67.65
123.45.67.66
123.45.67.67
123.45.67.68
123.45.67.69
123.45.67.70
123.45.67.71
123.45.67.72
123.45.67.73
123.45.67.74
123.45.67.75
123.45.67.76
123.45.67.77
123.45.67.78
123.45.67.79
123.45.67.80
123.45.67.81
123.45.67.82
123.45.67.83
123.45.67.84
123.45.67.85
```

Figure 9-11 Output of the code stated above

**Alternative way:**

The alternative way to generate a range of all the ip addresses from a CIDR address is by using netaddr Library.

To install netaddr:

*pip install netaddr*

**Script:**

*from netaddr import IPNetwork*

*for ip in IPNetwork('192.0.2.0/23'):*

   *print ip*

**Output:**

The output will look something like below:

```
from netaddr import IPNetwork

for ip in IPNetwork('192.0.2.0/23'):
    print ip
192.0.2.0
192.0.2.1
192.0.2.2
192.0.2.3
192.0.2.4
192.0.2.5
192.0.2.6
192.0.2.7
192.0.2.8
192.0.2.9
192.0.2.10
192.0.2.11
192.0.2.12
192.0.2.13
192.0.2.14
192.0.2.15
192.0.2.16
192.0.2.17
192.0.2.18
```

Figure 9-12 Output of the code to generate IP's

### 9.3.5 Waiting for a remote network service

If you are waiting for remote service then certain piece of code will work as below

*import socket*

*import errno*

*from time import time as now*

*def wait_net_service(server, port, timeout=None):*

  *s = socket.socket()*

  *end = now() + timeout*

  *while True:*

    *try:*

      *if timeout:*

        *next_timeout = end - now()*

        *if next_timeout < 0:*

          *return False*

        *else:*

```
            s.settimeout(next_timeout)

        s.connect((server, port))

    except socket.timeout, err:

        if timeout:

            return False

    except socket.error, err:

        if type(err.args) != tuple or err[0] != errno.ETIMEDOUT:

            raise

    else:

        s.close()

        return True
wait_net_service("10.1.10.96", 139, 120)
```

**Output:**

```
import socket
import errno
from time import time as now
def wait_net_service(server, port, timeout=None):
    s = socket.socket()
    end = now() + timeout
    while True:
        try:
            if timeout:
                next_timeout = end - now()
                if next_timeout < 0:
                    return False
                else:
                    s.settimeout(next_timeout)

            s.connect((server, port))

        except socket.timeout, err:
            if timeout:
                return False

        except socket.error, err:
            if type(err.args) != tuple or err[0] != errno.ETIMEDOUT:
                raise
        else:
            s.close()
            return True
wait_net_service("10.1.10.96", 139, 120)
True
```

Figure 9-13 Output of remote network service code

### 9.3.6 Finding the IP address for a specific interface on your machine

ip address for specific interface can be found using ifaddr Python library.

- Install ifaddr:
- Pip install ifaddr

**Script:**

*#find IP address*

*import ifaddr*

*adapters = ifaddr.get_adapters()*

*#receives all the network adapters with their IP addresses*

*for adapter in adapters:*

    *print "IPs of network adapter: " + adapter.nice_name*

*#class ifaddr.Adapter: nice_name is used for human readable name of the adapter.*

    *for ip in adapter.ips:*

*print ip.nice_name, "%s/%s" % (ip.ip, ip.network_prefix)*

*#class ifaddr.ip: ip for displaying ip address of the adapter. network_prefix represents the subnet mask.*

**Output:**

```
>>> import ifaddr
>>>
>>> adapters = ifaddr.get_adapters()
>>>
>>> for adapter in adapters:
...     print ("IPs of network adapter " + adapter.nice_name)
...     for ip in adapter.ips:
...         print ("  %s/%s" % (ip.ip, ip.network_prefix))
...
IPs of network adapter Intel(R) 82579LM Gigabit Network Connection
  ('fe80::f18f:f8fe:c66:5ce3', 0, 10)/64
  169.254.92.227/16
IPs of network adapter LogMeIn Hamachi Virtual Ethernet Adapter
  ('2620:9b::191b:2a19', 0, 0)/64
  ('fe80::11e3:18f4:4269:dd83', 0, 7)/64
  25.27.42.25/8
IPs of network adapter LogMeIn Hamachi Virtual Ethernet Adapter #2
  ('fe80::f014:715:1011:9b12', 0, 13)/64
  172.16.0.30/24
IPs of network adapter Microsoft Wi-Fi Direct Virtual Adapter
  ('fe80::b48b:c14a:b26c:5fa2', 0, 2)/64
  169.254.95.162/16
IPs of network adapter Npcap Loopback Adapter
  ('fe80::28ba:431d:2337:9004', 0, 4)/64
  169.254.144.4/16
IPs of network adapter Intel(R) Centrino(R) Advanced-N 6205
  ('fe80::bc8c:1de9:a7e1:918b', 0, 8)/64
  192.168.100.181/24
IPs of network adapter Software Loopback Interface 1
```

Figure 9-14 Output of Finding the IP address for a specific interface on your machine

## 9.3.7 Using the socket function, changing a socket to the blocking/non-blocking mode.

### 9.3.7.1 Blocking socket

By default, TCP sockets are placed in a blocking mode. This means that the control is not returned to your program until some specific operation is complete.
We can call setblocking(1) to set up blocking or setblocking(0) to unset blocking.

Now, run Block_server.py first and then Block_client.py. You'll notice that the server keeps on printing Hello Python. This will go on and on till all the data is sent. In this code the line All Data Received will not be printed for long time, because as the client has to send a large number of strings, which will take time, and until then the socket input-output will get blocked.

**Script:**

**Block_client.py**

```
>>> import socket
>>> s = socket.socket()
>>> host = socket.gethostname()
>>> port = 12345
>>> s.connect((host, port))
>>> print (s.recv(1024))
```

Figure 9-15 client server

**Block_server.py**

```
>>> import socket
>>> s = socket.socket()
>>> host = socket.gethostname()
>>> port = 12345
>>> s.bind((host, port))
>>> s.listen(5)
>>> while True:
...     c, addr = s.accept()
...     print ('Got connection from', addr)
...     c.send('Thank you for connecting')
...     c.close()
...
Got connection from ('172.16.0.30', 43247)
```

Figure: 9-16 Block server

**Output:**

```
Hello Python
Hello Python
Hello Python
Hello Python
Hello Python
Hello Python
Hello Python
Hello Python
Hello Python
Hello Python
Hello Python
Hello Python
Hello Python
Hello Python
Hello Python
Hello Python
Hello Python
Hello Python
```

Figure 9-17 Output of block_server code

### 9.3.7.2 Non – blocking socket

Now, if we run the non_blocking_client.py, you'll notice that the program will run for a small time, it will print the last line "All Data Received" and soon terminate.

What's going on here? Here the client did not send all the data. When we make a socket non-blocking by calling setblocking(0), it will never wait for the operation to complete. So, when we call the send() method, it will put as much data in the buffer as possible and return.

**Script:**

*import socket*

*sock = socket.socket()*

*host = socket.gethostname()*

*sock.connect((host, 12345))*

*sock.setblocking(0) # Now setting to non-blocking mode*

*data = "Hello Python\n" *100 # Huge amount of data to be sent*

*assert sock.send(data)     # Send data till true*

**Output:**

```
Hello Python
Hello Python
Hello Python
Hello Python
Hello Python
Hello Python
Hello Python
Hello Python
Hello Python
Hello Python
Hello Python
Hello Python
Hello Python
Hello Python
Hello Python
Hello Python
Hello Python
```

Figure 9-13 Output of non-blocking client

### 9.3.8  Ping 15 servers sequentially 192.158.10.1 - 192.168.10.15

The following script lets us ping to all the ip addresses on the network sequentially.

**Script:**

*import ipaddress*

*import subprocess*

```python
# Create the network
ip_net = ipaddress.ip_network(u'10.1.10.0/24')
# Get all hosts on that network
all_hosts = list(ip_net.hosts())
# Configure subprocess to hide the console window
info = subprocess.STARTUPINFO()
info.dwFlags |= subprocess.STARTF_USESHOWWINDOW
info.wShowWindow = subprocess.SW_HIDE
# For each IP address in the subnet,
# run the ping command with subprocess.popen interface
for i in range(len(all_hosts)):
    output = subprocess.Popen(['ping', '-n', '1', '-w', '500', str(all_hosts[i])],
stdout=subprocess.PIPE, startupinfo=info).communicate()[0]
    if "Destination host unreachable" in output.decode('utf-8'):
        print(str(all_hosts[i]), "is Offline")
    elif "Request timed out" in output.decode('utf-8'):
        print(str(all_hosts[i]), "is unreachable")
    else:
        print(str(all_hosts[i]), "is reachable")
```

## Output

```
('10.1.10.85', 'is unreachable')
('10.1.10.86', 'is unreachable')
('10.1.10.87', 'is unreachable')
('10.1.10.88', 'is unreachable')
('10.1.10.89', 'is unreachable')
('10.1.10.90', 'is unreachable')
('10.1.10.91', 'is reachable')
('10.1.10.92', 'is reachable')
('10.1.10.93', 'is unreachable')
('10.1.10.94', 'is reachable')
('10.1.10.95', 'is reachable')
('10.1.10.96', 'is reachable')
('10.1.10.97', 'is reachable')
('10.1.10.98', 'is unreachable')
('10.1.10.99', 'is unreachable')
('10.1.10.100', 'is unreachable')
('10.1.10.101', 'is unreachable')
('10.1.10.102', 'is unreachable')
('10.1.10.103', 'is unreachable')
```

Figure 9-14 Output of the code after pinging the service

### 9.3.9 Pool the services enabled on a server 192.168.1.5 (Interrupt)

a. **Operating System**

This program helps us to know what operating system our server runs on.

The connection variable is used if you want to connect to remote machine. If you want to get information from local machine, then use c=wmi.WMI(), and no need to use the connection variable.

To check for status os OS the code is below:

**Script:**

```
>>> import wmi
>>>
>>> c = wmi.WMI ()
>>> for s in c.Win32_Service ():
...     if s.State == 'Stopped':
...         print (s.Caption, s.State)
...
AllJoyn Router Service Stopped
Application Layer Gateway Service Stopped
Application Identity Stopped
Application Management Stopped
App Readiness Stopped
AppX Deployment Service (AppXSVC) Stopped
ActiveX Installer (AxInstSV) Stopped
BitLocker Drive Encryption Service Stopped
Computer Browser Stopped
Bluetooth Handsfree Service Stopped
Bluetooth Support Service Stopped
CDPSvc Stopped
COM+ System Application Stopped
Intel(R) Content Protection HECI Service Stopped
Offline Files Stopped
Dropbox Update Service (dbupdate) Stopped
Dropbox Update Service (dbupdatem) Stopped
Optimize drives Stopped
Device Install Service Stopped
DevQuery Background Discovery Broker Stopped
Microsoft (R) Diagnostics Hub Standard Collector Service Stopped
```

Figure:9-19 Os status

**Output:**

```
Microsoft Windows 10 Pro
OK
```

Figure 9-20 Output showing the operating system that is being used

### b. Processes Running

This program can be used to get all running process on local or remote machine. The results show the processId and Name.

**Script:**

```
>>> import wmi
>>> c = wmi.WMI ()
>>>
>>> for process in c.Win32_Process (name="notepad.exe"):
...     print (process.ProcessId, process.Name)
...
1288 notepad.exe
1100 notepad.exe
```

Figure 9-21 process running

**Output:**

```
(0, u'System Idle Process')
(4, u'System')
(88, u'Registry')
(324, u'smss.exe')
(424, u'csrss.exe')
(500, u'wininit.exe')
(516, u'csrss.exe')
(596, u'winlogon.exe')
(612, u'services.exe')
(644, u'lsass.exe')
(736, u'fontdrvhost.exe')
(744, u'fontdrvhost.exe')
(820, u'svchost.exe')
(844, u'svchost.exe')
(888, u'svchost.exe')
(932, u'svchost.exe')
(1000, u'dwm.exe')
(444, u'svchost.exe')
(492, u'svchost.exe')
(724, u'svchost.exe')
```

Figure 9-22 Output of the processes that are running

The program lets you know what processes are running on the server. You can pass in creation, deletion, modification, operation to watch_for method.

**Script:**

*import wmi*

*def get_p():*

   *connection = wmi.connect_server(server="ABJ-HP-23", user="username", password="password")*

*c = wmi.WMI()*

*watch_process = c.Win32_Process.watch_for("operation")*

*while True:*

   *new = watch_process()*

   *print (new.Caption)*

**Output:**

```
System Idle Process
Code.exe
python.exe
browsernativehost.exe
conhost.exe
conhost.exe
CodeHelper.exe
powershell.exe
conhost.exe
chrome.exe
python.exe
winpty-agent.exe
conhost.exe
ipython.exe
cmd.exe
chrome.exe
cmd.exe
Memory Compression
svchost.exe
vmtoolsd.exe
```

Figure 9-23 Output of the processes that are running

c. **Services**

- The program displays all the services running on the server.

**Script:**

```
>>> import wmi
>>> c = wmi.WMI()
>>> for service in c.Win32_Service():
...     print (service.Name)
...
AdobeARMservice
AJRouter
ALG
AppIDSvc
Appinfo
AppMgmt
AppReadiness
AppXSvc
AudioEndpointBuilder
Audiosrv
AxInstSV
BDESVC
BFE
BITS
BrokerInfrastructure
Browser
BthHFSrv
bthserv
CDPSvc
CertPropSvc
ClipSVC
COMSysApp
CoreMessagingRegistrar
cphs
```

Figure: 9-24 Output service running

- The above program displays all the services along with their status.

**Script:**

```
>>> import wmi
>>> c = wmi.WMI()
>>> for service in c.Win32_Service():
...     print (service.name, service.status)
...
AdobeARMservice OK
AJRouter OK
ALG OK
AppIDSvc OK
Appinfo OK
AppMgmt OK
AppReadiness OK
AppXSvc OK
AudioEndpointBuilder OK
Audiosrv OK
AxInstSV OK
BDESVC OK
BFE OK
BITS OK
BrokerInfrastructure OK
Browser OK
BthHFSrv OK
bthserv OK
CDPSvc OK
CertPropSvc OK
ClipSVC OK
COMSysApp OK
CoreMessagingRegistrar OK
cphs OK
```

Figure:9-25 output service status

- The above program lets us know the status of particular service.

**Script:**

```
>>> import wmi
>>> c = wmi.WMI()
>>> for service in c.Win32_Service(name="Dhcp"):
...     print (service.name, service.status)
...
Dhcp OK
```

Figure 9-26 output of the program stated above

### 9.3.10 When the service goes down (outage) on a server

- The program displays all the services in stop state or those that goes down.

**Script:**

```
>>> import wmi
>>> c = wmi.WMI()
>>> for service in c.Win32_Service(state="stopped"):
...     print (service.DisplayName)
...
AllJoyn Router Service
Application Layer Gateway Service
Application Identity
Application Management
App Readiness
AppX Deployment Service (AppXSVC)
ActiveX Installer (AxInstSV)
BitLocker Drive Encryption Service
Computer Browser
Bluetooth Handsfree Service
Bluetooth Support Service
CDPSvc
COM+ System Application
Intel(R) Content Protection HECI Service
Offline Files
Dropbox Update Service (dbupdate)
Dropbox Update Service (dbupdatem)
Optimize drives
Device Install Service
DevQuery Background Discovery Broker
Microsoft (R) Diagnostics Hub Standard Collector Service
Device Management Enrollment Service
dmwappushsvc
Delivery Optimization
```

Figure 9-27 Output of the program when a service goes down on a server

- To start a stopped service.

Following program lets you restart the stopped service.

**Script:**

```
>>> import wmi
>>> c = wmi.WMI()
>>> #write service name
... for service in c.Win32_Service(Name="Bluetooth Support Service"):
...     result, = service.StartService()
...     if result == 0:
...         print ("Service:", service.name, "started")
...     else:
...         print ("There was a problem starting service")
...     break
... else:
...     print ("Service not found")
...
Service not found
```

Figure 9-28 output of the program when a service is restarted

## 9.4 More Advanced Network Automation Scripts and Programs

This section discusses and show how move involved Network Automation tasks are achieved with Python Scripting

### 9.4.1 Finding whether an interface is up on your machine

Moving towards some advanced topic, we will find whether the interface is on machine or not.

**Script:**

*import socket*

*import subprocess*

*import sys*

*from datetime import datetime*

*# Clear the screen*

*subprocess.call('clear', shell=True)*

*# Ask for input*

*#remoteServer  = raw_input("Enter a remote host to scan: ")*

*remoteServer = socket.gethostname()*

*remoteServerIP = socket.gethostbyname(remoteServer)*

*print remoteServerIP*

*# Print a nice banner with information on which host we are about to scan*

*print "-" * 60*

```python
print "Please wait, scanning remote host", remoteServerIP
print "-" * 60
# Check what time the scan started
t1 = datetime.now()
# Using the range function to specify ports (here it will scan all ports between 1 and 1024)
# We also put in some error handling for catching errors
try:
    for port in range(1,1025):
        sock = socket.socket(socket.AF_INET, socket.SOCK_STREAM)
        result = sock.connect_ex((remoteServerIP, port))
        if result == 0:
            print "Port {}:        Open".format(port)
        sock.close()
except KeyboardInterrupt:
    print "You pressed Ctrl+C"
    sys.exit()
except socket.gaierror:
    print 'Hostname could not be resolved. Exiting'
    sys.exit()
except socket.error:
    print "Couldn't connect to server"
    sys.exit()
# Checking the time again
t2 = datetime.now()
# Calculates the difference of time, to see how long it took to run the script
```

*total = t2 - t1*

*# Printing the information to screen*

*print 'Scanning Completed in: ', total*

**Output:**

```
10.1.10.96
-------------------------------------------
Please wait, scanning remote host 10.1.10.96
-------------------------------------------
Port 135:          Open
Port 139:          Open
Port 445:          Open
Scanning Completed in:  0:17:06.266000
```

Figure 9-29 output of finding out the setup of the interface

### 9.4.2  Enumerating interfaces on your machine

You can Create a list of interfaces on your machine using psutil:

- Install psutil:
- Pip install psutil

**Script:**

```
>>> import psutil
>>> addrs = psutil.net_if_addrs()
>>> # addrs contains the list of the interfaces on your computer.
... print (addrs.keys())
dict_keys(['Ethernet', 'Hamachi', 'Hamachi - 369-336-078', 'Local Area Connection* 2', 'Npcap Loopback Adapter', 'Wi-Fi', 'isatap.{D0A33B7B-38BA-4011-84A1-4ADA328A83CB}', 'Local Area Connection* 4', 'isatap.{924EAE8C-47D2-4341-B97A-1FE8757DAD00}', 'isatap.{975A6B9F-ED57-44E1-BFF3-C3D2C51E02F8}', 'isatap.{D3E9C7EE-C9B2-4A08-8B8B-E7F14C06FAF0}', 'Loopback Pseudo-Interface 1'])
>>>
```

Figure 9-30 output of enumerating interface on a machine

### 9.4.3  ARP Monitoring

#### a. Using Scapy to monitor ARP traffic

Let's pretend that there is concern about someone potentially trying to use an ARP poisoning attack on our network. Using Scapy, we want to write a script that will listen to packets and print out all ARP requests and responses. For this, we use **Scapy sniff()** function and the filter argument like this:

**Script:**

*#arp tool using Scapy Python Library*

*from scapy.all import ***

*def arp_monitor_callback(pkt):*

   *if ARP in pkt and pkt[ARP].op in (1,2): #who-has or is-at*

      *return pkt.sprintf("%ARP.hwsrc% %ARP.psrc% %ARP.hwdst% %ARP.pdst%")*

*sniff(prn=arp_monitor_callback, filter="arp", store=0)*

**Output:**

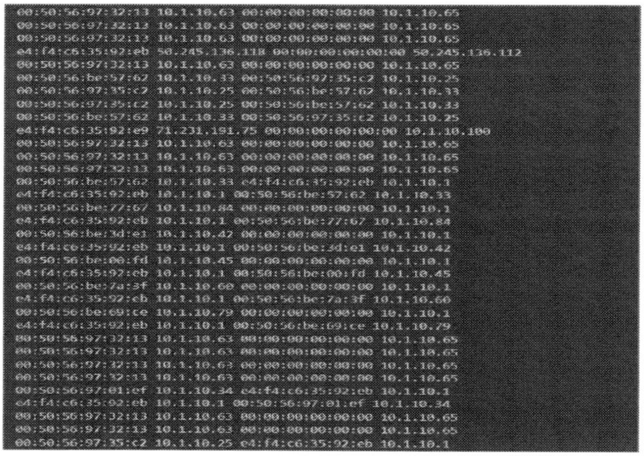

Figure 9-31 Demonstrating use of Scapy

**Script:**

*# ARP Tool 2*

*from scapy.all import ***

*def arp_display(pkt):*

   *if pkt[ARP].op == 1:  # who-has (request)*

      *return 'Request: {} is asking about {}'.format(pkt[ARP].psrc, pkt[ARP].pdst) #source ip is asking about destination ip's mac address*

   *if pkt[ARP].op == 2:  # is-at (response)*

*return '\*Response: {} has address {}'.format(pkt[ARP].hwsrc, pkt[ARP].psrc) #the destination ip responds back with its ip address.*

*sniff(prn=arp_display, filter='arp', store=0)*

This will create a live packet sniffer that will return any ARP requests that are seen on all interfaces. The entire method basically states that if a packet is both an ARP packet, and the operation of that packet is either who-has or is-at, then it will return a printed line stating the source MAC address and source IP address of that ARP packet. The method is applied to the sniff command using the prn function. Another important thing to notice is that 'store=0' is applied to the sniff command as well, and this is so that scapy avoids storing all the packets within its memory.

**Output:**

```
Request: 10.1.10.34 is asking about 10.1.10.1
*Response: e4:f4:c6:35:92:eb has address 10.1.10.1
Request: 10.1.10.63 is asking about 10.1.10.65
Request: 10.1.10.45 is asking about 10.1.10.60
*Response: 00:50:56:be:7a:3f has address 10.1.10.60
Request: 10.1.10.63 is asking about 10.1.10.65
Request: 10.1.10.95 is asking about 10.1.10.1
*Response: e4:f4:c6:35:92:eb has address 10.1.10.1
Request: 10.1.10.63 is asking about 10.1.10.65
Request: 10.1.10.33 is asking about 10.1.10.34
*Response: 00:50:56:97:01:cf has address 10.1.10.34
Request: 10.1.10.25 is asking about 10.1.10.33
*Response: 00:50:56:be:57:62 has address 10.1.10.33
Request: 10.1.10.25 is asking about 10.1.10.1
*Response: e4:f4:c6:35:92:eb has address 10.1.10.1
Request: 10.1.10.46 is asking about 10.1.10.60
*Response: 00:50:56:be:7a:3f has address 10.1.10.60
Request: 10.1.10.91 is asking about 10.1.10.1
*Response: e4:f4:c6:35:92:eb has address 10.1.10.1
Request: 10.1.10.79 is asking about 10.1.10.1
*Response: e4:f4:c6:35:92:eb has address 10.1.10.1
Request: 10.1.10.42 is asking about 10.1.10.1
*Response: e4:f4:c6:35:92:eb has address 10.1.10.1
Request: 10.1.10.41 is asking about 10.1.10.1
*Response: e4:f4:c6:35:92:eb has address 10.1.10.1
Request: 10.1.10.97 is asking about 10.1.10.1
Request: 10.1.10.60 is asking about 10.1.10.1
*Response: e4:f4:c6:35:92:eb has address 10.1.10.1
*Response: e4:f4:c6:35:92:eb has address 10.1.10.1
Request: 10.1.10.29 is asking about 10.1.10.1
*Response: e4:f4:c6:35:92:eb has address 10.1.10.1
Request: 10.1.10.46 is asking about 10.1.10.1
*Response: e4:f4:c6:35:92:eb has address 10.1.10.1
Request: 10.1.10.43 is asking about 10.1.10.60
*Response: 00:50:56:be:7a:3f has address 10.1.10.60
Request: 10.1.10.63 is asking about 10.1.10.65
```

Figure 9-32 Demonstrating the use of Scapy

### 9.4.4 Write a short Firewall Program in Python

The program given below is a firewall program that can you be used to block websites

**Script:**

*#LogicFinder Inc. 2018*
*#block websites*

*import time*

*from datetime import datetime as dt*

```python
# change hosts path according to your OS
hosts_path = "C:\Windows\System32\drivers\etc\hosts"
# localhost's IP
redirect = "127.0.0.1"
# websites That you want to block
website_list = ["www.facebook.com","facebook.com",
    "dub119.mail.live.com","www.dub119.mail.live.com",
    ]
while True:
    # time of your work
    if dt(dt.now().year, dt.now().month, dt.now().day,8) < dt.now() < dt(dt.now().year, dt.now().month, dt.now().day,16):
        print("Working hours...")
        with open(hosts_path, 'r+') as file:
            content = file.read()
            for website in website_list:
                if website in content:
                    pass
                else:
                    # mapping hostnames to your localhost IP address
                    file.write(redirect + " " + website + "\n")
    else:
        with open(hosts_path, 'r+') as file:
            content=file.readlines()
            file.seek(0)
```

  *for line in content:*

    *if not any(website in line for website in website_list):*

      *file.write(line)*

    *# removing hostnmes from host file*

    *file.truncate()*

  *print("Fun hours...")*

*time.sleep(2.5)*

**Output:**

```
Traceback (most recent call last):
  File "c:\Users\owner\Documents\python function\blockip.py", line 27, in <module>
    with open(hosts_path, 'r+') as file:
IOError: [Errno 13] Permission denied: 'C:\\Windows\\System32\\drivers\\etc\\hosts'
```

Figure 9-33 Output of firewall program in Python

### 9.4.5 Sniffing packets on your network

Sniffing packets involves capturing the packets that are transmitted over the network to trouble shoot problem. It is also used to collect statistics.

Following piece of code will make it clear how to do it

**Script:**

*#Sniff Packets*

*import socket,os*

*#create an INET, raw socket*

*if os.name == "nt":*

  *# for windows*

  *s = socket.socket(socket.AF_INET,socket.SOCK_RAW,socket.IPPROTO_IP)*

  *s.bind(("10.1.10.96",0)) # your interface ip*

  *s.setsockopt(socket.IPPROTO_IP,socket.IP_HDRINCL,1)*

    s.ioctl(socket.SIO_RCVALL,socket.RCVALL_ON)

else:

    s=socket.socket(socket.PF_PACKET, socket.SOCK_RAW, socket.ntohs(0x0800)) # for *nix

# receive a packet

while True:

    pkt=s.recvfrom(65565) # print output on terminal

**Output:**
**Error**

```
import socket,os

#create an INET, raw socket

if os.name == "nt":
    # for windows
    s = socket.socket(socket.AF_INET,socket.SOCK_RAW,socket.IPPROTO_IP)
    s.bind(("10.1.10.96",0)) # your interface ip
    s.setsockopt(socket.IPPROTO_IP,socket.IP_HDRINCL,1)
    s.ioctl(socket.SIO_RCVALL,socket.RCVALL_ON)
else:
    s=socket.socket(socket.PF_PACKET, socket.SOCK_RAW, socket.ntohs(0x0800)) # for *nix

# receive a packet
while True:
    pkt=s.recvfrom(65565) # print output on terminal

---------------------------------------------------------------------------
error                                     Traceback (most recent call last)
<ipython-input-8-b097d78b4146> in <module>()
      5 if os.name == "nt":
      6     # for windows
----> 7     s = socket.socket(socket.AF_INET,socket.SOCK_RAW,socket.IPPROTO_IP)
      8     s.bind(("10.1.10.96",0)) # your interface ip
      9     s.setsockopt(socket.IPPROTO_IP,socket.IP_HDRINCL,1)

C:\Users\owner\Anaconda2\lib\socket.pyc in __init__(self, family, type, proto, _sock)
    189     def __init__(self, family=AF_INET, type=SOCK_STREAM, proto=0, _sock=None):
    190         if _sock is None:
--> 191             _sock = _realsocket(family, type, proto)
    192         self._sock = _sock
    193         for method in _delegate_methods:

error: [Errno 10013] An attempt was made to access a socket in a way forbidden by its access permissions
```

Figure 9-34 output of sniffing packets code

### 9.4.6 Write a Python Script that can work as a packet sniffer

The below program shows how a simple packet sniffer program can be created in Python

#Packet Sniffer Program

#!/usr/bin/env python

# Python Network Programming Cookbook -- Chapter - 9

# This program is optimized for Python 2.6.

```python
# It may run on any other version with/without modifications.
import argparse
import pcap
from construct.protocols.ipstack import ip_stack

def print_packet(pktlen, data, timestamp):
    """ Callback for priniting the packet payload"""
    if not data:
        return
    stack = ip_stack.parse(data)
    payload = stack.next.next.next
    print payload

def main():
    # setup commandline arguments
    parser = argparse.ArgumentParser(description='Packet Sniffer')
    parser.add_argument('--iface', action="store", dest="iface", default='eth0')
    parser.add_argument('--port', action="store", dest="port", default=80, type=int)
    # parse arguments
    given_args = parser.parse_args()
    iface, port = given_args.iface, given_args.port
    # start sniffing
    pc = pcap.pcapObject()
    pc.open_live(iface, 1600, 0, 100)
    pc.setfilter('dst port %d' %port, 0, 0)
    print 'Press CTRL+C to end capture'
    try:
```

```
while True:

    pc.dispatch(1, print_packet)

except KeyboardInterrupt:

    print 'Packet statistics: %d packets received, %d packets dropped, %d packets dropped by the interface' % pc.stats()

if __name__ == '__main__':

    main()
```

### 9.4.7    Implementing Network Service Involving Sockets

Implement a network service involving sockets where servers and clients authenticate themselves and encrypt the transmitted data using SSL.

**Script**:

Download cacert.pem from the given link  https://wiki.python.org/moin/SSL

```
import socket

import ssl

HOST = "www.debian-administration.org"

PORT = 443

# replace HOST name with IP, this should fail connection attempt

#HOST = socket.getaddrinfo(HOST, PORT)[0][4][0]

#print(HOST)

HOST = socket.gethostbyname(HOST)

print(HOST)

# create socket and connect to server

# server address is specified later in connect() method

sock = socket.socket()

sock.connect((HOST, PORT))

# wrap socket to add SSL support
```

```
sock = ssl.wrap_socket(sock,
    # flag that certificate from the other side of connection is required
    # and should be validated when wrapping
    cert_reqs=ssl.CERT_REQUIRED,
    # file with root certificates
    ca_certs="C:\Users\owner\Downloads\cacert.pem"
)
# security hole here - there should be an error about mismatched host name
# manual check of hostname
cert = sock.getpeercert()
for field in cert['subject']:
    if field[0][0] == 'commonName':
        certhost = field[0][1]
        if certhost != HOST:
            raise ssl.SSLError("Host name '%s' doesn't match certificate host '%s'"
                               % (HOST, certhost))
```

**Output:**

```
104.28.5.9
Traceback (most recent call last):
  File "c:\Users\owner\Documents\python function\ssl.py", line 24, in <module>
    ca_certs="C:\Users\owner\Downloads\cacert.pem"
  File "C:\Users\owner\Anaconda2\lib\ssl.py", line 911, in wrap_socket
    ciphers=ciphers)
  File "C:\Users\owner\Anaconda2\lib\ssl.py", line 579, in __init__
    self.do_handshake()
  File "C:\Users\owner\Anaconda2\lib\ssl.py", line 808, in do_handshake
    self._sslobj.do_handshake()
SSLError: [SSL: SSLV3_ALERT_HANDSHAKE_FAILURE] sslv3 alert handshake failure (_ssl.c:590)
```

Figure 9-35 output of implementing network service

### 9.4.8 Identifying Bouncing Interfaces on a Network Device

Sometimes Interfaces can bounce. A program to get list of flapping/down interfaces on the network is:

*psutil.net_if_stats()*

- Return information about each NIC (network interface card) installed on the system as a dictionary whose keys are the NIC names and value is a named tuple with the following fields:

*isup: a bool*

- It indicates whether the NIC is up and running.

*duplex: the duplex communication type*

- It can be either NIC_DUPLEX_FULL, NIC_DUPLEX_HALF or NIC_DUPLEX_UNKNOWN.

*speed: the NIC speed expressed in megabits (MB)*

- If it can't be determined (e.g. 'localhost') it will be set to 0.

*mtu: NIC's maximum transmission unit expressed in bytes.*

**Script:**

```
>>> import psutil
>>> add = psutil.net_if_stats()
>>>
>>> for key,val in add.items():
...     print(key, "=>", val)
...
Ethernet => snicstats(isup=False, duplex=<NicDuplex.NIC_DUPLEX_FULL: 2>, speed=0, mtu=1500)
Hamachi => snicstats(isup=True, duplex=<NicDuplex.NIC_DUPLEX_FULL: 2>, speed=4294, mtu=1500)
Hamachi - 369-336-078 => snicstats(isup=True, duplex=<NicDuplex.NIC_DUPLEX_FULL: 2>, speed=4294, mtu=1500)
Npcap Loopback Adapter => snicstats(isup=True, duplex=<NicDuplex.NIC_DUPLEX_FULL: 2>, speed=1215, mtu=1500)
Loopback Pseudo-Interface 1 => snicstats(isup=True, duplex=<NicDuplex.NIC_DUPLEX_FULL: 2>, speed=1073, mtu=1500)
Wi-Fi => snicstats(isup=True, duplex=<NicDuplex.NIC_DUPLEX_FULL: 2>, speed=144, mtu=1500)
Local Area Connection* 2 => snicstats(isup=False, duplex=<NicDuplex.NIC_DUPLEX_FULL: 2>, speed=0, mtu=1500)
isatap.{D0A33B7B-38BA-4011-84A1-4ADA328A83CB} => snicstats(isup=False, duplex=<NicDuplex.NIC_DUPLEX_FULL: 2>, speed=0, mtu=1280)
Local Area Connection* 4 => snicstats(isup=False, duplex=<NicDuplex.NIC_DUPLEX_FULL: 2>, speed=0, mtu=1472)
isatap.{924EAE8C-47D2-4341-B97A-1FE8757DAD00} => snicstats(isup=False, duplex=<NicDuplex.NIC_DUPLEX_FULL: 2>, speed=0, mtu=1280)
isatap.{975A6B9F-ED57-44E1-BFF3-C3D2C51E02F8} => snicstats(isup=False, duplex=<NicDuplex.NIC_DUPLEX_FULL: 2>, speed=0, mtu=1280)
isatap.{D3E9C7EE-C9B2-4A08-8B8B-E7F14C06FAF0} => snicstats(isup=False, duplex=<NicDuplex.NIC_DUPLEX_FULL: 2>, speed=0, mtu=1280)
```

Figure 9-36 output of identifying bouncing interfaces

### 9.4.9 NetConf Agent Implementation

Here is a very simple netconf agent implementation using python Script

a. pip install ncclient
b. Install some Python dependencies
c. pip install ncclient pyang pyangbind xmltodict

**Script:**

from ncclient import manager

with manager.connect(host="10.1.10.43", port=830, username="user", hostkey_verify=False,

        device_params={'name':'csr'}) as m:

c = m.get_config(source='running').data_xml

with open("%s.xml" % host, 'w') as f:

    f.write(c)

**Output:**

```
SSHError                                  Traceback (most recent call last)
<ipython-input-11-c3fe5b2e81b0> in <module>()
      2
      3 with manager.connect(host="10.1.10.43", port=830, username="user", hostkey_verify=False,
----> 4                      device_params={'name':'csr'}) as m:
      5     c = m.get_config(source='running').data_xml
      6     with open("%s.xml" % host, 'w') as f:

C:\Users\owner\Anaconda2\lib\site-packages\ncclient\manager.pyc in connect(*args, **kwds)
    160         return connect_ioproc(*args, **kwds)
    161     else:
--> 162         return connect_ssh(*args, **kwds)
    163
    164

C:\Users\owner\Anaconda2\lib\site-packages\ncclient\manager.pyc in connect_ssh(*args, **kwds)
    125
    126     try:
--> 127         session.connect(*args, **kwds)
    128     except Exception as ex:
    129         if session.transport:

C:\Users\owner\Anaconda2\lib\site-packages\ncclient\transport\ssh.pyc in connect(self, host, port, timeout, unknown_host_cb, use
rname, password, key_filename, allow_agent, hostkey_verify, look_for_keys, ssh_config, sock_fd)
    392                     break
    393             else:
--> 394                 raise SSHError("Could not open socket to %s:%s" % (host, port))
    395         else:
    396             if sys.version_info[0] < 3:

SSHError: Could not open socket to 10.1.10.43:830
```

Figure 9-37 output of using NetConf agent configuration

**Script:**

from ncclient import manager

m = manager.connect(host='10.1.10.43', port=830, username='cisco',

        password='cisco', device_params={'name': 'csr'})

print m.connected

**Output:**

```
In [2]: python-input-13-c1c61a4c826> in <module>()
      2
      3 m = manager.connect(host='10.1.10.43', port=830, username='cisco',
----> 4                     password='cisco', device_params={'name':'csr'})
      5
      6 print m.connected

C:\Users\owner\Anaconda2\lib\site-packages\ncclient\manager.pyc in connect(*args, **kwds)
    160         return connect_ioproc(*args, **kwds)
    161     else:
--> 162         return connect_ssh(*args, **kwds)
    163
    164

C:\Users\owner\Anaconda2\lib\site-packages\ncclient\manager.pyc in connect_ssh(*args, **kwds)
    125     try:
    126
--> 127         session.connect(*args, **kwds)
    128     except Exception as ex:
    129         if session.transport:

C:\Users\owner\Anaconda2\lib\site-packages\ncclient\transport\ssh.pyc in connect(self, host, port, timeout, unknown_host_cb, use
rname, password, key_filename, allow_agent, hostkey_verify, look_for_keys, ssh_config, sock_fd)
    392                 break
    393             else:
--> 394                 raise SSHError("Could not open socket to %s:%s" % (host, port))
    395         else:
    396             if sys.version_info[0] < 3

SSHError: Could not open socket to 10.1.10.43:830
```

Figure 9-38 Output of NetConf Agent Implementation

## 9.5   Ideas for Additional Network Scripts and Programs

Here are some great Python Programming ideas which I encourage you to write. These will open your mind and help in learning more about the Python programming scripts.

### 9.5.1   Authenticating Clients

Implement a simple program to authenticate the clients connecting to servers in a distributed system.

*Hint: No need to use a complex protocol such as SSL.*

**Echo Client:**

*#!/usr/bin/env python3*

*import socket*

*HOST = '127.0.0.1'   # The server's hostname or IP address*

*PORT = 65432        # The port used by the server*

*with socket.socket(socket.AF_INET, socket.SOCK_STREAM) as s:*

  *s.connect((HOST, PORT))*

  *s.sendall(b'Hello, world')*

  *data = s.recv(1024)*

*print('Received', repr(data))*

***Echo Server****:*
*#!/usr/bin/env python3*

```python
import socket

HOST = '127.0.0.1'  # Standard loopback interface address (localhost)
PORT = 65432        # Port to listen on (non-privileged ports are > 1023)

with socket.socket(socket.AF_INET, socket.SOCK_STREAM) as s:
    s.bind((HOST, PORT))
    s.listen()
    conn, addr = s.accept()
    with conn:
        print('Connected by', addr)
        while True:
            data = conn.recv(1024)
            if not data:
                break
            conn.sendall(data)
```

The above script is sourced from : : https://realpython.com/python-sockets/)

### 9.5.2 Perform health check on a router

Perform a health check on a router and give an output stating if the BGP is up and for how long. The first example is using a basic health check test to determine if a route should be announced or withdrawn from BGP.

```python
# Script is written in Python 3
#!/usr/bin/env python3
from __future__ import print_function
import socket
from sys import import stdout
from time import import sleep
def is_alive(address, port):
```

```python
    """ This is a function that will test TCP connectivity of a given
    address and port. If a domain name is passed in instead of an address,
    the socket.connect() method will resolve.
    address (str): An IP address or FQDN of a host
    port (int): TCP destination port to use
    returns (bool): True if alive, False if not
    """
    # Create a socket object to connect with
    s = socket.socket()
    # Now try connecting, passing in a tuple with address & port
    try:
        s.connect((address, port))
        return True
    except socket.error:
        return False
    finally:
        s.close()

while True:
    if is_alive('thepacketgeek.com', 80):
        stdout.write('announce route 100.10.10.0/24 next-hop self' + '\n')
        stdout.flush()
    else:
        stdout.write('withdraw route 100.10.10.0/24 next-hop self' + '\n')
        stdout.flush()
    sleep(10)
```

Let's update our ExaBGP's `conf.ini` to run this python script:

process healthcheck {

   run /path/to/python3 /path/to/healthcheck.py;

   encoder json;

}

neighbor 172.16.2.10 {

   router-id 172.16.2.1;

   local-address 172.16.2.1;

   local-as 65000;

   peer-as 65000;

   api {

     processes [healthcheck];

   }

}

What if we want to check multiple end hosts and automate different prefix advertisements? Well, that could entail an entire application to manage and monitor the end host and prefix objects, but here's a quick and dirty modification of our `healthcheck.py` script:

```
#!/usr/bin/env python3

import socket

from collections import namedtuple

from sys import import stdout

from time import sleep

def is_alive(address, port):
```

```python
""" same as above, removed for brevity """
# Add namedtuple object for easy reference below
TrackedObject = namedtuple('EndHost', ['address','port','prefix', 'nexthop'])
# Make a list of these tracked objects
tracked_objects = [
    TrackedObject('thepacketgeek.com', 80, '100.10.10.0/24', 'self'),
    TrackedObject('8.8.8.8', 53, '200.20.20.0/24', 'self'),
]
while True:
    for host in tracked_objects:
        if is_alive(host.address, host.port):
            stdout.write('announce route {} next-hop {}\n'.format(host.prefix, host.nexthop))
            stdout.flush()
        else:
            stdout.write('withdraw route {} next-hop {}\n'.format(host.prefix, host.nexthop))
            stdout.flush()
    sleep(10)
```

### 9.5.3 ASIC errors on a network device

Perform a health check on a router and give an output if there are any ASIC errors.

```
pip install healthcheck
```

```python
from flask import Flask
from healthcheck import HealthCheck, EnvironmentDump

app = Flask(__name__)

# wrap the flask app and give a heathcheck url
health = HealthCheck(app, "/healthcheck")
```

```
envdump = EnvironmentDump(app, "/environment")
# add your own check function to the healthcheck
def redis_available():
    client = _redis_client()
    info = client.info()
    return True, "redis ok"
health.add_check(redis_available)
# add your own data to the environment dump
def application_data():
        return {"maintainer": "Frank Stratton",
                "git_repo": "https://github.com/Runscope/healthcheck"}
envdump.add_section("application", application_data)
```

Check functions take no arguments and should return a tuple of (bool, str). The boolean is whether or not the check passed. The message is any string or output that should be rendered for this check. Useful for error messages/debugging.

```
# add check functions
def addition_works():
        if 1 + 1 == 2:
                return True, "addition works"
        else:
                return False, "the universe is broken"
```

The above script is sourced from : : https://github.com/Runscope/healthcheck)

### 9.5.4 Generate configlets for Juniper routers

Write a program to generate configlets for Juniper routers for some specific task - router upgrades as an example.

We present two scripts which can be used to generate configs for Juniper routers

**First Script:**

```
#set($source-ip = $source-ip.get(0).split("/"))
security {
  log {
    mode stream;
    source-address $source-ip.get(0);
    transport {
      protocol udp;
    }
    stream SYSLOG-STREAM {
      severity info;
      format sd-syslog;
      category all;
      host {
        10.1.1.42;
        port 514;
      }
    }
  }
}
```

The above script is sourced from : : https://forums.juniper.net/t5/Junos-Automation-Scripting/Trying-to-populate-a-variable-in-a-configlet-with-the-IP-address/td-p/289725

**Second Script:**

```
from jnpr.junos import Device
from jnpr.junos.utils.config import Config
```

```python
from jnpr.junos.exception import *
import jcs
def main():
    usage = """
        This script disables the interface specified by the user.
        The script modifies the candidate configuration to disable
        the interface and commits the configuration to activate it.
    """
    print usage
    interface = jcs.get_input("Enter interface to disable: ")
    if not interface:
        print "invalid interface"
        sys.exit(1)
    config_xml = """
        <configuration>
            <interfaces>
                <interface>
                    <name>{0}</name>
                    <disable/>
                </interface>
            </interfaces>
        </configuration>
    """.format(interface).strip()
    dev = Device()
    dev.open()
```

```python
dev.bind( cu=Config )
# Lock the configuration, load configuration changes, and commit
print "Locking the configuration"
try:
    dev.cu.lock()
except LockError:
    print "Error: Unable to lock configuration"
    dev.close()
    return
print "Loading configuration changes"
try:
    dev.cu.load(config_xml, format="xml", merge=True)
except ConfigLoadError as err:
    print err
    print "Unable to load configuration changes: "
    print "Unlocking the configuration"
    try:
        dev.cu.unlock()
    except UnlockError:
        print "Error: Unable to unlock configuration"
    dev.close()
    return
print "Committing the configuration"
try:
    dev.cu.commit()
```

```
    except CommitError:
        print "Error: Unable to commit configuration"
        print "Unlocking the configuration"
        try:
            dev.cu.unlock()
        except UnlockError:
            print "Error: Unable to unlock configuration"
        dev.close()
        return
    print "Unlocking the configuration"
    try:
        dev.cu.unlock()
    except UnlockError:
        print "Error: Unable to unlock configuration"
    dev.close()
if __name__ == "__main__":
    main()
```

Device Configuration

To download, enable, and test the script:

Copy the script into a text file, name the file config-change.py, and copy it to the /var/db/scripts/op/ directory on the device.

### 9.5.5 Collecting Logs from Juniper Devices

Write a program to collect Junipers logs from Juniper devices automatically after/before crash.

Following script can be used to collect Logs from Juniper devices

```
from junos import Junos_Configuration
```

```
import jcs

def main():
    root = Junos_Configuration
    for element in root.xpath("./snmp/community"):
        if element.find("authorization") is None or element.find("authorization").text != 'read-write':
            jcs.syslog("172", "SNMP community does not have read-write access: " +
                element.find('name').text)

if __name__ == '__main__':
    main()
```

The above script is sourced from :
https://www.juniper.net/documentation/en_US/junos/topics/example/junos-script-automation-commit-script-generating-custom-system-log-message.html

### 9.5.6 Reporting errors on Connected Router Interfaces

Write a script to indicate if there are errors on connected router interfaces.

**First Script:**

```
#!/usr/bin/env python3

import getpass
import csv
import netmiko
import paramiko
from argparse import ArgumentParser

def main():
    parser = ArgumentParser(description='Arguments for running oneLiner.py')
    parser.add_argument('-c', '--csv', required=True, action='store', help='Location of CSV file')
```

```python
args = parser.parse_args()
ssh_username = input("SSH username: ")
ssh_password = getpass.getpass('SSH Password: ')
with open(args.csv, "r") as file:
    reader = csv.DictReader(file)
    for device_row in reader:
        try:
            ssh_session = netmiko.ConnectHandler(device_type='cisco_ios', ip=device_row['device_ip'],
                        username=ssh_username, password=ssh_password)
            print("+++++ {0} +++++".format(device_row['device_ip']))
            ssh_session.send_command("terminal length 0")
            print(ssh_session.send_command("sh ip int br"))
            ssh_session.send_command("terminal length 30")
            ssh_session.disconnect()
        except (netmiko.ssh_exception.NetMikoTimeoutException,
                netmiko.ssh_exception.NetMikoAuthenticationException,
                paramiko.ssh_exception.SSHException) as s_error:
            print(s_error)
if __name__ == "__main__":
    main()
```

The above script is sourced from : : https://community.cisco.com/t5/routing/basic-python-script/td-p/3227660)

**Second Script:**

```python
import paramiko
import sys
import os
import subprocess
with open('C:\Python27\Testing\Fetch.txt') as f:
    for line in f:
        line = line.strip()
        dssh = paramiko.SSHClient()
        dssh.set_missing_host_key_policy(paramiko.AutoAddPolicy())
        dssh.connect(line, username='cisco', password='cisco')
        stdin, stdout, stderr = dssh.exec_command('sh ip ssh')
        mystring = stdout.read()
        print mystring
        f = open('C:\Python27\Testing\output.txt', 'a+')
        f.write(mystring)
        f.close()
dssh.close()
```

Input file Fetch.txt looks like this,

10.0.0.1

10.0.0.2

10.0.0.3

10.0.0.4

10.0.0.5

OR

```python
import paramiko
import sys
import os
import subprocess
dssh = paramiko.SSHClient()
dssh.set_missing_host_key_policy(paramiko.AutoAddPolicy())
with open('C:\Python27\Testing\Fetch.txt') as f:
    for line in f:
        line = line.strip()
        with open(os.devnull, "wb") as limbo:
            ip = line
            result = subprocess.Popen(["ping", "-n", "1", "-w", "200", ip],
                        stdout=limbo, stderr=limbo).wait()
            if result:
                print ip, "Down"
            else:
                print ip, "Reachable"
        dssh.connect(line, username='cisco', password='cisco')
        stdin, stdout, stderr = dssh.exec_command('sh ip ssh')
        mystring = stdout.read()
        print mystring
        f = open('C:\Python27\Testing\output.txt', 'a+')
        f.write('\n' + ip + '\n' + mystring)
        f.close()
dssh.close()
```

### 9.5.7 Detecting Configuration changes using SNMPv3

Using SNMPv3 create a script that detects router configuration changes.

SNMP is an internet protocol that allows you to retrieve management information from a remote device or to set configuration settings on a remote device.

Examples: CPU load, RAID status

A SNMP system is generally considered to have 3 components:

1. **Agents**
   Agents expose management information on a device. Usually, this is a daemon running on the device. It is the server in a typical client/server configuration. In our case, this is the snmpd process running on our remote device.

2. **Managers**
   A manager is an application to retrieve information from the remote machine. A manager may be a web client, a command line program, or another daemon running on a monitoring machine. In our case, this is nagios.

3. **Management Information Bases (MIBs)**
   MIBs are hierarchical lists of variables available via snmp. Each variable has an Object Identifier (OID), for example, on a Dell system, 1.3.6.1.4.1.674.10892.1.700.20.1.6.1.1 is the chassis temperature.

**Installation**
1. # apt-get install snmp snmpd
2. 
3. By default, snmpd listens only on 127.0.0.1. If you wish to monitor your system remotely, you need to edit /etc/default/snmp. Add your host IP address to the SNMPDOPTS line:
4. #SNMPDOPTS='-Lsd -Lf /dev/null -u snmp -I -smux -p /var/run/snmpd.pid 127.0.0.1'
5. SNMPDOPTS='-Lsd -Lf /dev/null -u snmp -I -p /var/run/snmpd.pid localhost,gracie'
6. At this point you should be able to query system information via snmpget and snmpwalk:

$ snmpget -v2c -c public localhost 1.3.6.1.2.1.1.3.0

The above script is sourced from : https://www.math.wisc.edu/~jheim/snmp/

### 9.5.8 Detecting Man-in-the-middle attack

Create a tool to monitor ARP for the purposes of detecting a Man-in-the-middle attack

These tools are intended to detect various kinds of man-in-the-middle (M-I-T-M) attacks, or more practically, verify that you are not being subject to a M-I-T-M attack.

Here are the scripts you could probably use right now:

1. `ssl-grab-cert.sh` will download the SSL certificate from an HTTPS server.
2. `ssl-cert-info.sh` will print the interesting bits of a downloaded certificate.
3. `ssl-mitm-check.sh`
4. Downloads an SSL certificate and compares it to a local, trusted copy, using fingerprints.
5. You should make a trusted copy of a certificate first, using `ssl-grab-cert.sh`.
6. Will also try to detect a captured network, wildcard certs, subjectAltNames with DNS entries, and do the right thing.
7. `transparent-proxy-check.sh` has a server-side dependency to work.
8. `content-tampering-check.sh` also has a server-side dependency.

The above script is sourced from : https://github.com/chorn/mitm-detector

### 9.5.9 Using NetFlow to track utilization

Use NetFlow to track utilization of a given link over time and generate invoices using burstable billing

Using the Advanced Reporting Module for Scrutinizer NetFlow & sFlow Analyzer and a customized Billing configuration, you can monitor the bandwidth usage of your customers and also provide a data export to your current billing application.

The Advanced Reporting Module allows you to restrict your customers to view specific devices and/or interfaces in Scrutinizer.

The Billing configuration is generally a customized solution using the enhanced features of the Advanced Reporting Module and importing that data into your billing application.

A custom data file (i.e. saved report filter) is created and exported every hour, giving the most granular data (1 minute intervals) available. The data file can include but is not limited to:

- Time Stamp
- Rate: bytes / second
- Peak: same as above when reporting at 1 minute intervals
- Totals: total bytes per minute

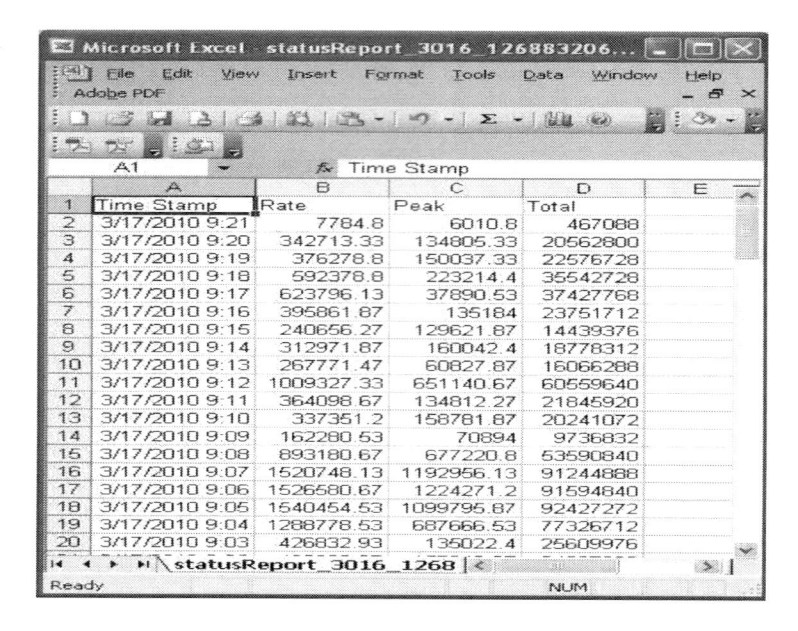

|  | A | B | C | D |
|---|---|---|---|---|
| 1 | Time Stamp | Rate | Peak | Total |
| 2 | 3/17/2010 9:21 | 7784.8 | 6010.8 | 467088 |
| 3 | 3/17/2010 9:20 | 342713.33 | 134805.33 | 20562800 |
| 4 | 3/17/2010 9:19 | 376278.8 | 150037.33 | 22576728 |
| 5 | 3/17/2010 9:18 | 592378.8 | 223214.4 | 35542728 |
| 6 | 3/17/2010 9:17 | 623796.13 | 37890.53 | 37427768 |
| 7 | 3/17/2010 9:16 | 395861.87 | 135184 | 23751712 |
| 8 | 3/17/2010 9:15 | 240656.27 | 129621.87 | 14439376 |
| 9 | 3/17/2010 9:14 | 312971.87 | 160042.4 | 18778312 |
| 10 | 3/17/2010 9:13 | 267771.47 | 60827.87 | 16066288 |
| 11 | 3/17/2010 9:12 | 1009327.33 | 651140.67 | 60559640 |
| 12 | 3/17/2010 9:11 | 364098.67 | 134812.27 | 21845920 |
| 13 | 3/17/2010 9:10 | 337351.2 | 158781.87 | 20241072 |
| 14 | 3/17/2010 9:09 | 162280.53 | 70894 | 9736832 |
| 15 | 3/17/2010 9:08 | 893180.67 | 677220.8 | 53590840 |
| 16 | 3/17/2010 9:07 | 1520748.13 | 1192956.13 | 91244888 |
| 17 | 3/17/2010 9:06 | 1526580.67 | 1224271.2 | 91594840 |
| 18 | 3/17/2010 9:05 | 1540454.53 | 1099795.87 | 92427272 |
| 19 | 3/17/2010 9:04 | 1288778.53 | 687666.53 | 77326712 |
| 20 | 3/17/2010 9:03 | 426832.93 | 135022.4 | 25609976 |

Figure 9-39 Status Report

Any NetFlow or sFlow exported field can be included (bits, packets, percent, IP/MAC addresses, VLAN ID, applications, ToS, Autonomous System, etc.) if required. The billing application or script can then read in the files exported by Scrutinizer at a definable interval.

You should also know that Flexible NetFlow using a Permanent Cache can also be used for importing data into your billing application.

If your billing application is based on 95th percentile measurements, this information is also available in the Traffic Volume report displayed below.

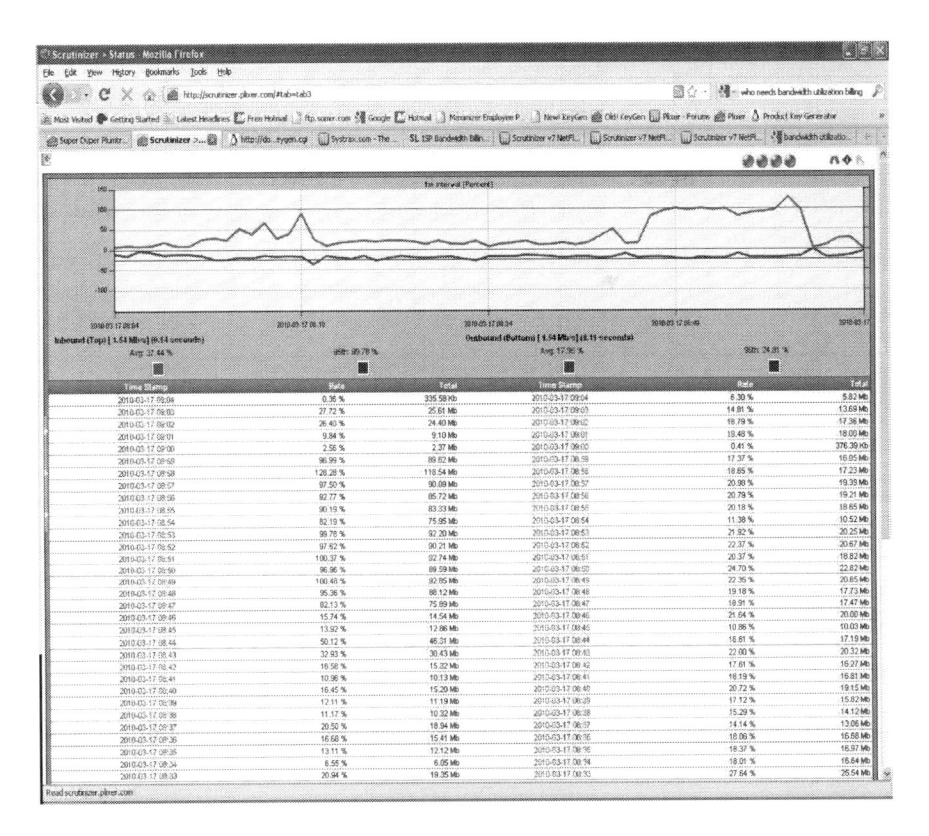

Figure 9-40 Utilization Chart

95th percentile billing allows for the top 5% of spikes in a given period to be dropped from the utilization reported. In the example above, 95th percentile for Inbound is 99.78% and Outbound is 24.81%. This report is based on a one hour timeframe, providing both Inbound and Outbound traffic for the T1 interface.

The above script for NetFlow analysis is sourced from :
https://www.plixer.com/blog/scrutinizer/using-cisco-netflow-for-bandwidth-utilization-billing-systems/

### 9.5.10 Server's Virtualization Parameters

Develop a Python script to probe a server's virtualization parameters? There are hundreds of BIOS settings, some should be disabled/enabled for VMWare/OpenStack.

*import sys*

*import os*

*def main():*

   *print os.name*

```python
if __name__ == '__main__':
    try:
        if sys.argv[1] == 'deploy':
            import paramiko
            # Connect to remote host
            client = paramiko.SSHClient()
            client.set_missing_host_key_policy(paramiko.AutoAddPolicy())
            client.connect('remote_hostname_or_IP', username='john', password='secret')
            # Setup sftp connection and transmit this script
            sftp = client.open_sftp()
            sftp.put(__file__, '/tmp/myscript.py')
            sftp.close()
            # Run the transmitted script remotely without args and show its output.
            # SSHClient.exec_command() returns the tuple (stdin,stdout,stderr)
            stdout = client.exec_command('python /tmp/myscript.py')[1]
            for line in stdout:
                # Process each line in the remote output
                print line
            client.close()
            sys.exit(0)
    except IndexError:
        pass
    # No cmd-line args provided, run script normally
    main()
```

The above script is sourced from:

https://stackoverflow.com/questions/20499074/run-local-python-script-on-remote-server

### 9.5.11 Querying OIDs using SNMP

Query a specific OID in SNMP

```python
#!/bin/python
# listinterfaces.py
#
# Copyright (c) 2014 Michael Shoup mike@shouptech.com
#
# License: MIT - see http://opensource.org/licenses/MIT

__version__ = "0.1"

from pysnmp.entity.rfc3413.oneliner import cmdgen
import sys

class SnmpError(Exception):
    def __init__(self, errorIndication, errorStatus=None):
        self.errorIndication = errorIndication
        self.errorStatus = errorStatus

def print_interfaces(varBindTable):
    # Build up a list of interfaces, and figure out maximum width of columns
    interfaces = []
    indexColMax = 5
    descriptionColMax = 11
    for row in varBindTable:
        index = row[0][1].prettyPrint()
        description = row[1][1].prettyPrint()
```

```
        if len(index) > indexColMax:
            indexColMax = len(index)
        if len(description) > descriptionColMax:
            descriptionColMax = len(description)
        interfaces.append([index, description])
    # Print the interfaces in a formatted manner
    print('| {} | {} |'.format('index'.center(indexColMax),
        'description'.center(descriptionColMax)))
    print('-' * (7+indexColMax+descriptionColMax))
    for interface in interfaces:
        print('| {} | {} |'.format(interface[0].ljust(indexColMax),
            interface[1].ljust(descriptionColMax)))

def query_community(version, community, host, port=161, protocol='udp'):
    gen = cmdgen.CommandGenerator()
    # Specify TCP or UDP
    if protocol == 'tcp':
        transportTarget = cmdgen.TcpTransportTarget((host,port))
    else:
        transportTarget = cmdgen.UdpTransportTarget((host,port))
    # Query device for ifIndex and ifDescr. This should be enough to ascertain
    # which interfaces to use.
    errorIndication, errorStatus, errorIndex, varBindTable = gen.nextCmd(
        cmdgen.CommunityData(community, mpModel=(1 if version=='2c' else 0)),
        transportTarget,
        cmdgen.MibVariable('IF-MIB', 'ifIndex'),
```

```python
                       cmdgen.MibVariable('IF-MIB', 'ifDescr'),
                       lookupValues=True)
# Raise exceptions if errors occur
if errorIndication:
    raise SnmpError(errorIndication)
else:
    if errorStatus:
        raise SnmpError(errorIndication, errorStatus)
    print_interfaces(varBindTable)
def query_v3(authName, authPass, host, port=161, authProto='md5',
             privProto='des', privAuth=None, protocol='udp'):
    gen = cmdgen.CommandGenerator()
    # Specify TCP or UDP
    if protocol == 'tcp':
        transportTarget = cmdgen.TcpTransportTarget((host,port))
    else:
        transportTarget = cmdgen.UdpTransportTarget((host,port))
    # MD5 or SHA for auth protocol
    if authProto == 'sha':
        genAuthProto = cmdgen.usmHMACSHAAuthProtocol
    else:
        genAuthProto = None
    # DES or AES for priv protocol
    if privProto == 'aes':
        genPrivProto = cmdgen.usmAesCfb128Protocol
```

```python
        else:
            genPrivProto = None
        # Generate user data
        if privAuth:
            userData = cmdgen.UsmUserData(authName,
                                         authPass,
                                         privAuth,
                                         authProtocol=genAuthProto,
                                         privProtocol=genPrivProto)
        else:
            userData = cmdgen.UsmUserData(authName,
                                         authPass,
                                         authProtocol=genAuthProto)
        # Query device for ifIndex and ifDescr. This should be enough to ascertain
        # which interfaces to use.
        errorIndication, errorStatus, errorIndex, varBindTable = gen.nextCmd(
            userData,
            transportTarget,
            cmdgen.MibVariable('IF-MIB', 'ifIndex'),
            cmdgen.MibVariable('IF-MIB', 'ifDescr'),
            lookupValues=True)
        # Raise exceptions if errors occur
        if errorIndication:
            raise SnmpError(errorIndication)
        else:
```

```python
        if errorStatus:
            raise SnmpError(errorIndication, errorStatus)
        print_interfaces(varBindTable)

if __name__ == "__main__":
    import argparse
    # Set up command line arguments
    parser = argparse.ArgumentParser(
        description='List interfaces from SNMP capable device.')
    parser.add_argument('-v', '--snmpversion', default='1',
        choices=['1','2c','3'],
        help='SNMP version to query with. If not specified,' +
        ' uses v1.')
    parser.add_argument('-c', '--community',
        help='SNMP community string (v1 or v2c only).')
    parser.add_argument('-V', '--version', action='version',
        version='%(prog)s v'+__version__)
    parser.add_argument('-n', '--port', default=161,
        help='Port to query (default 161)')
    parser.add_argument('-P', '--protocol', default='udp',
        choices=['tcp','udp'],
        help='Protocol to use. (default udp)')
    parser.add_argument('-u', '--user',
        help='Username for USM based queries (v3 only).')
    parser.add_argument('-p', '--password',
        help='Password for USM based queries (v3 only).')
```

```
parser.add_argument('-a', '--authprotocol',
    choices=['md5','sha'], default='md5',
    help='Auth protocol for USM. (default md5) (v3 only)')
parser.add_argument('-X', '--privauth',
    help='Privacy pass phrase used for encrypted v3')
parser.add_argument('-x', '--privprotocol',
    choices=['des','aes'], default='des',
    help='Privacy protocol used for encrypted v3')
parser.add_argument('host', type=str,
    help='Specify the host/IP address to query')
args = parser.parse_args()
# Determine which query function to call.
if args.snmpversion == '1' or args.snmpversion == '2c':
    if args.community:
        query_community(args.snmpversion
            args.community,
            args.host,
            args.port,
            args.protocol)
    else:
        print("v1 or v2c specified, but no community provided.",
            file=sys.stderr)
elif args.snmpversion == '3':
    query_v3(args.user,
        args.password,
```

*args.host,*

*args.port,*

*args.authprotocol,*

*args.privprotocol,*

*args.privauth,*

*args.protocol)*

> The above script is sourced from :
> https://gist.github.com/shouptech/e9c0dc44f643d3206749)

### 9.5.12   Monitor Network using Python

Create a program to Monitor Network Performance

Following script can be used to Monitor a Network using Python

*import time*

*import psutil*

*def main():*

  *old_value = 0*

  *while True:*

    *new_value = psutil.net_io_counters().bytes_sent + psutil.net_io_counters().bytes_recv*

    *if old_value:*

      *send_stat(new_value - old_value)*

    *old_value = new_value*

    *time.sleep(1)*

*def convert_to_gbit(value):*

  *return value/1024./1024./1024.*8*

*def send_stat(value):*

  *print ("%0.3f" % convert_to_gbit(value))*

*main()*

The above script is sourced from : https://stackoverflow.com/questions/15616378/python-network-bandwidth-monitor

### 9.5.13 Playing with ciscoconfparse Python Library

Using Python library named ciscoconfparse that helps you parse Cisco hierarchical configurations parse BGP and OSPF configurations

We would let you investigate Ciscoconfparse on your own

### 9.5.14 Monitoring windows registry Changes

Create an application to automatically track changes to the windows registry

There is a _winreg library in python that reading from and writing to the Windows Registery.

```
from _winreg import *


print r"*** Reading from SOFTWARE\Microsoft\Windows\CurrentVersion\Run ***"
aReg = ConnectRegistry(None,HKEY_LOCAL_MACHINE)
aKey = OpenKey(aReg, r"SOFTWARE\Microsoft\Windows\CurrentVersion\Run")
for i in range(1024):
    try:
        n,v,t = EnumValue(aKey,i)
        print i, n, v, t
    except EnvironmentError:
        print "You have",i," tasks starting at logon..."
        break
CloseKey(aKey)

print r"*** Writing to SOFTWARE\Microsoft\Windows\CurrentVersion\Run ***"

aKey = OpenKey(aReg, r"SOFTWARE\Microsoft\Windows\CurrentVersion\Run", 0, KEY_WRITE)
```

*try:*

   *SetValueEx(aKey,"MyNewKey",0, REG_SZ, r"c:\winnt\explorer.exe")*

*except EnvironmentError:*

   *print "Encountered problems writing into the Registry..."*

*CloseKey(aKey)*

*CloseKey(aReg)*

This is an example of reading and writing.

The above script is sourced from : https://stackoverflow.com/questions/34738317/how-to-track-changes-in-specific-registry-key-or-file-with-python

## 9.5.15 Assignment Questions

## Assignment 1

**9.1** Write a program using NTP to compare the current computer time with NTP time?
**9.2** Write a short code to create a simple HTTP file server?
**9.3** Write a python script to interact with HTTP services as a client?
**9.4** Write a code to create TCP server and TCP client?
**9.5** Write a script to create UDP server and UDP client?
**9.6** How can you find the IP address for a specific interface on your machine?
**9.7** Write a program to get all running processes on local or remote machine?
**9.8** Write a program to display all services in a stop state on a server?
**9.9** How can you create a list of interfaces on your machine?
**9.10** Write a python script using Scapy library to monitor ARP traffic?

# Chapter 10
# Network Automation and Automation tools

## 10.1 Objectives

- To understand Network Automation and various tools available for Network Automation.
- To use the Network Automation tools such as Ansible, Pramiko
- To be able to identify the commercially available Network Automation Tools
- To use Python to develop Network Automated tasks
- Provide direction in developing network libraries

## 10.2 Introduction

Networking plays an important role in organizational growth in the current world by enabling the sharing of resources. Within a network, there are some repetitive tasks and routines that enable it to perform its roles, these tasks include; configuration, provisioning, diagnosis, detection, remediation and management. These tasks are so repetitive that it may be a painful experience if a human was involved. An automated network is, therefore, a network that performs these repetitive tasks with minimal involvement of a human being; networking tools such as program codes are deployed to manipulate processes, servers and hardware components. With automation, an organization is able to change job functions, processes an even the organizational culture.

## 10.3 What kind of networks can be automated?

A network resource that is API or CLI controlled is legible for automation; these include WANs, LANs, Data Centers, Cloud networks.

### 10.3.1 Network automation categories

a) *Script-driven automation of network:* In this type of automation, a programming language or a script is used for the execution tasks with procedures that are consistent. Some of these tools are Perl and TCL but most currently used are ruby and python.
b) *Software-based/ intelligent network automation*: This is a platform that helps do away with hand scripting. It is a porthole with templates used to execute tasks.
c)

## 10.4 Reasons and benefits for network automation

Automation is important for enterprises by offering needed solutions. This in return causes reliability, flexible, autonomous, scalability, portable and the human cost is reduced dramatically. The enterprises of today need systems which are easy to use, secure, have low costs and which is centrally controlled.

A Centrally Controlled Network or system Configuration is an organizational requirement if prosperity is the driving force, this has the effect of not only cutting costs but most importantly increased the efficiency of operation. Some of these activities include patching, the configuration of the firewall, and Syslog being managed from a central location. Another important reason for automation is the ease of use of application and systems, playing a role in eliminating complexities or difficulties in the system. This has the effect the reducing operational costs on such activities or even attends to other important matters. Hence lower tasks time. Cost is an integral aspect of organizational growth; therefore, the system adopted must be cheap for cost reduction.

The world of today is full of threats to enterprises' informational resources. Security, therefore, is paramount to any automation system. This can be achieved if the automation tool is able to perform upgrades of software and security patches. Another section that should always be made secure is the central servers as well as processes. Another reason to automate it to enable host configuration flexibility. This has the effect of having the ability to install different software packages to members of the same station. It also enables a host by host OS and software configuration on systems.

Automation should make it possible for network autonomy. An autonomous network helps minimize human intervention. Portability of devices and applications is very important for a good business. Portability makes it possible for the running of cross multiple Oss at will. The networking world is flooded with many different types of equipment from different vendors, different standards which undergo change every other time and the many interface variations. Management of such a network with multi-vendor devices in even more complicated and near possible for a human being in the case of a large network say 100 routers as well as switches. Automation comes in such cases; such systems will be able to give alerts and information regard to utilization of network resources, error alerts, packet losses, jitters in the network and much more. These activities are referred to as performance monitoring. SLA tests are also a key role of the automated systems because of the reporting feature they possess after result processing for the network.

Using automation tools networks are now able to automatically save the network configurations, perform policy and security standards adherence checks, identify the network topology, minimize downtime and reduce the chances of failure of the network. These processes have the effect of making the network more consistent as far as deployment is concerned, compliant, secure, resilient, up to date, minimal human errors and most importantly effective and efficient utilization of network resources.

Network automation reduces complexities of the network considerably because it will effectively handle configuration management, this has the effect of resulting in a fewer person-hours requirement for the infrastructure operations, administration and management. This immediately reduces the costs of operations. Most importantly automation allows an organization to be able to shift a workforce towards a more strategic and tactical work to enable the running of the business. This is possible because the workforce has been shifted from the repetitive, manual and mundane network tasks but the introduction of automation. Resources can, therefore, be shifted to these tactical tasks which are of higher order some of which include application delivery updating.

Automation is also necessary for the agility of the network; this is the ability to respond to changes, this is possible as a result of analytics making a user capable of knowing what is happening in the network with respect to resource utility and performance real-time. The agility makes an organization able to compete competitively in the current world.

Network automation allows the description of the network components both logical and physical in a format that is human readable. This is referred to as I infrastructure as a code. These are appealing interfaces which are easy to use.

Network automation is also key to the subject of policy enforcement achievability. This is possible due to the ability of an automated network to continuously check for drifts in configurations and compliance during the validation process of a network infrastructure.

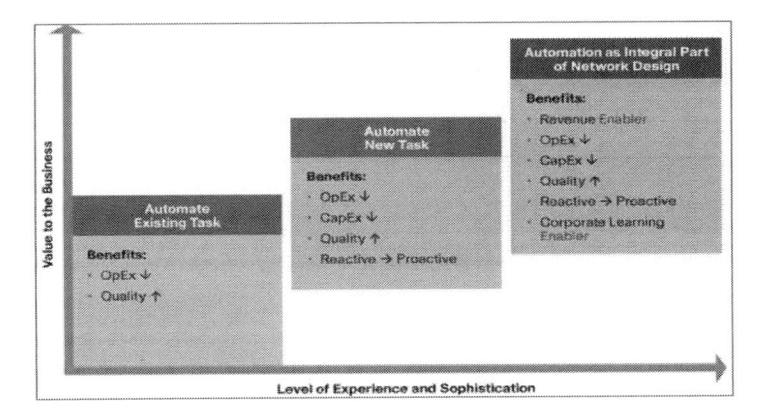

Figure 10-1 Impacts of Automation on the Business

## 10.5 What Makes Automation Of Network A Possibility?

Current network has the ability to accept automation as a result of the following reasons, the existence of generic routers and switches, the SDN capabilities of current routers and the current technology called infrastructure as code.

**Generic Routers:** A generic router has the ability to receive configurations from any line of code. The vendor specificity is slowly but surely fading away. The current routers can put a line between hardware and software just like PCs and Mobile handset.

**SD:** Generic routers can accept software-defined networking deployment due to the hardware-software separation. The software is the key components for network automation and they provide control of the three separate layers of the network which include management, control and data plane. The layering also makes it possible for the automation.

**Infrastructure as a service:** This is a concept that enables the management and control of servers as well as resources. It is a process that considers development standards, testing mechanisms and implementing them by scripting the codes into the servers with a goal of replication the protocols in the whole network as it is being scaled

## 10.6 How to automate network management?

A network is an interconnection of nodes and other devices like switches, routers. The interconnection requires management and administration for good functionality. The function of the administration of such networks becomes an issue as the network is being scaled up by an increased number of nodes increase necessitating the aspect of network automation. This involves the use of specific tools like python, puppet. These tools enable a seamless administration of distributed networks. This evolution of management of a network takes the following route. Firstly, a centralized network management should be adopted, this enables the administration of the network through a single interface.

This interface otherwise called a controller enables an IT team to manage the network efficiently from a single point; abstraction should also be credited for this possibility to deploy automation tools. Secondly, the enterprise should be willing to implement automation. This will include the use of network tools which can be in the form of programming languages like python and API. Some of these tools are open source while others are vendor offered. Thirdly, it is important to take advantage of the software toolkits like python to automate through its libraries like JSON and RESTful. Cisco ACL also is a viable tool for network automation it comprises SDK and a tool to build around it. Lastly, given the presence of a variety of tools and the choice by an enterprise to automate the networks, a self-driven network should be configured based on network policy. The enterprise ill realizes that automation is the only way to go to enable a near excellent functioning network with minimal errors and with high performance.

## 10.7 Steps to achieve a fully automated network

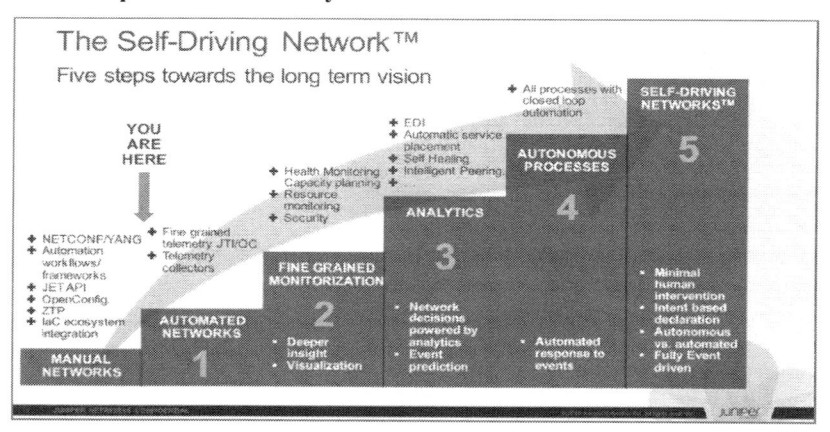

Figure 10-2 Pictorial presentation

| STEP | EXPLANATION |
|---|---|
| Maturation cycle | This is the router configuration using the APIs by deploying configuration scripts. |
| Maturity Chart | The man aims of this stage s to ensure the network health through the processes like traffic, performance and routine monitoring. |
| Analytics | This stage performs the following functions; performing simple aggregation, machine learning, collected metrics presentation, prediction of events and detection of network anomalies among others. |
| Autonomous process. | This stage is purposely for effecting the changes observed during the analysis face. |
| Culmination of technologies | At this stage, the network operations are solely done through automaton by the involvement of artificial intelligence and rule-based control. |

Table 19 Steps and their description

## 10.8 Using Python and its libraries for network automation

Python is a very powerful tool for network automation; this function is made possible by the existence of the many libraries. Python library consists of functions or methods that give a programmer the ability to implement some functionality without having to write the lines of code thereby enabling the completion of actions during programming work easier and faster, examples of such tools include NTPlib, Scapy, Paramiko among others. These libraries contain components like functions, exemption and collection modules.

## 10.9 Should you build or buy network automation tools?

A network is regarded as a useful link between a business and the clients, therefore it should always be reliable and with the ability to meet the needs of the clients conveniently, without which the business risks low returns.

It is projected that by the year 2020, internet users will be 4.1 billion with a corresponding 26.3 billion devices used on the internetwork. This is in the response to the advancements in cloud computing, IOT, network mobility and analytics. The described scenarios will by default require automation to up its game in order attract usage because networks ought to be more scalable, transformation oriented by the ability to support applications, agile, reliable, interoperable most significantly secure.

The topmost budget constraints regarding technology acquisition ion organizations are security and compliance, appropriate skills marching the change as well as the structure of the given organization. Although automation of the organizational network is costly, it comes with more returns. To begin with, it will reduce staff time tremendously by taking up tasks that would have other ways been administered by paid individuals, network errors that in many cases result to the organization losing money will be reduced to a negligible level.

Automation will then surely make a business stay ahead due to the ability to adaptability to the business needs, automation has a return on investment when properly deployed approximated at about 350% within a period of 5 years with a payback of 6 months. The business benefits of network automation will be in terms of the following; low operational costs as a result of the elimination of the slow manual processes. This will not only have the effect of enhancing the capability of the network, reducing network errors by humans but also help achieve a return on investment. The network will be able to provide employees and the clients with the information, applications and data they require at the appropriate time or rather conveniently.

The organizational employees and clients will have a simple way to access the network, network resources and services due to reduced complexities of operation by the deployment of abstraction. The network will be faster, resilient and capacity of utilization will increase. As a result, saves on man hours, resource utilization and reduces error costs. This simplification could be achieved through the use of an automation tool called juniper.

Another benefit is the increase in savings for a given business. With automation, the network costs will reduce by a projected value of slightly above 30% taking the case of Juniper deployment. With increased returns in an organization the ability to increase savings will be within the reach of the business because the network will be flexible, reliable, speedy and efficient meeting the needs of the clients, therefore, more ROI because in the business world of today networking is everything and with automation, everything falls in place.

As discussed, automation is the only option for businesses that want to pursue success. As for the debate of whether the company needs to buy, built or settle on a hybrid of the two ways in the acquisition of automation tools. The following considerations should be made, the business needs, the sufficiency and capability of personnel to handle the automation tool required and to orchestrate the deployment of the chosen technology of automation, whether or not the vendor provides the personnel, risks of chosen technology and the mitigation plans, the timelines of the benefits of deploying a given technology, the knowledge and the readiness of the business to commence the given technology. In view of the above items, a business can make a choice of whether to outsource or built their own technology to enable their network automation.

## 10.10    Do we need expensive tool to do meaningful automation?

Automation deployment in an organisation requires a skilled workforce to handle the technology, a network infrastructure that can accept the tools of change and lastly the tools of automation themselves. The institution will have to bear these costs. Concerning tools of automation given these other factors solved other considerations should be made as follows; the orchestration or arrangement of the domains which includes services, policy, maintenance and device layers.

The other is the onramp or the processes of accessing the automation services, which considers the ownership of the network automation, defined processes of the network management processes as well as the platform or the defined tools for use.

The tools vary from proprietary to open source, the choice of a tool depends on the defined processes and requirements of the tool, some of the open source tools are Ansible, puppet, chef and salt. These are powerful tools for the deployment of network automation.

This subject is contentious, the most direct answer is no due to a large variety of open source tools available for automation, which are equally powerful and capable of handling automation. On the other hand, for an extensive architecture with sophistications in the workflows some institutions may opt for proprietary tools, which are sometimes not very expensive to acquire and deploy or in some cases, Institutions can deploy both proprietary and open source tools for automation. Therefore, to sum up, one does not need expensive tools for automation purposes.

## 10.11    Outstanding automation tools and libraries vendor specific APIs:
### 10.11.1    Ansible

It's a python-based CLI tool used for network administration across a variety of platforms like the Linux servers, Cisco devices and much more. Ansible does this network administration through running of a YAML-based playbook file which provides a description of the tasked to be performed and the corresponding module for the operation of each task. Ansible is more advantageous to use compared to some other tools because, with an SSH connection, it can manage a variety of devices from different vendors without the need for further installation of applications in the target device.

### 10.11.2    Puppet

It is a ruby- based automation tool useful for the administration of servers across different platforms like Cisco IOS and Linux, these devices include switches and routers, this tool, on the other hand, requires an application installed in the node of interest requiring management and is mostly used to manage the interfaces and VLANs. This tool consists of a puppet master and an agent in the target device, it employs its own sysadmin accessible declarative and a configuration language to initiate pull definitions periodically from the puppet master server to the nodes, this is purposed to compare the configurations of these two ends.

### 10.11.3 Chef

This is also a ruby based tool for automation whose configurations revolve around the knowledge of Git, conceptually it bears resemblance to puppet as it also involves the installation of a master server and an agent on the nodes to be managed. The installation of the agent can be performed by 'knife', a tool that employs secure shell during the deployment process after which the nodes undergo authentication with the master using certificates.Chef used the cooking theme with recipes for tasks. The only point to pass on is that this tool is confined to the management of devices which possess the ability to support agent installation.

### 10.11.4 NetConf

This is a network configuration protocol that uses an extensible markup language to delimit a simple means through which network resources are managed. These tasks include management of devices, retrieval, manipulation and updates of configuration data. This protocol sends notifications about network configurations of any kind over NETCONF if the operation successfully occurs.

### 10.11.5 Salt

This is a non-proprietary automation tool that is based on a master-minions topology just like puppet and chef. It also faces the challenges the later faces but with a little point of deviation. Salt clients are also known as minions have the capability to be installed on a newer system running their OS in a container. The proxy- minions enable the control and management of devices that lack the ability to run the standard salt-minion and in some cases, an interface needs to be created for use. Napalm-salt is a framework of automation that communicates with network devices. It is always advisable to use the same tool to manage servers as well as the network when using salt.

### 10.11.6 Git / GitHub / Gitlab

Git is an automation tool that has the ability to keep track of changes made in lines of code to the given files by a programmer by the provision of version control and repositories of code. GitHub is a platform that offers the ability for the programmers to define, upload and privately store at a fee or share code for free with others who with then have the ability to download the code and use it in their local machines. Gitlab is a tool that grants the ability for the installation of a server of Git within once network infrastructure as well as a cloud-based service and therefore controlling access to the server and its access.

### 10.11.7 Jenkins

It is a non-proprietary tool used to verify the correctness of a code before it made live and operational from repositories like Git as well as start the process of deployment of the code through tools like Ansible. It is coded and run in Java with a little inclusion of Groovy, ruby as well as Antlr file. Every line of code is executed one by one with a definition of points of the check along the way.

### 10.11.8 NETMIKO

Netmiko is an important paramiko based library for network automation across several networking platforms, it is key to the management of secure shell in the networking devices. The library is important for the following reasons; establishing an SSH connection with success, to enable the simplification of show commands, output data retrieval, configuration commands, commit actions. Below is a sample code for a simple SSH session Example: 'show ip int-brief' command to a Cisco router

```
>>> from netmiko import ConnectHandler
>>> cisco_881 = {
...     'device_type': 'cisco_ios',
...     'ip': '10.10.10.227',
...     'username': 'pyclass',
...     'password': 'password',
... }
```

Figure 10-3 Code snippet

### 10.11.9 REST

The acronym stands for Representational State transfer and it is purposed to handle multiple call types and to return varied data format and with the ability to effect structural data changes given a correct implementation. REST by design separates data from methods and resources hence can be used over an array of protocols without the need to install additional software and libraries but the tool employs the existing protocols like in the case oh HTTP when applied for web API.

### 10.11.10 REST

The acronym stands for Representational State. REST is a data-driven application platform or architecture that depends entirely on the stateless communication protocol like HTTP. It presents data in machine-readable structures formats some of which are XML and YAML. It follows the OOP paradigms, OOP is the short form of object-oriented. Rest takes many formats at the description stage because it has no unit standard. The REST HTTP requests for RES include the following: POST, GET, PUT, and DELETE.

### 10.11.1 SOAP

This is a functional driven messaging framework which is strongly types and relies upon XML to a greater extent in combination with schemas. The framework employs the web service description or definition language also abbreviated as WSDL which is defined in programming as a method signature for web services to provide an explicit co definition of every operation and services it provides. Each input value is given a definition after which the defined value is tied to type which includes a string, integer or even other complex objects.

The WSDL is sometimes explained as the contract that exists between a service provider and a client consuming the service. SOAP having separated data and application, its messages which are XML formatted can be transported over near all protocols including TCP, JMS among others. This message must be inclusive of a single root element which acts as an envelope as in the case of an XML document. The envelope constitutes two parts, the header and the body while the rest part is described as the web service definition.

SOAP was developed before the development of WSDL, so in reality, the SOAP should operate without the WSDL in other ways it should be optional. Practical y is it sometimes a hard nut to crack without it proves difficult to interface with a web service that possess no WSDL. The WSDL though optional dictates the specific order of the appearance of elements also, it also dictates the allowed attributes and elements.

### 10.11.2 JSON

This stands for JavaScript Object Notation, and it's a tool for storing information in an organized, easy-to-access manner. In a nutshell, it gives us a human-readable collection of data that we can access in a logical manner.

### 10.11.3 YAML

This is a regarded as a standard for data serialization toolkit. It is usable for all languages for programming. It is, however, important to note that this is not a Markup language and in addition is human readable hence user-friendly to a larger extent.

Simplicity is the founding principle of this tool. This tool is not core and is very usable for a description of data and grants the permissions to run configuration settings.

### 10.11.4 NAPALM

This toolkit is a library of python which provides a unified API across a network infrastructure composed of devices from different vendors. This tool is aimed to interface and enable communication between devices from a competing vendor through a unified API. With this tool configuration of devices can be made without the care of the OS platform and the type of device in question. Some of the code snippet used by Napalm is like

| Code snippet | Function |
| --- | --- |
| load_merge_candidate() | Creation of the wanted configuration in the device |
| load_replace_candidate() | Full configuration command |
| compare_config() | Confirming the necessity of the change of configuration |
| commit_config() | Applying the configuration change |
| discard_config() | Rolling back the configuration |

Table 20 Codes and their functions

This tool can be installed using the pip, with the incorporation of some other necessary applications, this will enable the programmer to create their own code snippets to be used for network automation. Sample Napalm code snippet for configuring a device with an access list

```
from napalm.base import get_network_driver
driver = get_network_driver('iosxr')
dev = driver(hostname='r1', username='admin',
        password='admin')
dev.open()
dev.load_merge_candidate(filename='ACL_SAMPLE.cfg')
dev.commit_config()
dev.close()
```

Figure 10-4 Code snippet

## 10.12 Vendor specific Automation Tools and APIs

### 10.12.1 Cisco Prime Infrastructure

This is a Cisco tool for performing network management and administration; it supports lifecycle administration of the whole network infrastructure from a single platform or graphical user interface. The tasks like provisioning, optimization, monitoring, troubleshooting both on the wired and the wireless platforms or devices can be handled from the single UI of Cisco Prime Infrastructure, the resounding result is that there is the tremendous reduction in costs of deployment and operations therefore very economical.

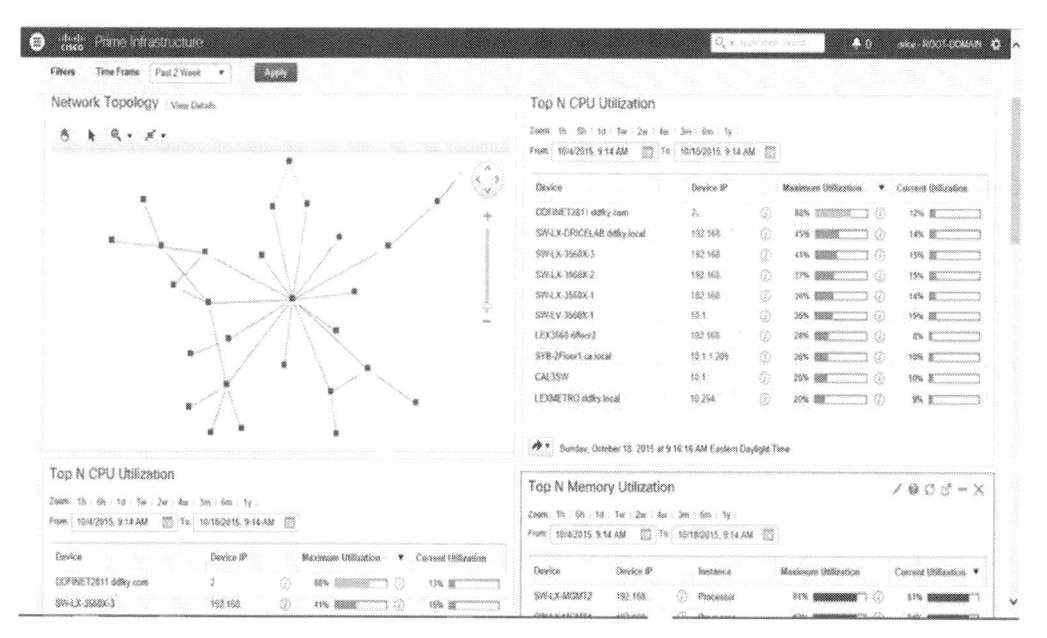

Figure 10-5 Cisco Prime Infrastructure

The table below gives a description of the UI organization into a lifecycle workflow. It also encompasses the high-level tasks areas

| Area of Task | Definition or description | User |
|---|---|---|
| The dashboard | Enable the observation of the dashboards, which provides a quick overview of nodes, the information about their performance, and the various occurrences in the network. | Operators and engineers of the Network |
| The monitor | This section is important for the day to day management and administration of the network and devices. The tasks offered by this section are the troubleshooting, maintenance, configuration, operations that are related to inventory of the nodes in the network. In a nutshell, it comprises the tools to manage the networks and the dashboard for the view | Designers, engineers and architectures of the network |
| Configuration | At this section the design of patterns and features are done, these are key to the deployment of the lifecycle, plug and profiles as well as mobility services. These include templates of configuration found in the design area, the designs may be self-created or can be adopted from the already defined templates. | Designers, engineers and architectures of the network |
| The inventory | The inventory section is responsible for the management of devices and operations, the tasks performed include addition, configuration archives, auditing of configurations of the devices. Other tasks include running discovery as well as software image management. | Designers, NOC operators and SOs of the network |
| The maps | This section is for the view of maps and network topology. | Designers, NOC operators and SOs of the network |
| The Services | This section is responsible for the services of control, visibility and access mobility. It also plays a role in features of IWAN | Designers, NOC operators and SOs of the network |
| The Report | This section deals in reports. The tasks range from, creation, viewing the already saved ones as well as the running of the scheduled reports | Designers, NOC operators and SOs of the network |
| The administration | This is a management interface through which settings of such as system configuration, data collection, access control for messages is performed. The engineer is also at liberty to view and do an approval of a job, making the specification of health rules and for management of licenses. Configuration and updates can also be performed. | Engineers |

Table 1 Description of UI organizations

## 10.12.2 Juniper PyEZ

The Juniper PyEZ is a framework designed for both programmers and non-programmers to automate the usage of devices that are running on Junos operating system, this automation gives the user the power to manage the devices remotely. It is important to note that this tool does not need its users to be a software guru, these can use devices like the mobile phones or tablets on the native python shell for server management, these devices act as a point of control for the remote management of the OS. The python shell provides a friendly tool for such operations.

For the programmers, this python package gives a provision for installing some other widgets to enable these types of users to customize their needs depending on their objectives. Another advantage for this is the fact that Juniper PyEZ is not specific to any version of the OS or family of product

This python package has performed the following key functions;

Availing information about the following regarding the device: Serial number, version of the software among others.

Allows a user to retrieve the run-state information regarding a device using its views.

Apart from making configuration changes which are structured as well as those which are unstructured, the configuration data can also be accessed by users through the views as well as tables.

Enable the secure copy feature for both files and updates on software packages

Juniper PyEZ has an architecture gives the capability of offering services to both programmers and non-programmers.

## 10.12.3 Cisco CrossWorks for Service Providers

This is a solution framework that is geared towards achieving a network infrastructure which is more agile and more predictable. The Cisco CrossWorks does this with the help of the following; data analytics, machine learning and telemetry. This framework provides closed-loop workflow and health monitoring. These in conjunction enable automation and smart remediation based on machine learning.

The Cisco Cross Network technology enables the following advancement to be made on a network infrastructure; maximization of network resource utilization, the creation of a reliable network with increased uptime. These have a larger effect of reducing operational costs and man-hours due to, network, device and service activation and assurance, event management based on machine learning, operations that are work follow define.

In the event of the deployment of this technology some of the expectations which come in handy are; the ability to tread the network code as an application s software; modification of the network errors by the use of the KPI deployment during the self-service monitoring and lastly the simplification of software provisioning, deployment of the network; reuse of the existing library plays which the technology also as allows for customization, building and partner service of plays as well as configuration of management.

The Cisco CrossWorks has the following layers in its architecture; open application ecosystem, common data

| LAYER | FUNCTION |
|---|---|
| Open application ecosystem | Solves specific problems of operations |
| Data Source and Processing | Aggregation, distribution, analysis and storage of databases |
| Deployment and Collection Service | Important for deploying configuration and acquiring data for events, flow data and operational data. |

Table 2 Layers and their functions

The above functionality is possible due to the existence of smart sensors, smart alerts and smart remediation. This framework helps reduces the cost of integration, hardware creates an infrastructure which is highly scalable and network telemetry traffic also reduces.

### 10.12.4 PYCSCO

The pycsco a very easy to use the module written to support NX-OS off-box scripting. It requires the installation of PyYaml. It is that it very easy to use. Below is a sample a Nexus Python scripting with the Requests module.

```
from pycsco.nxos.device import Device
# Login
IP = "<ip of nexus>"
USER = "admin"
PW = "password"
# Device1 login session
DEVICE1 = Device(username=USER,password=PW,ip=IP)
```

Figure 10-6 Code snippet

### 10.12.5 Cisco pyIOSXR.

pyIOSXR is a python library to help interact with Cisco devices running IOS-XR, in the spirit of pyEOS for Arista EOS devices and pyEZ for JUNOS devices.

Below is a Debugging Connection sample

```
>>> from pyIOSXR import IOSXR
>>> import sys
>>> device=IOSXR(hostname="router", username="cisco", password="cisco", port=22, timeout=120, logfile=sys.stdout
```

### 10.12.6 Arista EOS API eAPI.

This automation tool is used for building management plane applications, making it easy to develop solutions that interface with the device configuration and state information. It is designed to assist network engineers, operators and developers to build eAPI applications faster without having to deal with the specifics of the eAPI implementation, it is designed to run either locally on the EOS node or remotely using the HTTP/S transport capabilities of eAPI and provides an easy to use Python library for building robust management plane applications.

## 10.13 PYTHON ENVIRONMENTS AND PROJECTS USED FREQUENTLY WITH NETWORK AUTOMATION TOOLS

### 10.13.1 Modules and Packages

Modular programming is key to automation, it enables simplicity, ability to maintain a program, reusability and scoping. The aspects that support this aspect are the existence of packages and modules. There are several advantages to modularizing code in a large application and packages are all constructs in Python that promote code modularization.

### 10.13.2 Python Modules

Python modules can be written in languages like python, C and can exist as a built-in module is intrinsically contained in the interpreter but in all cases, the accessibility is the same.

### 10.13.3 Python Packages

Packages are usable to put together modules of the same kind together because as the number of modules grows, it becomes difficult to keep track of them all if they are dumped into one location. The packages will allow for a hierarchical structuring of the module namespace using dot notation. In the same way that modules help avoid collisions between global variable names, packages help avoid collisions between module names.

Creating a package is quite straightforward since it makes use of the operating system's inherent hierarchical file structure.

### 10.13.4 Pip

Pip is easy to install, upgrade and remove package management system in python used to install and manage software packages, such as those found in the Python Package Index. Below are sample codes.

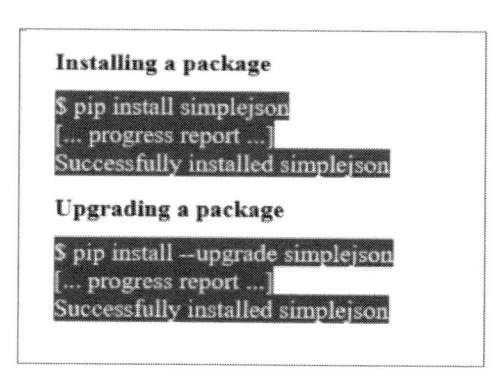

```
Installing a package
$ pip install simplejson
[... progress report ...]
Successfully installed simplejson

Upgrading a package
$ pip install --upgrade simplejson
[... progress report ...]
Successfully installed simplejson
```

Figure 10-7 Code snippet of uploading Pip package

### 10.13.5 Virtualenv

This is an isolated working copy of Python which allows you to work on a specific project without worry of affecting other projects. It enables multiple side-by-side installations of Python, one for each project. It doesn't install separate copies of Python, but it does provide a clever way to keep different project environments isolated.

### 10.13.6 Anaconda

Anaconda is a Python interpreter which acts as a single installer for several platforms. It eliminates the issues of package installation and management.

## 10.14 Other Tools Used to Support Network Automation

### 10.14.1 CFEngine

CFEngine is an infrastructural automation framework that ensures a continuous operation of the network. It is an important tool to engineer and network administrators to keep to the high levels of service of the IT infrastructure ensuring compliance and high-level service delivery. This tool has the proprietary version as well as the opensource version. It can handle a high number of the smallest server emended devices of up to tens of thousands. T has a star topology which includes hosts which are points of execution of policy instructions and nodes

This tool has the responsibility of ensuring compliance, it does this role by offering a definition of the configuration of the IT infrastructure and the desired state, these ensure compliance. This tool offers the following advantages to the users like autonomy which is ensured by the agents which are autonomously charged with the responsibility of implementing the desired state as well as the continues back reporting as it runs on virtually every node in the network. The tool can also be described to be everywhere, its capable of being installed in the smallest embedded devices in the servers, in the cloud, and on mainframes making causing the possibility of handling a larger number of nodes.

Other advantages of this platform are security, scalability and scalability. The developers of this tool put security as a concern in all aspects of all the steps of development, rendering it very secure. This tool as also been tested as far as stability is concerned it has been applied in mission-critical production environments for over 20 years and given the many years of deployment it can be regarded as the most stable and secure of all the competing automation tools. This tool is also very scalable which grows with the network infrastructural growth this proves that this tool is very easily scalable, from statistics it has been running on near 200,000 serves of over 12 separate data centres of the largest IT infrastructures in the globe.

### 10.14.2 Prometheus

Prometheus is a non-proprietary reliable toolkit built for the purpose of providing alerts as well as system monitoring. It is important to point out that this tool has a vibrant community of users this has resulted in this toolkit is a standalone tool and maintenance is done independently of the users. This tool has most of its components coded in Go this has the result of making the tool relatively easy in terms of building and deployment. In the monitoring task, Prometheus proves a highly dynamic and service oriented in addition to the property of being machine centric. These properties make this toolkit formidable for both multi-dimensional querying and data collection micro services and services

This toolkit has several functional strengthen which are outlined as follows; this toolkit is reliable, accurate, detailed and dependable. These merits are possible as a result of the following features and components and the architecture.

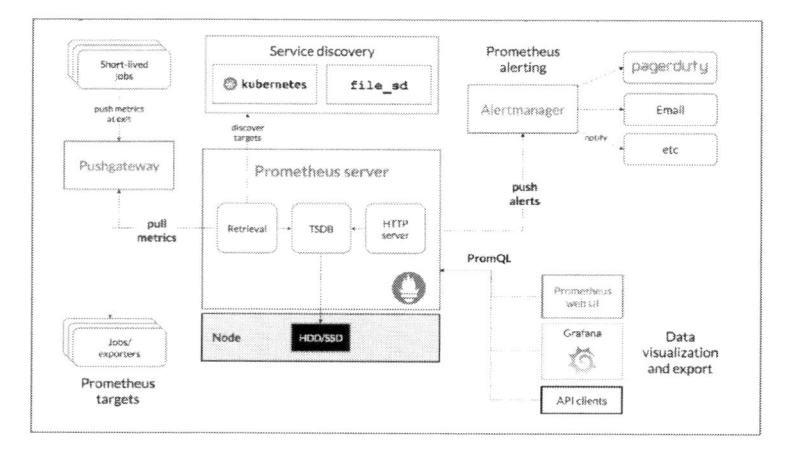

Figure 10-8 Architecture of Prometheus server

**Features**

1. It supports a multi-mode in terms of graphing and dashboard
2. A static configuration or in other cases a service discovery facilitate discovery of targets
3. The pull model and HTTP are important for a collection of time series
4. The autonomy of nodes of the single servers makes it non-reliant on a distributed storage architecture
5. This toolkit offers a data model which is multi-dimensional and possesses a time series data which is the metric name and key identifier. This directionality is further aided by the query language which is flexible

**Components**

1. Possesses the main server which is responsible for storage of time series data and scrapping.
2. Has a variety of support tools.
3. Alerts are also managed by the alert manager.
4. Application code is instrumented by the client libraries
5. It also comprises of a service called push gateway which is responsible for the support of jobs which are short-lived.
6. The services like statsD and Graphite have a special purpose exporter.
7. The above features structure, as well as features, make this toolkit suitable for the recording of a time series which is exclusively numeric. It is also very reliable as a result of a result of an isolated server.

### 10.14.3 Vagrant

This is an easy to use command line tool or utility that is tasked with the management of a virtual machine life circle. The workflows focus on automation, this tool is key to the reduction of setup time in a development environment thereby increasing the parity of production.

This tool, apart from being easy to use during configuration, it is reproducible and most importantly very portable. In a team environment, the vagrant provides a world standard in terms of technical standards with the easy to use workflow which is consistent and line to enable productivity maximization and team flexibility. The following line of code is used to forward port 80 of a box to port 8080 on the host.

*Config.vm.network "forwarded_port" , guest: 80, host: 8080*

### 10.14.4 Rancher

This is a non-proprietary application which makes it possible for the running of containers during production by companies. This un necessitated the writing of containers from scratch because with the rancher there is a software stack which is necessary to produce containers, this tool manages multiple Kubernetes clusters. The rancher can provision and manage cloud Kubernetes services like GKE, EKS, and AKS or import existing clusters. Rancher implements centralized authentication (GitHub, AD/LDAP, SAML, etc.) across RKE or cloud Kubernetes services.

Rancher offers an intuitive UI, enabling users to run containers without learning all Kubernetes concepts up-front. Rancher includes an application catalogue, enabling one-click deployment of Helm and Compose templates. Rancher implements integrated alert and logs aggregation and turn-key CI/CD pipelines.

Rancher makes it easy to manage containerized environments from deploying and scaling multiple Docker clusters to integrating the container networks and storage. The simple yet powerful user interface provides complete visibility into your infrastructure and the applications running on top of it. You can easily select, configure and deploy infrastructure services through the Rancher interface, enabling repeatable deployments of customer environments.

### 10.14.5 Solar Winds

Solar winds are a network automation manager used for managing bulk configurations to both wireless nodes and wired nodes. This tool has inbuilt workflows which are deployed for tasks of scheduling, managing approvals and reviews as well as bulk pushing of configurations after the template designs are created and standardized.

This toolkit is also key in the network infrastructure monitoring after which alerts of inappropriate configurations issued for corrective measures to be made in order to reverse the problems, which can be done in a few minutes. During this monitoring process, the tool gives a comprehensive report of the changes in the network configuration detailing who made these changes, what time, on which node in addition to deletion and additions information.

Another key area where the tool is deployed is for compliance auditing ensuring that the requirements for security policies and standards are met and gives alerts if any. Lastly, this tool is important in because it automates backups of configuration, this is done in layer 2 as well as 3 nodes in the network infrastructure.

The above functions have an effect of saving money for the institutions by avoiding fines as a result of non-compliance. It also prevents issues in the network resulting in misconfigurations and most importantly, the corrective measures can be configured in the network in a short time and in bulk reducing downtime.

## 10.15 Conclusion

Research has it that, human errors account for at least 40% of network failures and in some cases even higher. These errors occur during the processes of verification and validation of the network resources. It is also proven through research that these errors can be minimized to near nonexistence with the deployment of automation. This only shows one thing, that automation is the way to go.

The document discusses the python libraries in terms of definition function and examples, some of the libraries discussed are NTPlib which is responsible for time synchronization, Contract responsible for declaring and parsing binary data; Xmlrpclib for describing method results and calls, Paramiko which gives functionality to both server and customer, Supervisor that control as well as monitoring of processes among others. It is therefore important to conclude that python library methods are key in automation of networks

Using automation tools networks are now able to automatically save the network configurations, perform policy and security standards adherence checks, identify the network topology, minimize downtime and reduce the chances of failure of the network. These processes have the effect of making the network more consistent as far as deployment is concerned, compliant, secure, resilient, up to date, minimal human errors and most importantly effective and efficient utilization of network resources making the organizations reap big in term of ROI.

A Centrally Controlled Network or system Configuration is an organizational requirement if prosperity is the driving force, this has the effect of not only cutting costs but most importantly increased the efficiency of operation. Some of these activities include patching, the configuration of the firewall, and Syslog being managed from a central location. Another important reason for automation is the ease of use of application and systems, playing a role in eliminating complexities or difficulties in the system. This has the effect the reducing operational costs on such activities or even attends to other important matters. Hence lower tasks time. Cost is an integral aspect of organizational growth; therefore, the system adopted must be cheap for cost reduction.

It is evident that automation is the only option for businesses that want to pursue success. As for the debate of whether the company needs to buy, built or settle on a hybrid of the two ways in the acquisition of automation tools. The following considerations should be made, the business needs, the sufficiency and capability of personnel to handle the automation tool required and to orchestrate the deployment of the chosen technology of automation, whether or not the vendor provides the personnel, risks of chosen technology and the mitigation plans, the timelines of the benefits of deploying a given technology, the knowledge and the readiness of the business to commence the given technology. In view of the above items, a business can make a choice of whether to outsource or built their own technology to enable their network automation. Another benefit is the increase in savings for a given business. With automation, the network costs will reduce by a projected value of slightly above 30% taking the case of Juniper deployment. With increased returns in an organization the ability to increase savings will be within the reach of the business because the network will be flexible, reliable, speedy and efficient meeting the needs of the clients, therefore, more ROI because in the business world of today networking is everything and with automation, everything falls in place.

## 10.16 Summary

To summarize, any institution's business success is very dependent on the kind of network infrastructure it possesses. An effective and efficient network is superb in terms of reliability, speed agility flexibility making it key to the provision of access and communication between employees themselves, between applications, hardware both within and outside the business network. This can only be achieved through automation using the appropriate tools that the entity will feel fit for use after consideration. This is of course with a little investment.

## 10.17 Assignment Questions

### Assignment 1

| | |
|---|---|
| **10.1** | What kind of networks can be automated? |
| **10.2** | What are the categories of network automation? |
| **10.3** | Describe the benefits of automating networks? |
| **10.4** | How to automate network management? |
| **10.5** | Describe some of the tools used for network automation? |
| **10.6** | What is NAPALM? |
| **10.7** | What is Juniper PyEZ? |
| **10.8** | Describe Cisco Cross Network technology? |
| **10.9** | What is Cisco pyIOSXR? |
| **10.10** | What is modular programming and its advantages? |

### Assignment 2

| | |
|---|---|
| **10.11** | Define "module" And "package" |
| **10.12** | How Memory Is Managed In Python? |
| **10.13** | What Python frameworks do you know? |
| **10.14** | What tools that help Python development do you know? |
| **10.15** | The following is displayed by a print function call: yesterday today tomorrow. Please write an example of a print function. |
| **10.16** | What are the rules for legal Python names? |
| **10.17** | Explain how Python does Compile-time and Run-time code checking? |
| **10.18** | What is a "unittest" in Python? |
| **10.19** | Define "slicing". |
| **10.20** | What are generators in Python? |
| **10.21** | How do you convert a number into a string? |
| **10.22** | What are the built-in type does python provides? |
| **10.23** | Mention what are the rules for local and global variables in Python? |
| **10.24** | How can you share global variables across modules? |
| **10.25** | Explain how can you make a Python Script executable on Unix? |

# Appendix 1: Online Courses and Books in Python

There are limited number of online resources and books available to further enhance your Python and Programming learning experience for Network Automation however there are many courses available online to learn general Python Programming. The Appendix I provide references to such online courses and book. We would like to remind them.

### A. Online Courses Teaching General Python Programming Scripting

1. Complete Python Bootcamp: Go from zero to hero in Python 3
   https://www.udemy.com/complete-python-bootcamp

2. Learn Python Programming Masterclass
   https://www.udemy.com/python-the-complete-python-developer-course

3. The Python Bible™ | Everything You Need to Program in Python
   https://www.udemy.com/the-python-bible/

4. Learn Python the Hard Way
   https://learnpythonthehardway.org/book/

5. A Byte of Python
   https://python.swaroopch.com/

6. Google's Python Class
   https://developers.google.com/edu/python/

7. Automate the Boring Stuff with Python
   http://automatetheboringstuff.com/

8. Automate the Boring Stuff with Python
   https://www.coursera.org/specializations/python

9. Applied Data Science with Python Specialization
   https://www.coursera.org/specializations/data-science-python

10. Programming for Everybody (Getting Started with Python)
    https://www.coursera.org/learn/python

11. The Official Python Tutorial
    http://docs.python.org/tutorial/

12. Dive Into Python
    http://www.diveintopython.net/toc/index.html

13. Python Official Documentation
    https://www.python.org/doc/

## B. Network Automation Courses using Python

Courses in Network Automation are limited as this filed is complex and very involving. Here we list some very well know Network Automation courses available today

1. Python for Network Engineers
   https://www.logicfinder.net/python

2. Python for Network Engineers
   https://pynet.twb-tech.com/

3. Master Network Automation with Python for Network Engineers
   https://www.udemy.com/master-python-network-automation-for-network-engineers/

4. Network Programming & Automation
   http://www.networktocode.com/network-programming-automation/

5. Practical Python Cisco Network Automation
   https://ine.com/products/practical-python-cisco-network-automation

6. Python Programming for Network Engineers
   https://www.networkershome.com/python-programming-for-network-engineers/

7. Network Automation using Python for Engineers
   https://academy.ehacking.net/p/network-automation-python-engineers

8. Network Automation using Python for Engineers
   https://www.lynda.com/GNS3-tutorials/Network-Automation-Quick-Start/769296-2.html

9. Python Network Programming for Network Engineers by David Bombal
   https://pythoncoursesonline.com/python-programming-network-engineers/

10. Ansible Network Automation
    https://pynet.twb-tech.com/class-ansible-a.html

## C. General Python Learning Books

There are quite a few books available on Amazon on Python Programming language,

1. Learning Python 5th Edition Written by Mark Lutz and David Ascher
2. Python Programming: An Introduction to Computer Science Second edition by John Zelle's
3. Python Cookbook by David Beazley and Brian K. Jones
4. Python Essential Reference by David M. Beazley,
5. Python In A Nutshell by Alex Martelli
6. LearnPython
   http://www.learnpython.org/
7. How To Think Like A Computer Scientist
   http://interactivepython.org/runestone/static/thinkcspy/index.html

## D. Books on Network Automation

1. Mastering Python Networking
   https://www.amazon.com/Mastering-Python-Networking-solution-%20automation/dp/1784397008

2. Network Automation using Python 3: An Administrator's Handbook
   https://www.amazon.com/Network-Automation-using-Python-Administrators-ebook/dp/B07HQZWKCG

3. Python Automation Cookbook: Explore the world of automation using Python recipes that will enhance your skills
   https://www.amazon.com/Python-Automation-Cookbook-Explore-automation-ebook/dp/B07F2L2CDC>

4. Network Programmability and Automation: Skills for the Next-Generation Network Engineer 1st Edition
   https://www.amazon.com/Network-Programmability-Automation-Next-Generation-Engineer/dp/1491931256

5. Practical Network Automation: Leverage the power of Python and Ansible to optimize your network
   https://www.amazon.com/Practical-Network-Automation-Leverage-optimize/dp/1788299469/

6. Violent Python: A Cookbook For Hackers, Forensic Analysts, Penetration Testers And Security Engineers Written by TJ O'Connor
   https://www.amazon.com/Violent-Python-Cookbook-Penetration- Engineers/dp/1597499579

# Appendix 2: Selected Bibliography

## Chapter 1

- On-Box Python for Cisco Devices – the Why, What, and How
  https://www.infoworld.com/article/3208727/development-tools/how-to-use-on-box-python-scripts-for-cisco-devices.html

- Network Automation Using Python: BGP Configuration
  https://networkcomputing.com/networking/network-automation-using-python-bgp-configuration/1423704194

- Network automation tools: Should you build or buy?
  https://searchnetworking.techtarget.com/Network-automation-tools-Should-you-build-or-buy

- Network Automation – Now!
  https://blogs.cisco.com/enterprise/network-automation-now

- Network Automation for Config Change Management and Compliance
  https://www.solarwinds.com/topics/network-automation

- Cisco Crosswork for Service Providers
  https://www.cisco.com/c/en/us/products/cloud-systems-management/crosswork-network-automation/index.html

- Best Network Configuration Management Tools and Software
  https://www.ittsystems.com/best-network-configuration-management-tools-and-software/

- Python 2 vs Python 3: Practical Considerations
  https://www.digitalocean.com/community/tutorials/python-2-vs-python-3-practical-considerations-2

- The Key Differences Between Python 2 and Python 3
  https://blog.appdynamics.com/engineering/the-key-differences-between-python-2-and-python-3/

- Python 3.3: Trust Me, It's Better than 2.7
  https://www.youtube.com/watch?v=f_6vDi7ywuA&feature=youtu.be

- What are the pros and cons of Python 2.7.6 versus 3.3?
  https://www.quora.com/What-are-the-pros-and-cons-of-Python-2-7-6-versus-3-3#!n=12

- WHAT SHOULD I LEARN AS A BEGINNER: PYTHON 2 OR PYTHON 3?
  https://learntocodewith.me/programming/python/python-2-vs-python-3/

- Why Network Engineers must learn Python Scripting
  http://wajidhassan.com/research-teaching/python/

- Try Python!
  https://try-python.appspot.com/

# Chapter 2

- Antiga, L., Piccinelli, M., Botti, L., Ene-Iordache, B., Remuzzi, A., & Steinman, D. A. (2008). An image-based modelling framework for patient-specific computational hemodynamics. Medical & biological engineering & computing, 46(11), 1097.
- Bergstra, J., Bastien, F., Breuleux, O., Lamblin, P., Pascanu, R., Delalleau, O., ... & Bengio, Y. (2011). Theano: Deep learning on GPUs with python. In NIPS 2011, big learning Workshop, Granada, Spain (Vol. 3, pp. 1-48). Microtome Publishing.
- Bjørndalen, J. M., Vinter, B., & Anshus, O. J. (2007, July). PyCSP-Communicating Sequential Processes for Python. In Cpa (pp. 229-248).
- Dalcın, L., Paz, R., Storti, M., & D'Elıa, J. (2008). MPI for Python: Performance improvements and MPI-2 extensions. Journal of Parallel and Distributed Computing, 68(5), 655-662.
- Dolomanov, O. V., Bourhis, L. J., Gildea, R. J., Howard, J. A., & Puschmann, H. (2009). OLEX2: a complete structure solution, refinement and analysis program. Journal of Applied Crystallography, 42(2), 339-341.
- Edwards, S. H., Tilden, D. S., & Allevato, A. (2014, March). Pythy: improving the introductory python programming experience. In Proceedings of the 45th ACM technical symposium on Computer science education (pp. 641-646). ACM.
- Hammond, M., & Robinson, A. (2010). Python Programming on Win32: Help for Windows Programmers. " O'Reilly Media, Inc.".
- Helmus, J. J., & Collis, S. M. (2016). The Python ARM Radar Toolkit (Py-ART), a library for working with weather radar data in the Python programming language. Journal of Open Research Software, 4.
- Kraft, P., Vaché, K. B., Frede, H. G., & Breuer, L. (2011). CMF: a hydrological programming language extension for integrated catchment models. Environmental Modelling & Software, 26(6), 828-830.
- Poolman, M. G. (2016). Scrumpy: metabolic modelling with Python. IEE Proceedings-Systems Biology, 153(5), 375-378.
- Rivers, K., & Koedinger, K. R. (2017). Data-driven hint generation in vast solution spaces: a self-improving python programming tutor. International Journal of Artificial Intelligence in Education, 27(1), 37-64.
- Sanner, M. F., Duncan, B. S., J. CARRILLO, C., & Olson, A. J. (2009). Integrating computation and visualization for biomolecular analysis: an example using python and AVS. In Biocomputing'99 (pp. 401-412).
- Seitz, J. (2009). Gray Hat Python: Python programming for hackers and reverse engineers. No Starch Press.
- Sieg, A., Mobasher, B., & Burke, R. (2010, September). Improving the effectiveness of collaborative recommendation with ontology-based user profiles. In Proceedings of the 1st International Workshop on Information Heterogeneity and Fusion in Recommender Systems (pp. 39-46). ACM.
- Sukumaran, J., & Holder, M. T. (2010). DendroPy: A Python library for phylogenetic computing. Bioinformatics, 26(12), 1569-1571.
- Zelle, J. M. (2014). Python programming: an introduction to computer science. Franklin, Beedle & Associates, Inc.

## Chapter 3

- Beazley, D., & Jones, B. K. (2013). Python Cookbook: Recipes for Mastering Python 2. " O'Reilly Media, Inc.".
- Lutz, M. (2014). Python Pocket Reference: Python In Your Pocket. " O'Reilly Media, Inc.".
- Ramalho, L. (2015). Fluent Python: clear, concise, and effective programming. " O'Reilly Media, Inc.".
- Sarkar, D. (2016). Python Refresher. In Text Analytics with Python (pp. 51-3.7.4.1). Apress, Berkeley, CA.
- Tipalty, K. (2018). Quora. Retrieved from https://www.quora.com/What-are-sequences-and-what-are-collections-in-Python-Where-does-list-tuple-string-dictionary-set-etc-fit-in
- VanRossum, G., & Drake, F. L. (2010). *The python language reference.* Amsterdam, Netherlands: Python Software Foundation.

## Chapter 4

- Rivers, K., & Koedinger, K. R. (2017). Data-driven hint generation in vast solution spaces: a self-improving python programming tutor. International Journal of Artificial Intelligence in Education, 27(1), 37-64.
- Olsen, R. (2017). Python: Learn Python (Advanced) in 7 Days and Ace It Well. Hands-on Challenges INCLUDED! (Volume 2).
- Alvaro, F. (2016). PYTHON: Easy Python Programming for Beginners, Your Guide to Learning Python.
- Shaw, Z. A. (2016). Learn Python the Hard Way (2013). URL http://learnpythonthehardway.org/book.
- Chan, J. (2015). Learn Python in one day and learn it well: Python for beginners with the hands-on project: the only book you need to start coding in Python immediately. CreateSpace Independent Publishing.

## Chapter 5

- Denis, G., 2014. The While and Do While Loops. Programming, 5(2), pp. 40-55.
- Donald, E. K., 2010. Loop Statements. Art of Computer Programming, 4(1), p. 40.
- Harold, A., 2016. Loops. Structure and Interpretation of Computer Programs, 5(4), pp. 20-30.
- Steve, M., 2013. Loops. Code Complete, 7(7), pp. 17-28.
- Thomas, H. C., 2012. Loop Statements.. Introduction to Algorithms, 10(7), pp. 30-50.

## Chapter 6

- Adams, R. (2018). Smack Python Programming: a completely friendly way to learn Python Fast for Beginners.
- Bae, D. Y., & Mascarenas, D. D. (2016). Control of Delta Robot and Development of Servo Hook using Python Programming (No. LA-UR-16-21840). Los Alamos National Lab. (LANL), Los Alamos, NM (United States).
- Barupal, D. K., Fan, S., & Fiehn, O. (2018). Integrating bioinformatics approaches for a comprehensive interpretation of metabolomics datasets. Current opinion in biotechnology, 54, 1-9.
- Edwards, S. H., Tilden, D. S., & Allevato, A. (2014, March). Pythy: improving the introductory python programming experience. In Proceedings of the 45th ACM technical symposium on Computer science education (pp. 641-646). ACM.
- Fangohr, H., O'Brien, N., Prabhakar, A., & Kashyap, A. (2015). Teaching Python programming with automatic assessment and feedback provision. arXiv preprint arXiv:1509.03556.

- Gold, S. (2016). Python: Python Programming Learn Python Programming in A Day-A Comprehensive Introduction to The Basics Of Python & Computer Programming.
- Havill, J. (2016). Discovering computer science: interdisciplinary problems, principles, and Python programming. Chapman and Hall/CRC.
- Helmus, J. J., & Collis, S. M. (2016). The Python ARM Radar Toolkit (Py-ART), a library for working with weather radar data in the Python programming language. Journal of Open Research Software, 4.
- Marin-Sanguino, A. (2016). Book Review: Python Programming for Biology. Frontiers in Genetics, 7, 66.
- Nelli, F. (2015). Python Data Analytics: Data Analysis and Science using pandas, matplotlib and the Python Programming Language. Apress.
- Olsen, R. (2017). Python: Learn Python (Advanced) in 7 Days and Ace It Well. Hands-On Challenges INCLUDED! (Volume 2).
- Ozer, R. (2017). Intermediate Python Programming: The Insider Guide to Intermediate Python Programming Concepts.
- Rivers, K., & Koedinger, K. R. (2017). Data-driven hint generation in vast solution spaces: a self-improving python programming tutor. International Journal of Artificial Intelligence in Education, 27(1), 37-64.
- Yim, A., Chung, C., & Yu, A. (2018). Matplotlib for Python Developers: Effective techniques for data visualization with Python.
- Zhao, G., Zhao, S., Zou, C., & Wang, Z. (2017, August). Exploration of teaching method of Python Programming based on the case of a technical problem. In Computer Science and Education (ICCSE), 2017 12th International Conference on (pp. 600-603). IEEE.

## Chapter 7

- Cornu, B., Seinturier, L., & Monperrus, M. (2015). Exception handling analysis and transformation using fault injection: Study of resilience against unanticipated exceptions. Information and Software Technology, 57, 66-76.
- Haraldsson, S. O., Woodward, J. R., & Brownlee, A. I. (2017, May). The use of automatic test data generation for genetic improvement in a live system. In Search-Based Software Testing (SBST), 2017 IEEE/ACM 10th International Workshop on (pp. 28-31). IEEE.
- Haraldsson, S. O., Woodward, J. R., Brownlee, A. E., & Siggeirsdottir, K. (2017, July). Fixing bugs in your sleep: how genetic improvement became an overnight success. In Proceedings of the Genetic and Evolutionary Computation Conference Companion (pp. 1513-1520). ACM.
- Johansson, R. (2014). Introduction to scientific computing in Python. GitHub. com/jrjohansson/scientific-python-lectures.
- Vitousek, M. M., Kent, A. M., Siek, J. G., & Baker, J. (2014, October). Design and evaluation of gradual typing for Python. In ACM SIGPLAN Notices (Vol. 50, No. 2, pp. 45-56). ACM.

## Chapter 8

- Cielen, D., Meysman, A., & Ali, M. (2016). Introducing data science: big data, machine learning, and more, using Python tools. Manning Publications Co.
- McKinney, W. (2015). pandas: A Python data analysis library. see http://pandas.pydata.org/. Google Scholar.
- Hernández, C. X., Harrigan, M. P., Sultan, M. M., & Pande, V. S. (2017). MSMExplorer: Data visualizations for biomolecular dynamics. J. Open Source Softw, 2, 12.

- Barnard, L., & Mertik, M. (2015). Usability of visualization libraries for web browsers for use in scientific analysis. International Journal of Computer Applications, 121(1).
- McLeod, C. (2015). A Framework for Distributed Deep Learning Layer Design in Python. arXiv preprint arXiv:1510.07303.
- Sweet, J. A., Walter, B. L., Gunalan, K., Chaturvedi, A., McIntyre, C. C., & Miller, J. P. (2014). Fiber tractography of the axonal pathways linking the basal ganglia and cerebellum in Parkinson disease: implications for targeting in deep brain stimulation. Journal of neurosurgery, 120(4), 988-996.
- Blackledge, M. D., Collins, D. J., Koh, D. M., & Leach, M. O. (2016). Rapid development of image analysis research tools: bridging the gap between researcher and clinician with pyOsiriX. Computers in biology and medicine, 69, 203-212.
- Springer, D., Schnurrer, W., Weinlich, A., Heindel, A., Seiler, J., & Kaup, A. (2014, October). Open source HEVC analyzer for rapid prototyping (HARP). In Image Processing (ICIP), 2014 IEEE International Conference on (pp. 2189-2191). IEEE.
- McGuffee, J., & Salan, S. (2018). Engaging constructivist oriented learners with Python. Journal of Computing Sciences in Colleges, 33(5), 63-69.
- Schubert, O. T., Gillet, L. C., Collins, B. C., Navarro, P., Rosenberger, G., Wolski, W. E., ... & Aebersold, R. (2015). Building high-quality assay libraries for targeted analysis of SWATH MS data. Nature protocols, 10(3), 426.
- Chen, V. (2017). Awesome Python: A curated list of awesome Python frameworks, libraries, software and resources.
- Chen, V. (2017). Awesome Python: A curated list of awesome Python frameworks, libraries, software and resources.
- Helmus, J. J., & Collis, S. M. (2016). The Python ARM Radar Toolkit (Py-ART), a library for working with weather radar data in the Python programming language. Journal of Open Research Software, 4.
- Sun, Q., Berkelbach, T. C., Blunt, N. S., Booth, G. H., Guo, S., Li, Z., ... & Wouters, S. (2018). PySCF: The Python-based simulations of chemistry framework. Wiley Interdisciplinary Reviews: Computational Molecular Science, 8(1), e1340.
- Yoo, J. Y., & Yang, D. (2015). Classification scheme of unstructured text document using TF-IDF and naive bayes classifier. Advanced Science and Technology Letters, 111(50), 263-266.
- Li, M., Cai, Z., Yi, X., Wang, Z., Wang, Y., Zhang, Y., & Yang, X. (2016, August). ALLIANCE-ROS: a software architecture on ROS for fault-tolerant cooperative multi-robot systems. In Pacific Rim International Conference on Artificial Intelligence(pp. 233-242). Springer, Cham.
- Perkel, J. M. (2015). Programming: pick up Python. Nature News, 518(7537), 125.

# Chapter 9

- Network Programming In Python
  https://www.studytonight.com/network-programming-in-python/blocking-and-nonblocking-socket-io

- Python Script to Get Windows System Information Using WMI
  https://topnetworkguide.com/python-script-to-get-windows-system-information-using-wmi/

- Using Scapy in a Python Script
  https://thepacketgeek.com/scapy-p-07-monitoring-arp/

- Python Scripting with Scapy
  https://www2.mmu.ac.uk/media/mmuacuk/content/documents/school-of-computing-mathematics-and-digital-technology/blossom/PythonScriptingwithScapyLab.pdf

- Psutil Documentation
  https://psutil.readthedocs.io/en/latest/

- Python Library for NETCONF Clients
  https://ncclient.readthedocs.io/en/latest/

- Configuration of a Networking Device using NETCONF
  https://www.fir3net.com/Networking/Protocols/how-to-operate-a-device-using-netconf-and-python.html

## Chapter 10

- D. F. Macedo, D. Guedes, L. F. M. Vieira, M. A. M. Vieira and M. Nogueira, (2017) "Programmable Networks—From Software-Defined Radio to Software-Defined Networking," in IEEE Communications Surveys & Tutorials, vol. 17, no. 2, pp. 1102-1125
- P. Chaignon, K. Lazri, J. Francois and O. Festor, (2017) "Understanding disruptive monitoring capabilities of programmable networks," 2017 IEEE Conference on Network Softwarization NetSoft, Bologna, pp. 1-6.
- Tischer R., Gooley J. (September 9th, 2016) Programming and Automating Cisco Networks, Cisco Press, Cisco" DevNet" Open Source Dev Center -
  https://developer.cisco.com/site/opensource/Netmiko,https://pynet.twbtech.com/blog/automation/netmiko.html
- Edelman J., Lowe S., Oswalt M. (2017) Network Programmability and Automation, O'Reilly Media, Inc., 12. GNS3 emulator, https://www.gns3.com/ Network Automation
- S. Lowe, J. Edelman, M. Oswalt, (December 2015) "Network Programmability and Automation, Skills for the Next-Generation Network Engineer", O'Reilly Media,
- K. Jambunatha, (2015), "Design and implement Automated upgrade remote network devices using Python," IEEE International Advance Computing Conference (IACC), Banglore, pp. 217-221.
- Negus C., Henry W. (September 21st, 2015) Docker Containers: From Start to Enterprise, Prentice Hall, Docker Container, https://www.docker.com/what-container
- S Zamfir, T Balan, F Sandu, (2015) "Automating Telecom Equipment for Cloud Integration", Review of the Air Force Academy.
- S. Bendel, T. Springer, D. Schuster, A. Schill, R. Ackermann and M. Ameling, (2013) "A for the Things based on XMPP,". IEEE International Conference on Pervasive Computing and Communications Workshops (PERCOM Workshops), San Diego, CA, 2013, pp. 385-388.

Printed in Poland
by Amazon Fulfillment
Poland Sp. z o.o., Wrocław